W9-AAD-771

Also by the Author

Psychology in Clinical Practice

Managing People, Influencing Behavior

What You Fear Is Who You Are:
The Role of Fear in Relationships
www.whatyoufear.com

THE MANAGER:

Understanding and Influencing People

By

David W. Thompson, Ph.D.

MTR CORP
CHICAGO, IL

Copyright 2004 by MTR Corp.

All rights reserved. No part of this book may be reproduced
in any manner without written permission of the publisher.

Printed in the United States of America

MTR Corp.
PO Box 10128
Chicago, IL 60610
312.642.0652
WWW.MTRCORP.NET

ISBN 0-9705-1851-X

To those managers who
emotionally reinforce the successes and
self confidence of others

Table of Contents

SECTION 5
CHANGING OTHERS

SECTION 6
INTERVIEWING

SECTION 7
THE ART OF CONSTRUCTIVE FEEDBACK

SECTION 8
THE MANAGERIAL PROCESS: CASE STUDIES

ADDENDUM

PREFACE

TRUTH IS AN ELUSIVE QUALITY for at least two reasons. First, appearances to the contrary, it is difficult to determine the relevant variables influencing a given event. The most effective approach seems to be scientific experimentation. This book is based on principles derived from controlled experiments; its conclusions, consequently, should not fall victim to the frequent and realistic criticism that they are merely another of the many transient management fads.

Second, truth is often elusive because it may conflict emotionally with ideals and attitudes we have long held to be "good." This book is based on the experimental work of Pavlov and Skinner, two names that can strike emotional terror in the hearts of many people. One might well ask whether such terror (or disgust) can result from a confrontation with truth. The answer seems to be yes, as the experiences of Socrates or Copernicus or Galileo could confirm. Indeed, Diogenes might have searched in vain, not only for someone who spoke truth, but also for someone who sought truth.

It is hoped that readers will judge this book by the criterion of truth – that is, by the effectiveness and workability of the concepts presented, not by their compatibility with values they have held most of their lives. Few standards of truth are more stringent than whether a concept actually works. Fortunately, it seems to this writer at least, managers in private industry, because of the competitive nature of their area, are more concerned with a concept working than are people in any other sector of our economy.

This book is complex, but then so too is the nature of its subject, human behavior. Readers are urged, consequently, to try the exercises interspersed throughout the book.

Studying scientific principles in the abstract rarely encourages us to make them an integral part of our repertoire. Using the principles in real-life situations does. The book has been divided, somewhat arbitrarily, into shorter chapters. The goal here is to encourage the reader to think about the points being made before going on to other issues and being frustrated by the nuances and ramifications covered.

One of the crucial principles of this book centers on the idea that those people in our inner circle have an enormous influence on us, what we believe and feel about ourselves and the world around us. I would like to mention four such people in my life:

Rex N. Olsen, a person of formidable mental acuity who has saved me from many a blunder.

Robal Johnson, a demanding person by any measure, but a person whose demands elicit the best from others, a factor that so often returns the best to them.

Krysten Thompson, my daughter and the subject of so many of my ideas and hypotheses; that she has not been hospitalized for multiple personality syndrome is amazing.

Nancie Thompson, my wife; one of the main thrusts of this book is to get readers to surround themselves with people who love their confidence, thus reinforcing and strengthening their love and respect for themselves – no one does it better.

The best prediction of future behavior is past behavior. The history of humankind is a history of war and conflict. Yet, while the future may be a repetition of the past behaviorally, it will not be a repetition in its effects. This is primarily due to the technology that has so rapidly developed in the physical sciences, a technology that now can result in devastating consequences, be it through the principles of physics, chemistry, or biology. The only hope would seem to lie in developing and applying scientific principles in the behavioral sciences that are as effective as those in the physical sciences. Many of these principles are now known. Our survival may well rest on our acceptance of them and our determination to apply them toward socially constructive,
rather than destructive, ends.

David W. Thompson, Ph.D.

SECTION 1

THE MANAGERIAL FOCUS

What are the reasons for success in an organization?

What should be the manager's primary focus?

How important is managing people in today's organizations?

CHAPTER 1

MANAGING PEOPLE

Survival Depends on Profits

Survival is the basic goal of any organization. In political organizations, survival depends on votes. In corporations, survival depends on profits. The manager, therefore, should be concerned with profits and what causes them to rise, fall, or stay the same – this much is obvious. Profits, however, are a consequence, a result, an effect. To focus on profits is to focus on an event that cannot be changed by direct action. Indeed, few managers, outside of CEOs, can be held accountable for profits. Thus, it is in NOT recognizing and focusing on the relevant causes of profits that managers can easily go astray.

Factors Influencing Profits

Three factors have an impact on profits: The first is weather conditions. If an extreme drought or severe cold weather affect crop production, food prices will rise and disposable income will gravitate away from other goods; these effects will ripple through the economy and influence the profits of many organizations. But few managers can influence weather, hence its potential consequences should be noted, but the study of its causes left to others.

The second factor that affects profits is the behavior of people outside an organization. If the Fed loosens interest rates, or OPEC tightens the oil supply, or a competitor makes a startling advance in technology, the profits of an organization can be greatly affected. These events must be

3

monitored closely because they can, at times, overwhelm the other two factors influencing profits. But, again, a manager generally has little influence on the behavior of people outside their organization.

The third factor influencing profits is the behavior of people inside the organization. This is because the activities that determine profits – judgment calls, decisions, changes in policy, new ideas for product lines, dependability in sales calls, conscientious maintenance of equipment, production efficiencies, and other meaningful events – originate ultimately in the behavior of the people in the organization.

Performance Vs. Behavior

Many managers make the common mistake of concentrating solely on the results of behavior rather than on the behavior itself and its causes. They may focus, for example, on the number of sales calls made, the errors in a submitted report, or the inadequate design of a particular product. And, indeed, the manager should use quantitative measures of profits and their precursors, such as production and sales figures, as an indication of effective, or ineffective, behavior patterns of people in the organization. So the results of behavior can be a good starting point in the managerial process, but it is only the first step (and usually the easiest).

The next step is determining the factors that influenced the quantitative measures, especially in an adverse manner. This determination will not be complete until it is made in terms of the constructive (or non-constructive) behavior of the people in the organization. Herein lies the manager's principal responsibility, the behavior of their subordinates. This can be an emotionally and intellectually difficult process and therefore is often avoided. Also, many managers, unfortunately, are so concerned with their own boss that their focus is too often directed upward on pleasing their superior rather than downward on constructively influencing the behavior of their subordinates.

Avoiding the Difficulties of Managing Others

Why do managers tend to avoid responsibility for the behavior of subordinates? First, in a society in which everyone is created equal, accepting responsibility for changing or modifying the behavior of someone else is akin to playing God, and that can be frightening. (Indeed, it is a responsibility that leads many to consider managing people an unnatural act). The mere idea of authority over others makes many managers uncomfortable. Second, there are enormous complexities involved in the behavior of people. It is much easier to focus on a written report than on the vagaries that led an individual to slant that report one way or another.

There are, however, as many complex variables in determining and measuring the objectives and effects of behavior as there are in measuring behavior itself. Some of these variables are controllable; many are not. Suppose, for example, two salespeople are achieving only 80 percent of their sales quota. Many managers will focus only on the "missing 20 percent," often in an accusatory manner. As a result, they may create a higher level of motivation in their two subordinates – motivation that, unfortunately, does not last. The subordinates, on the other hand, will tend to focus on the uncontrollable variables that they claim are influencing their poor performance. Perhaps their best customer moved, or a competitor has a close relative on a customer's staff. These statements may be true, but there is little that anyone (especially the salesperson) can do about them.

The Manager's Proper Focus

Discussions dealing only with the 20 percent or with the uncontrollable variables have little long-term effect and waste valuable time. For the salesperson, such discussions merely shift the manager's attention away from his or her shortcomings to innocuous factors that the manager can do little about. Too often, the manager is only too happy to go along with this approach, thereby avoiding a possible confrontation. The manager's

5

proper focus, however, should be on the *behavior of the subordinate* that is contributing to the "missing 20 percent." It is here that a manager can have an impact.

The manager may determine, for example, that one salesperson loses sales because she is too abrasive with customers, another because he is too meek and passive. These are variables that the manager can influence. Toning down abrasiveness and replacing meekness with confidence – even to a small degree – should help bridge the gap between sales and quota. More important, sales should improve for the long term; the manager should no longer have to deal constantly with new problems caused by the same old ineffective behavior of his/her salespeople.

To summarize: Many variables influence the profits of an organization. While a number of these variables cannot be controlled (for example, general economic conditions, government intervention), one of the most important – the behavior of the people in the organization – is always susceptible to managerial influence. Too many managers spend too much time focusing on effects or on causative factors over which they have little control. Many managers could increase profits substantially by recognizing and accepting the enormous influence the behavior of their subordinates has on results and the enormous influence their own behavior can have on the behavior of their subordinates.

Managing People Increasingly Important

Oddly enough, advanced technology has further emphasized the importance of management. In the past, most interactions were of a man-machine variety. Automation in the plant and computerization in the office, however, have led to an enormous increase in the need for person-person interactions. Because of automation, one factory worker can now produce 2,000 units instead of 50 per day. Because of computerization and the Internet, one office worker can now handle effectively many more transactions than before. The effect has been to place much more responsibility on people in lower-level positions, since the consequences of their behavior has been so magnified. This increased responsibility requires more frequent manager-subordinate interactions because small errors can have far greater implications. In short, because of its multiplying effect through computers and automation, the behavior of any given individual can have much more impact than formerly, and the need for managerial monitoring and influence is correspondingly increased.

Summary

The abuse of managerial power in private industry has stemmed more from its lack of use than from its misuse. Because, as we shall see, fear leads us to assiduously avoid certain behaviors that may lead to unpleasant interactions, many managers shrink from making judgments and taking actions that involve people. But judgments and actions involving millions of dollars of inventory, capital investments, or potential mergers also involve and have a direct impact on people. In fact, any judgment, whether it concerns inventory or people, is intrinsic to a managerial position and can never be avoided. When managers refuse to give subordinates honest, adequate, and frequent feedback or to fire incompetent people, they are actually making judgments and having an impact on the behavior of all employees.

Managers most often attempt to avoid their responsibilities because carrying them out effectively can result in interactions that are unpleasant. To be more accurate, ineffective management most often occurs because effective management requires interactions that are frequently fraught with fear. It is true that fear is often a close companion throughout much of our lives, but rarely more so than in the proper implementation of the responsibilities inherent in managerial positions. And so it is to the topic of fear that we now turn.

Why is fear such an important factor in managing people?

Whose fear is more important, the manager's or the subordinate's?

How do we know what another person's fears are?

How do we know what our fears are?

What are the signs of confidence in someone?

CHAPTER 2

MANAGING FEAR

Three Basic Managerial Responsibilities

Managing people is a task more difficult emotionally than intellectually. That is partially due to the fact that managing people involves one of the most pervasive motivators and influencers of human behavior – fear! Fear, as we shall see, leads us to engage in certain behaviors excessively and to excessively avoid other behaviors. The pervasive influence of fear can be demonstrated by looking at three basic functions of a manager.

First, no decision a manager makes is more important than the selection-promotion decision. Managers are expected to surround themselves with highly competent subordinates – people who are independent, attack problems aggressively, and take the initiative in speaking up for their ideas.

Managers may give lip service to selecting such people, but it is emotionally difficult for them to actually do so. Most managers, consciously or not, tend to surround themselves with people who won't cause trouble, who will follow orders with a minimum of back talk, and who avoid mistakes that might reflect on the manager. Some managers may be reluctant to select or promote the subordinate who is ideal from a profit point of view, consequently, because such an individual can be personally threatening to them, eliciting the manager's fear of

9

confrontation, of being treated with disrespect, of being seen as inadequate or incompetent in comparison.

A second basic managerial function is to fire incompetent subordinates quickly. The inability to carry out this responsibility, especially at high levels of an organization, probably accounts for more business failures than all other factors combined. The cause, of course, is that firing someone is probably the most emotionally difficult task required of managers. It also elicits the fear of confrontation, of being disliked, criticized, or even being physically hurt. The idea of an organization layoff of 100 production people is often much easier for the sales manager to accept than is firing three incompetent salespeople, even though the salespeople's incompetence may well be the cause of the production department layoffs.

A third basic function of managers is the development of subordinates by constructively changing their behavior. Virtually all such change requires external feedback. No one is in a stronger position or as responsible for this feedback than a manager. But discussing personal shortcomings with another human being is, again, one of the most emotionally difficult managerial responsibilities. Hence, feedback in most organizations is criminally lacking. Indeed, it is assiduously avoided. This is why most companies insist on a performance review every six or twelve months. Little is known, however, about what actually takes place during a typical performance review. At best, little behavioral change will occur as a result of talking with a subordinate about his/her behavior and attitudes as infrequently as once or twice a year.

[Highly motivated managers can help create an atmosphere that encourages feedback by periodically asking their boss, "What do you feel is my greatest shortcoming in the work setting?" This should be done in a soft, gentle tone, on an informal, spontaneous basis, when everything is going well and there aren't any open conflicts festering in the background.

It is also a question managers should frequently ask their subordinates. Accepting any responses to this question with appreciation often provides

10

excellent feedback, opens up communication generally, and frequently prevents "surprises" in a relationship by bringing festering problems to the fore in a constructive environment. (As we shall see later, the answers to this question will often indicate the fears driving the speaker. Briefly, for example, if a manager is told she is too tactless, it may mean her subordinate is fearful of being criticized, a factor she must take into account in her interactions with him.)]

It should be noted that all three of these basic managerial decisions depend on the manager's ability to accurately evaluate the assets and liabilities of people. Few skills are as important to an organization as the expertise of assessing people. It is crucial in sales, counseling, and almost any managerial interaction.

The Inadequacy of Management Training

As we've seen so far, management consists of many emotionally difficult tasks that are often avoided, and most of these responsibilities are avoided because they involve interpersonal interactions. This avoidance is not surprising since the focus of most of our fears center on the behavior of other people.

Most management training is of little help. Too many programs merely describe the ideal of human behavior but give little information on how to achieve that ideal, especially when it is one's own fears that prevent them from doing so. Thus, the study of such ideal behaviors can prove frustrating and actually lessen the confidence of the "average" manager since they know, for some reason, that they cannot seem to engage in these ideal behaviors.

Few would disagree that delegating authority, reinforcing competence in others, or "relationships of trust and respect" are goals to strive for. How to reach those goals with an overly suspicious, overly critical, and negative subordinate is another question. Indeed, delegating authority to someone else if we are a perfectionist and dread not being in control is the real issue for management training programs. Implementing ideal managerial solutions is often fraught with, and frustrated by, fear-driven inhibitions.

It is these fears that good managers and good management training programs address. And it is developing confidence in people that superb managers and superb training programs encourage. (Discussing good common sense managerial practice, with the implication that those who don't engage in them are ineffective, can only lessen a participant's confidence, thus increasing their need for more management training.).

The Principles of Influencing Behavior

There is an alternative to management training, however, for the manager who is willing to master certain principles for guiding behavior. Politicians, teachers, marketing experts, advertisers, parents, labor leaders, and managers all influence the behavior of others in order to achieve their goals. An important goal of this book is to set forth the principles by which the behavior of other people is influenced. Consciously using these principles implies manipulation – the conscious shaping of people's behavior. Labeling a set of principles as manipulative, however, does not deny their validity. Moreover, a statement of principles is not an attempt to tell a manager how he *should* manage, but rather, how he *does* manage. The purpose here is not necessarily to describe the ideal; it is to describe reality.

As we have seen, most people, particularly most managers, seldom recognize the dramatic impact of their behavior on their subordinates. The same vice president who admits he is different under the new CEO will still minimize and, indeed, scoff at the supposed impact he has on people below him. We are often more readily aware of the influence other people have on us than we are of the influence we have on other people.

This book will attempt to reverse that orientation by specifying the principles that control a human being's behavior. A word of caution: As previously mentioned, the principles may seem manipulative. Moreover, managerial-subordinate interactions are complex. Although the principles themselves seem simple, their different combinations in real-life situations, the difficulty of evaluating actual behavior, and the manager's own emotional involvement and especially their fear in a given situation often make their use difficult. (This is always true in science; E=MC2 is quite simple, but building an atomic reactor based on this principle can be complex indeed).

Fortunately, managers are not expected to be thinking constantly of these principles as they deal with subordinates. They should apply the principles when a subordinate obviously, frequently, and repetitively displays an ineffective behavior pattern.

There are limits to a manager's ability to influence behavior. The manager is most effective in applying principles in situations that involve little emotion. Thus, for example, when dealing with indecisiveness on the part of a subordinate, the manager should think about and plan his own behavior, much as she/he would when dealing with less important matters, such as inventory. Such planning and detachment is impossible in an emotionally charged situation, such as might occur should a subordinate insult the manager in the presence of others. In this situation, the manager will inevitably respond spontaneously according to the immediate dictates of his own feelings, and well he should.

The Question of Sincerity

Inevitably, the question of sincerity arises when managers are expected to consciously plan their behavior so that its impact on their subordinate's behavior will be constructive and increase profits. It's as though thinking about what to say to someone makes one suspect. This is especially true if the way to influence people is spelled out in specific, concrete terms.

This writer assumes sincerity on the manager's part. If, for example, the manager is asked to compliment his subordinate, it is assumed that the manager will select an area in which she/he feels the subordinate actually deserves a compliment. Sincerity is self-revealing, and so is its opposite. If we think a man dresses poorly, it will do us little good to compliment him falsely on his good taste in clothes. There are too many subtle ways, especially tone of voice, in which our insincerity is revealed. Let the reader be aware that attempts to manipulate the behavior of others in ways that are not truly felt are often doomed to failure in most day-to-day managerial interactions. (This is not to say that manipulation is impossible, as the success of many politicians, actors, salespeople, etc. would attest.)

Evaluating Others

One important function of this book is to offer a manager the tools to more truly know others. To do so accurately and fairly, we should focus only on a person's frequent, repetitive behavior patterns. Each of us will do a few things "out of character" periodically. But these aberrant forays are not the stuff of realistic assessments, especially in the workplace, where frequent, repetitive behaviors have ample opportunity to show themselves.

If a person is frequently dependable, we would best describe them as dependable, even though they may occasionally miss a meeting or deadline. If a person is most often cheerful and enthusiastic, we would describe them as such, despite their periodic, but rare, complaining. Evaluating other people, consequently, is most accurately accomplished by describing them in terms of their frequent, repetitive behavior.

The Role of Fear in Behavior Patterns

The reader will see that fear is touched on frequently throughout this book. Why? Because its presence in driving behavior, especially inappropriate behavior, is so pervasive. What role should it play in our evaluations of others? An integral one. Why? Because we're going to evaluate people in terms of their *frequent, repetitive* behavior. And fear always leads to *excessive, inappropriate* behavior. And what meets our criterion of frequent, repetitive as precisely as excessive? One does not know another person nor can they describe them accurately, consequently, until and unless one knows that person's fears. Consider the following two examples:

"You know, I always get a little nervous when I have to make a presentation to a group of people." This statement is neither excessive nor inappropriate; hence it is not fear driven.

"I was at a party the other night. I never saw so many wimps in my life. I could have taken on any three of them at the same time." This behavior is excessive and inappropriate; hence it is fear driven.

Why Is Fear-Driven Behavior Excessive?

The goal of fear-driven behavior is to prevent some specific response (depending on the fear) from others; it might be criticism, confrontation, intimacy, being controlled, being seen as a failure, disappointing others, being ignored, being the center of attention, and so forth. But since the behavior that we fear others might engage in could occur at any time, we have to be on guard all the time. Thus does our fear-driven behavior become excessive and inappropriate.

In the foregoing example, is the person who sees everyone as a wimp intent on being seen as tough and strong? No, fear-driven behavior is intended to prevent some behavior in others. This individual is driven to avoid having others see him as weak and frightened (he may have been

15

ridiculed as a "sissy" in earlier years). And since someone could see him as weak and frightened at any time, he must convince others he is tough all the time; thus his "macho" behavior becomes excessive.

Evaluating Ourselves

Evaluating the fears of others is best done in terms of noting their excessive, inappropriate behavior patterns. But this does not apply to evaluating ourselves. Why? Because we rarely would admit to any of our behavior being excessive! If we accused the gentleman in the previous example of being a little too concerned with his physical prowess in the eyes of others, he would probably deny it, accurately arguing that, "You weren't there; you didn't see these people." After all, if we truly felt any of our behavior was excessive, we'd probably put an end to it.

How do we objectively assess our own fears? By first noting that fear also leads people to excessively avoid certain behaviors. Thus, a relevant exercise might consist of determining which managerial behaviors are most effective and appropriate, but which, at the same time, we have difficulty engaging in:

- Can we ask people around us, especially our subordinates, what our greatest shortcoming is? If not, maybe we fear being criticized.
- Do we select and promote competent, aggressive subordinates? If not, maybe we're overly competitive and fear being seen as a failure by others.
- Are we doing realistically critical evaluations of subordinates and giving them frequent feedback on their performance? If not, maybe we fear being disliked.
- Do we fire incompetent people readily? If not, maybe we fear confrontation.
- Are we appropriately warm, emotionally expressive, and sensitive to the needs of people around us? If not, maybe we fear doing so might make us feel vulnerable, leading to too much intimacy.

- Do we avoid making decisions for too long? Maybe this is another instance in which we are too fearful of being criticized.
- Do we avoid making demands on others, seeking and listening to the views of those around us, delegating authority, praising competence when it is quite apparent, being comfortable with ambiguity, persuasively arguing our point, taking risks, etc.? Maybe we should explore the behavior we're trying to prevent in others by our avoidance of these important managerial behaviors.

Thus, it is hoped that a greater understanding of the principles by which behavior is influenced will enhance our insight into our own behavior and that of the people with whom we interact frequently, thereby making us more effective managers. This may require rigorous self-diagnosis. It can be frightening. It can also be immensely rewarding. The manager will then be better able to adapt her/his own behavior such that its impact on subordinates will help develop a greater self-awareness and effectiveness on their part, an effectiveness that will be reflected in the increased profits of the organization.

Building Confidence

Above all, however, the goal of this book is to help the reader become comfortable with increasing the confidence of others, especially subordinates. Almost all managerial problems are driven by someone's fear, that of the manager or that of the subordinate.

Fearful people tend to do the wrong thing at the wrong time in the wrong way. Confident people tend to do the right thing at the right time in the right way. The latter have a most uncommon trait, common sense. Learning the principles of management is of little value when the fears preventing their implementation are not alleviated first. Few things, consequently, are as important as managers being held responsible for increasing the confidence of their subordinates. This is most effectively accomplished by increasing the likelihood of people being comfortable with liking and respecting themselves. As we shall see, many of us fear doing so.

The Sign of Confidence

How do we know when a person is truly confident? When they have a *wide response repertoire*; that is, a competent, confident person is capable of responding differently at different times with different people, each when appropriate.

People who are always indecisive are fear-driven; they have a narrow response repertoire. But individuals who are always decisive are also fear-driven; they, too, have a narrow response repertoire. The confident person is mostly decisive but is capable of being indecisive, of saying, "I don't know" or "I'd like to think about that a while" when this behavior is warranted. They have a wide response repertoire and can be decisive or indecisive, as appropriate.

The person who is always positive and enthusiastic is fear-driven. They have a narrow response repertoire, probably because they fear being disliked. The person who is always negative and critical is fear-driven. They have a narrow response repertoire, possibly because of a fear of intimacy, of being liked! The confident person has a wide response repertoire; they can be critical or positive, each when appropriate.

Summary

Few things will be more accurately reflected in the success and profits of an organization than the confidence of employees. As we shall see, however, there are strong forces, some realistic, some institutional, many interpersonal, *strengthening our fear of liking and respecting ourselves.* Why so many people are threatened by confidence in others is an issue that will be addressed (and, we hope, answered) periodically throughout this book. The people who are confident, who like and respect themselves, are the people who can focus on the needs of customers, who can take appropriate risks, who have an excellent results orientation, who are constructively competitive with those outside their organization and highly cooperative with fellow employees, who have the flexibility to adapt to changing environments, and who will speak up forcefully on moral and ethical issues. These are the productive people who can be trusted with responsibility and authority and who will contribute the most to the success of an organization.

SECTION 2

CLASSICAL ASSOCIATIONS

THE INFLUENCE OF PAIRINGS

What is the most direct way to influence someone's attitudes?

Should I express my feelings to subordinates?

How does a person change someone else's attitudes toward me?

How might one subordinate try to influence my attitudes toward
another subordinate?

Why don't people listen to me?

CHAPTER 3

INFLUENCING OTHERS WITH PAIRINGS: Part 1

Since managers are responsible for the behavior of subordinates, it would seem important that they know some of the principles by which attitudes, feelings, and behavior are influenced. Again, it should be noted that few things have as much impact on a person as the behavior of other people.

We will look at two approaches toward influencing changes in others – classical learning and operant learning. Classical learning involves the association of events or stimuli. These associations, or pairings, can have a profound impact on a person's attitudes and feelings toward situations, ideas, and other people. If done correctly, these pairings are unusually powerful, yet people are rarely aware of them.

Classical learning is one of the most effective and frequently used ways of influencing attitudes, opinions, beliefs, and behavior. Advertisers, politicians, and government officials, without being aware of it, frequently try to use classical learning principles to influence our behavior. For example, a person sitting passively in front of a television set and watching a series of ads concerning a particular toothpaste or detergent can be persuaded to decide to purchase the product.

Yet few people are really aware of the principles of pairings or associations, and fewer still use them consciously. Thus, ads and government pronouncements are often "hit or miss" in their effectiveness. To explain classical influences adequately, we must introduce and define two terms, "reinforcers" and "aversive stimuli".

Reinforcers

Most of the stimuli that we encounter in our daily lives are neutral and have little impact on our behavior. One class of stimuli has a noticeable impact on our behavior, however; those stimuli are called reinforcers. A reinforcer is any stimulus that a person seeks out, likes, and wants to experience. Hence, a reinforcer might be the sight of a beautiful woman, the sound of a Mozart concerto, the taste of delicious food, the feel of a fine fabric, or the smell of an exotic perfume.

One of the most important categories of reinforcers consists of auditory stimuli experienced in the form of "words". This type of communication is uniquely human. Hence, the phrase "You are doing a fine job" can be a strong reinforcer for which we subsequently will put forth a good deal of effort. Actions do not speak louder than words, words are actions, and their impact on our behavior can be enormous. (That's why uttering the word "fire" in a theatre is illegal; its impact on people is potentially chaotic and can cause injury and death.)

What people say to each other and how they say it probably has more influence than any other kind of interaction in an organization. Verbal interactions can make or break a company, from the articulation of CEO attitudes and philosophies to the salesperson's behavior with customers.

Aversive Stimuli

Aversive stimuli, those we attempt to avoid or stop have the opposite effect on our behavior. Aversive stimuli might include the sight of blood, the sound of a sudden, loud noise, the taste of some foods, the feel of running one's fingernail down a blackboard, the smell of a noxious odor. Again, verbal stimuli are among the most important in influencing behavior. For example, the phrase "If you continue with those negative attitudes, I'll have to fire you" directed by a manager to a subordinate can be strongly aversive.

Only Stimuli We Experience Directly are Important

There are two important reasons to be aware of the fact that stimuli must be directly experienced. First, there are many competent people whose abilities are not matched by their self-confidence; this is most often due to the fact that people's competence is rarely acknowledged in their own presence. The manager who speaks glowingly of his/her subordinate's abilities to everyone except the subordinate will often have a competent, but insecure, subordinate. Many misunderstandings between managers and subordinates occur because managers silently respond to their own inner positive feelings about their subordinate, while the subordinate responds – uncomfortably – to her manager's silence. (This is also a major problem in many personal relationships; we assume the other person must know how we feel.)

The employee's insecurity, or fear, will manifest itself in a destructive fashion. Why? Because fear always leads a person to engage in some behaviors excessively (e.g., constantly seeking reassurance) and to excessively avoid certain behaviors that are sometimes needed (e.g., decisiveness). Each excessive reaction always leads to detrimental, unrealistic effects.

[At this point, the reader is asked to try to express his/her admiration of someone's strength directly to that person, the more obvious the strength, the better. It will often be noted that the recipient of the praise might well be taken aback in an embarrassed "Aw, shucks" manner to the reinforcer. This tends to make the whole process uncomfortable for everyone; it is best, consequently, to move quickly on to another topic after expressing admiration for their asset.]

The second reason for emphasizing the sensory aspect of stimuli is more subtle, but just as important. At times, managers will discuss individuals who are not present. The only possible justification for this is the manager's desire to change the behavior of the person to whom they are talking.

The question "How do you think Jim is doing?" is relevant only insofar as the manager is attempting to change his subordinate's behavior in relation to Jim. Obviously, long conversations about Jim's shortcomings will have no impact on Jim if they occur in his absence. (Only stimuli that impact our senses can influence us.) What may be interesting gossip to a manager and his audience of the moment can also be destructive unless the manager's focus is on influencing his listener's behavior. This focus will only be evident if the manager, during a discussion of Jim's deleterious behavior, for example, intends to ask his listener (Jim's manager), "What are *you* going to do about it?"

[When people start talking to us about someone not present, we might periodically ask ourselves why they are doing so. Is this frequent, repetitive behavior on the speaker's part? Are they trying to change our attitudes in a positive or negative way toward the person being discussed? The vast majority of the time, unfortunately, a negative direction will be indicated.]

Influencing a Person's Likes and Dislikes

It is quite apparent that a stimulus can be a reinforcer to one person and an aversive stimulus to another. Alligators or snakes may be aversive to some people, neutral to others, and quite reinforcing to still others. Males and females often find different things reinforcing and/or aversive, as do people raised in a rural as opposed to an urban setting. The question confronting us is, "How does a neutral stimulus become a reinforcer or an aversive stimulus?"

Any stimulus paired or associated with a reinforcer becomes more reinforcing. Any stimulus paired or associated with an aversive stimulus becomes more aversive.

Advertisers try to convey to us that using a particular mouthwash, for example, leads to a kiss by the men or women of our dreams. Pictures of an automobile are often paired with the attention and admiration of all the neighbors. In everyday experience, a person who becomes ill while drinking orange juice will usually respond warily to future offers of orange juice, even after they have been told their illness was due to something they ate hours before.

Politicians taking the "high road" try to pair themselves with reinforcers: "I promise you a more efficient government that will allow us to lower taxes." As election time comes to a close, however, many politicians seek any road to victory, often using negative campaigning techniques, i.e., pairing their opponent with aversives: "My opponent played a large role in the fraud and waste of taxpayer funds."

Third Party Pairings

The most important pairings, however, take place during conversations. Frequently, we pair a stimulus (often another person) with what to our listener is a reinforcer or an aversive stimulus without any conscious awareness on the part of either party.

Suppose, for example, one person tells another, "George Towers has been criticizing your report to the rest of the staff." The speaker has paired the stimulus "George Towers" with a stimulus aversive to the listener. If George Towers walked into the room at that moment, he might well notice a cold reaction on the part of the recipient of this pairing. This is a typical third party pairing.

The opposite effect will take place, of course, if someone is paired with reinforcers. The statement, "You know, Mary Allen thinks you're the most effective salesperson in our company," increases the likelihood that the listener will respond favorably to Mary Allen when they next interact.

[The reader may wish to try pairing someone not present with a reinforcer or an aversive stimulus to someone who is present. For added drama, the reader might make the pairing to an individual when they know that the person not present will soon be arriving – then note the reaction of the person who 'caught' the pairing when the 'target' arrives.]

Difficulties Using Reinforcers

What type of third party pairing is used most frequently, a reinforcer or an aversive stimulus? Usually and unfortunately, it's an aversive stimulus. Why?

- First, because fear is so pervasive, there are usually a wide variety of aversives (as opposed to reinforcers) available that could be effectively used to influence others.
- Second, again because fear is so pervasive, people are more motivated and practiced in using aversives to influence others.
- Third, few of us want someone we like to like someone else; we want to reserve that reaction for ourselves. That often means we have to use aversives to lessen any positive feelings they may have for another party.
- Fourth, conversely, most of us often feel safer if other people dislike those whom we dislike. ("The enemy of my enemy is my friend.")
- Fifth, because most people don't like and respect themselves, they don't often respond well to reinforcers and are more readily impacted by aversives.

Pairings to Influence the Manager

Managers are often subjected to aversive pairings about one of their subordinates from another subordinate. This is especially true in the case of subordinates who are insecure or in highly competitive departments in which a "macho" manager encourages competition between and among subordinates. These types of aversive pairings are also indicative of a manager being too critical, thus fostering a "cover your ass" environment.

If aversive pairings are being used frequently and repetitively by employees, then the manager must be listening closely, even sympathetically, to them, thus encouraging people to use them; and, indeed, some managers do like to see subordinates angry with each other. This, of course, ensures a lack of cooperation and constructive communication among subordinates.

- When should the manager ignore third party aversive pairings? When they're infrequent and/or when they're all coming from only one or two people.
- When should the manager be concerned about the third party complaints of subordinates? When they're frequent and repetitive and coming from a number of people about a number of their colleagues.
- Whose behavior should the manager be concerned with in the latter instance? His/her own.

[The reader might wish to pair a colleague with aversives to their manager and then note their manager's reaction. Does their superior give them "short-shrift" or encourage elaboration? The reader might also consider the frequency with which people pair others with aversives to their manager; an objective consideration of their manager's response to such pairings might well be in order. To be fair, the reader might also consider the frequency with which colleagues pair their manager with aversives to the reader, and how the reader reacts when they do.]

Managers should pay close attention to the aversive stimuli used in aversive pairings by subordinates because the speaker is really indicating what she or he feels the manager dislikes and/or is insecure about. In many instances, they are right! The subordinate, for example, who tells his manager that another subordinate "makes too many mistakes" may believe that his manager finds being criticized for poor performance in his department quite aversive. Similarly, pairing another subordinate with not being a team player may indicate that the speaker feels his manager finds independent behavior by a subordinate aversive.

Reinforcing or Aversive: To Whom?

The universal goal of making these sounds we call words is to influence the people to whom we are talking. Too often, we are frustrated when trying to reach that goal. A major reason for our inability to influence people (thus, for a manager's inability to influence subordinates) is that we don't focus on who they are, where their fears and frustrations lay, what they truly like or dislike. Instead, we try to influence people under the assumption, generally incorrect, that what is reinforcing and/or aversive to us must be reinforcing and/or aversive to them.

Evaluating and thereby knowing who a subordinate really is--and then adapting to the knowledge gained from that evaluation--separates the average manager from the superb manager. Because of the almost universal assumption that "what is reinforcing to me should be reinforcing to everyone," managers too often pair others with stimuli that elicit the opposite reaction of what was intended.

Consider the following comments by a director of sales: "We just hired a fellow, Clayton Smith, for the area sales manager position that was open. Clayton looks like a real comer. He's a young, aggressive guy who set sales records at Ryerton Manufacturing three years running. I think Clayton is going to move up fast in this company." Addressed to a profit-oriented company president, these pairings may be quite reinforcing and will probably lead the president to look favorably on Clayton Smith when they meet. The same comments made to another area sales manager who is highly competitive and/or insecure, could well have the opposite effect.

Virtually all of the joys and pains of life come from external sources, particularly from the behavior of other people. Developing greater sensitivity to other people and to our impact on those people *from their point of view* is an essential goal for any individual, especially for a manager who is being held accountable for the behavior of subordinates.

Consider this example: "I'm seen as an unusually competent consultant. In fact, I'm often asked by CEOs of multi-billion dollar corporations for advice and guidance. I'm sought after by many organizations to give speeches and seminars. Frankly, I have a good deal of influence in business circles." Who is this reinforcing to? The speaker. Who is this aversive to? The new female employee the manager is trying to impress. To assume that what's reinforcing to us must also be reinforcing to everyone else often makes us our own executioners.

[The reader might wish to think about a phrase that would be most reinforcing to hear from their boss. Is this phrase reinforcing to other subordinates of this manager? Are there colleagues who would react with indifference or even hostility to the same phrase ("He's such a phony!")? Every group of people is diverse; this diversity will be recognized and responded to appropriately by highly competent managers.]

Why do people react to me as they do?

Can I deal effectively with more than one person at a time?

Isn't internal competition good, especially if we reward the winners?

Why are some people's ideas always being attacked?

How do managers' fears influence their team and the company?

CHAPTER 4

INFLUENCING OTHERS WITH PAIRINGS: Part 2

Who We Are to Others

Some readers may object to the assumed impact of pairings, feeling it depends on who is using them, who is doing the speaking. They are absolutely correct. Since *any* stimulus paired with a reinforcer or an aversive stimulus becomes reinforcing or aversive, it stands to reason that the person who frequently uses reinforcers in their interactions with others will pair themselves with the same reinforcers; thus, they will become attractive and be sought out as someone who is liked. Conversely, the person who frequently uses aversive stimuli, even though they are pairing something or someone else with them, will also pair themselves with the aversives and become aversive to others. In short, you are to others what you use to influence them, reinforcers or aversives.

The speaker who said, "John Akerman thinks you're the best salesperson in our company," is not only pairing John Akerman with a reinforcer, she is also pairing herself with the same reinforcer. By using this reinforcer, the speaker has increased the probability that the listener will like her and will seek her out for further interactions. She has become a reinforcer to the listener.

On the other hand, the speaker who said, "George Towers is trying to discredit you with the rest of the staff," is pairing himself with the same

33

aversive stimulus he associates with George Towers. The listener may "thank" the speaker for giving him this news, but he does not like him the more for it. Indeed, if the speaker paired the names of a few more people (and himself in the process) with aversive stimuli, the listener would soon try to avoid him, that is, react to him as he would to any aversive stimulus (this is one reason the messenger so often met a terminal fate).

Being required to interact with several subordinates at the same time greatly complicates the manager's role. By focusing his/her attention on the proper pairings for one subordinate, the manager can inadvertently have a negative impact on another subordinate.

The Difficulty of Dealing with More than One Person Simultaneously

Sam is the president of a company. His favorite employee and heir-apparent, Bill, likes Sam's attention and the status he gets from his relationship with Sam. Indeed, Bill too often goes out of his way to interact with Sam, sometimes about trivial things that don't require Sam's attention. Since Bill's behavior is excessive, we know that it's fear-driven, in this case it's Bill's fear of being insignificant to Sam.

Now suppose Mary joins the company as a new vice president and within several months has won Sam's confidence. Over a two-week period Sam makes the following comments in Bill's presence:

> "That was an excellent idea, Mary, really innovative."
> "That is an important issue; let's hold off our discussion until Mary gets here."
> "Mary, could we get together for a few hours after this meeting?"
> "Mary, I'll take you out to the airport tonight; there are some things I'd like to go over with you."
> "Refer any questions on that matter to Mary while I'm away next week."

Subsequently, Sam cannot understand why Bill suddenly turns on him and fights ideas he had originally endorsed. When his 'Mary focused' behavior is pointed out to him, he protests, correctly, that none of these comments reflects badly on Bill. He also denies any change in his feelings toward Bill, giving as proof the fact that he has, within the last two days, recommended Bill as his replacement to the Board of Directors.

Yet, every comment referring to Mary not only has paired Mary with aversive stimuli to Bill, but also has paired the speaker, Sam, with the same aversive stimuli. Thus, Sam himself has become aversive to Bill, as evidenced by Bill's sudden opposition to Sam's ideas.

How should managers act in meetings? Neutrally, using reinforcers or aversives as little as possible. They should focus on facts, statistics, and data. As we have seen repeatedly, different things are reinforcing and/or aversive to each person. The only really effective time to reinforce or reprimand someone is when you're alone with that person. To do so in groups is dangerous and often destructive.

Who Gets Paired With Aversives

In the foregoing example, there is little doubt that Bill will soon be pairing Mary with aversives to Sam, as he will anyone else who might gain the president's favorable attention. If these pairings are successful, enormous harm can be done to the company, especially the fact that highly competent people can be looked on unfavorably by the president and leave the company. Indeed, it is the competent people who are most likely to pose a threat to fearful people in an organization, hence subjected to the most aversive pairings by those fearful employees. This is one reason managers must cut off aversive pairings by subordinates. Managers must make their own judgments about the competence of people. Anyone who thinks they will not be influenced by pairings is doing everyone, including themselves, a disservice. And those managers who encourage bickering and backbiting will be unable to build effective, results-oriented teams.

[The reader might try to pair someone with a reinforcer on one occasion and an aversive to the same person on another occasion. Noting the listener's reaction to both types of pairings can prove interesting. Which pairing does the listener respond more favorably to, i.e., with more emotion and rapt attention? If the listener is your manager and he/she responds more favorably to the aversive pairing, you might want to consider updating your resume.]

Acknowledging That Special Employee

There is little doubt that most people would respond favorably to a superior singling them out for special consideration (reinforcer), especially in front of their colleagues. Yet, these same reinforcers may be quite aversive to others in the audience, a fact that will eventually result in animosity directed toward the "special" employee, usually in the form of aversive pairings.

Managers have long known that punishing people in front of others is taboo. But reinforcing someone in front of others can be just as destructive. Telling Alice she is a most beautiful woman may be quite reinforcing to her, but hardly to the speaker's wife if she happens to be present. Telling your youngest son he's really athletic and you can't wait to watch him play in the big game may be quite reinforcing to him, but somewhat destructive of his brother's confidence if it is done in front of him.

Consider these comments by a CEO in handing out an award for best sales performance in front of the sales force: "John has done an outstanding job. John's performance is an example that could help all of us focus our efforts and develop more determination and perseverance in the face of obstacles. John has also shown us what dependability is and how we could all focus more effectively on our customers' needs. John, why don't you come up here and say a few words." What's the impact on the rest of the audience? A few are proud of John, more couldn't care less, and *most dislike him*. Indeed, the subsequent pairings heard around the company went something like this: "With John's quota, my ten-year-old could've set records." "John really had a windfall on his accounts." "John ought to share his award with Bill; he did most of the groundwork in John's territory."

Is it possible to find something that is reinforcing to everyone at the same time? Possibly, but not likely. And if we think something is truly reinforcing to everyone, it's usually so trite that its impact is minimal. Managers are paid to know what is reinforcing and aversive to their subordinates. That each person is so different is the main reason we have managers; they have the flexibility to treat each person differently AND appropriately.

Reinforcers, like aversives, should be expressed in one-on-one interactions, privately and away from others. Then the reinforcers used can be truly meaningful and motivating to the employee. (If such things as sales contests truly motivated all employees, we'd probably need far fewer managers.)

[The reader might wish to consider their true feelings when someone else is being given an award or public recognition. Better, the reader might wish to give someone a strong reinforcer in front of several other people and note reactions, including the sarcastic humor.

The author has been frequently (and viciously) attacked in many seminars for suggesting the idea that some people are not especially pleased at recognition when it is given to others. At the risk of being labeled rigid, the author bravely stands firm.]

Emotions Versus Facts

It is important to note that pairings can take precedence over rational considerations, including the facts or logic of a situation. All organizations experience this phenomenon frequently.

There are positive and negative aspects to any idea, any situation, any proposal put forth. If the individual making the proposal is aversive to us, our attention will automatically focus on the negative aspects of her ideas, since the ideas are paired with the individual presenting them. If, conversely, an individual is a strong reinforcer to us, our attention will focus on the positive aspects of her ideas.

If two people dislike each other intensely, meetings will be frequently disrupted by their attacking each other's ideas. A manager, on the other hand, can almost ensure a subordinate's complete agreement with his proposal if, just before a meeting on the proposal, he tells the subordinate, "You've done such an outstanding job, I've recommended you for the job in you wanted in London. I told your boss you really deserved it." The listener is now more likely to focus on the positive aspects of the speaker's proposal in the meeting because of the strong reinforcer pairings that just occurred, even though the pairings do not objectively reflect on the proposal itself.

The reactions of subordinates to their managers are determined, to a large extent, by whether the manager has paired herself/himself with stimuli aversive or reinforcing to the subordinate. An indecisive, overly detailed, micro-manager (probably because he fears criticism), for example, can become an intense aversive stimulus to a fast-paced, impulsive subordinate. Such a manager incurs the subordinate's dislike by pairing himself frequently with such phrases as, "Why don't we wait for more information before we go ahead," or "Let's hold off on that until George gives us his input." To a cautious, indecisive subordinate, however, this manager is, with the same statements, probably pairing himself with reinforcers.

In the former instance, if the manager does this too often and is aversive enough, his ideas will frequently be opposed by the impulsive, now frustrated, subordinate. In the latter case, if the manager is reinforcing enough, his ideas will be fully supported by the cautious subordinate, regardless of the content of the ideas. The impulsive subordinate will probably leave the company while more cautious individuals are sought out, hired, and promoted by the manager. Thus, the manager surrounds himself with a cautious cadre, each of whom is comfortable with the others and none of whom has a sense of urgency nor a desire to change anything. *An appraisal of a manager's behavioral impact on others is absolutely crucial before managerial responsibilities are assigned.*

Pairing Products and Services with Reinforcers

Many companies train their sales personnel to associate their product with rational, logical factors, such as low price and high quality. A more individualized approach is called for, as we've seen, since few people are influenced by these rational, logical factors. Consider the following two examples of pairings by computer salesmen to an ambitious vice president of administration in a large company:

> Salesman: If you buy our IT system, we will give you the highest quality performance at a price level that will save your company a good deal of money.
>
> Salesman: I should warn you that with our IT system you will become the central point of your company, since all the important information in the company will have to go through your department.

Again, the most important factor in selling (and managing) successfully is knowing who your audience is, what is reinforcing and what is aversive to them. Too much time is spent trying to influence people, too little on understanding who they are. As a result, most of our efforts to influence others are inefficient, miss the target, and often require back-pedaling. Interviewing skills, consequently, are essential in any area of life, but especially to the manager. These skills force us to focus on the other person, hence they should be the first step in virtually any interaction.

Doesn't everyone like compliments?

Do my aversive pairings reflect my fears?

What pairings will most diminish my confidence?

How do I know if I like and respect myself?

Can I ignore the influence of others, especially my boss?

CHAPTER 5

DEVELOPING EFFECTIVE PAIRINGS: Part 1

The Wide Range of Reinforcers and Aversive Stimuli

The greatest *intellectual* difficulty in using reinforcers and aversive stimuli effectively lies in deciding what truly is a reinforcer or an aversive stimulus to an individual. The fact is, *any stimulus can be either a reinforcer or an aversive stimulus* depending on the person and the situation. The range of reinforcers and aversive stimuli is virtually limitless, often self-destructive, and rarely compatible with reality. If the manager feels the principles set forth here do not work, it will more often than not be because an incorrect analysis has been made as to what is or is not a reinforcer or an aversive stimulus in a given individual.

Pain as a reinforcer is not an uncommon phenomenon in human behavior. This is particularly true in the sexual area, in which case the people are called masochistic. Most studies show that some people can be quite physically aggressive in sexual behavior. If the pain to their partner resulting from this aggressiveness is interspersed (paired) with words of love, devotion, and an orgasm, pain can then become a reinforcer. This will be especially true if the partner is in need of a good deal of affection; that is, words of love and devotion are strong reinforcers to her/him. The purpose here is not to titillate the reader, but rather, to show that common assumptions about reinforcers and aversives are often fraught with error.

An example: Attention from his mother is a strong reinforcer to Bobby. The child only elicits his mother's attention, however, by engaging in destructive behavior. This destructive behavior elicits both a negative emotional reaction and the attention the child so desperately seeks. This pairing may well result in a negative emotional reaction from a female becoming a strong reinforcer to Bobby, a reinforcer that may remain with him for the rest of his life.

A father is a strong reinforcer to his daughter. Her pleas for his time and attention are met with periodic rejections and reinforcement pairings: "I can't play with you now, honey, but Sunday just you and I will go for a ride in the car." "I won't be able to come home for your birthday party, but I'll get you a surprise gift you'll really love." Soon signs of rejection become reinforcing to the girl. In later years, she has little time for the individual who sends her flowers and candy along with his pleas for a date, but she actively pursues the young man who rejects her with such comments as, "I won't be able to take you to the dance Friday." By rejecting her the young man is actually pairing himself with stimuli strongly reinforcing to the girl.

All of these examples are meant to illustrate how useless and even misleading it is to assume that a wide range of reinforcers or aversive stimuli means the same thing to everyone. "Atta boys" may be loved by some, completely neutral to many, and actually aversive to more than a few people.

[The reader is encouraged to look back at some "failed" relationships and try to objectively determine what was truly reinforcing or aversive to the other party. Should you have seen that earlier? Could you have handled the situation more effectively?]

Making Reinforcers Into Aversives

Nothing is reinforcing to all people and everything (including death) is reinforcing to some people. Making what should be reinforcing, such as a compliment, aversive is most often accomplished via a "but" or "however" pairing. This is done by pairing compliments with aversive stimuli. Consider the impact of the following four comments ("but" pairings) by a new manager to his subordinate over a two-week period:

- "You did an excellent job on that report, Jim, but I wish you'd pay more attention to organizing your material; it was really sloppy."
- "I was really delighted that you got an order from Micron Company, although the order you got was much smaller than I'd anticipated."
- "That was an excellent presentation, Jim, but it would be a lot better if you didn't talk with your hand in front of your mouth so much and you really slur too many words."
- "You're one of the best salesmen we have, Jim, even though you have an awful lot to learn."

Soon the subordinate finds his manager's compliments of little value and, when he receives one, waits for the "other shoe" to drop. To others, he might well describe his manager as "insincere" or "a phony". (During a seminar on giving feedback, the participants were told that violent consequences would attend any use of "but" or "however". In presenting his feedback, one participant said to the recipient, "Earl, you have excellent analytical skills; on the other hand...").

One of the favorite pairings of CEOs in their inspirational year-end speeches: "Everybody did a great job this year, but let's see if we can do even better next year!"

[Because the reader is now familiar with "but" pairings, they are encouraged to jump in with a lively emotional reinforcer just before the "but". Your manager: "You know, that comment you made at the meeting was good, but ..." Your quick interruption: "Hey! Thank you very much! Your opinion is really important to me and I can't tell you how much that means to me!" Only the most vicious of managers would continue with a negative after you've paired yourself with those reinforcers.]

Fear Drives Destructive Aversive Pairings

Managers who pair compliments with aversive stimuli are often highly competitive people, so competitive that genuine accomplishments by their subordinates are aversive, rather than reinforcing, to them. They are driven by a strong underlying fear of being seen as a failure, especially in comparison to others, especially their subordinates. They are quick to punish failure and reluctant to praise or even acknowledge accomplishments by their subordinates. This is one of the strongest reasons for not promoting the best salesperson to a managerial position; their competitiveness may motivate them constructively in sales contests, but destructively in managerial interactions. Their fear of acknowledging anyone else's success means they are unlikely to fulfill a basic responsibility of any manager, building the confidence of those who report directly to them.

It is quite important that one look closely at the fears of their potential manager before accepting a position under him/her. Indeed, the success or failure of any long-term manager-subordinate relationship will be determined, to a large extent, by the fears of those involved. If a manager fears confrontation, subordinates may feel they are not getting the support they need in their interactions with senior management. If a manager fears being disliked, it is doubtful their direct reports will hear meaningful feedback, hence their opportunity to grow personally will be minimal.

One of the most destructive and yet pervasive areas of aversive pairings involves sexist and racial issues. Boys usually play with boys and girls with girls. Their comfort with each other is not only due to familiarity, but also to the frequent "other-sex" aversive pairings experienced. "Girls are just a bunch of sissies." "Boys are such dorks." These aversive pairings increase a person's fears when interacting with members of the opposite sex. These fears often continue into adulthood and are quite prevalent in movies and television shows. Thus, they are also frequently accompanied by same-sex bonding and camaraderie. (One sexist view, however, seems true to the author: Women are probably less inhibited using reinforcers, men using aversives.)

44

Aversive racial pairings are quite common because they play so readily to the fears of people, both reflecting and encouraging those fears (even giving examples here would be too inflammatory). Suffice it to say, racial (and religious) conflicts will continue until the leaders of one group start pairing members of other groups with reinforcers, rather than aversives, a highly unlikely prospect.

[Evaluating one's own fears is difficult. However, readers are encouraged to think about those behaviors they fear most from others. Then consider the pairings you might use because of those fears:

- Do you, for example, fear being seen as weak and pair yourself with frequent "macho" kinds of things?
- Do you fear members of the opposite sex and subtly pair them with aversives?
- Do you fear being controlled and pair authority figures with aversives?
- Do you fear being seen as a failure and pair yourself with "great feats" reinforcers?
- Do you fear being alone and pair shy people who don't seek you out with aversives?
- Do you fear criticism and pair performance reviews with aversives (waste of time)?

In sum, what aversive pairings do you use and what fears might you be guarding against by using them?]

Watch Your Audience

Again, the admonition of knowing your audience cannot be emphasized too often. Consider the following comment to two different managers about one of their subordinates: "Jim Camden is kind of a meek, shy person." One manager fears being insignificant to people and likes people needing her, hence she enjoys and is quick to help subordinates in trouble; she has a "social worker" philosophy toward running her department. She is likely to seek out Jim Camden, to interact frequently with him, to provide him with aid and support. This is because "meek, shy" people who need her help are reinforcing to this manager and the abovementioned comment has paired Jim Camden with reinforcers.

The second manager, however, looks for independence and an aggressive initiative in her subordinates. The same comment has increased the probability she will prod, push, and eventually fire Jim Camden. The same statement, therefore, can elicit opposite reactions from two different people.

Likewise, it is wrong to assume that a chief executive officer always finds profits strongly reinforcing. Many chief executives find firing an incompetent vice president (fear of confrontation) quite aversive; this may well supersede the reinforcing influence of profits on their actions, a fact that quickly leads to mediocrity at the top and a philosophy that rapidly permeates the organization. Indeed, many chief executives find the admiration and respect of incompetent subordinates far more reinforcing than increased corporate profits. Also, the indifference or even disdain of competent people directed at an incompetent CEO may be so aversive to that CEO that few such employees are to be found in the company, even after profits have fallen precipitously.

The assumption that profits are the most intense reinforcer to a chief executive officer is misleading, unrealistic, and often destructive to an organization. (The fact that most Board members are beholden to the CEO, hence won't take corrective action, is probably the weakest link in most corporations.)

Effectiveness with people requires us to look at our audience, not ourselves. If you dislike Jim Roberts and are trying to convince someone that Jim is no good, you're likely to say something such as, "Jim Roberts is a jerk." This may be aversive to Jim Roberts (and you), but may have little impact on anyone else. Saying to someone, on the other hand, "Jim Roberts thinks you're a jerk," may be more effective.

[The two most influential people in a person's life are typically their spouse and their boss. Evaluating them should be an ongoing process. Accuracy in this area is crucial for happiness in this life.]

"You" Pairings

One of the most potentially damaging or beneficial pairings is what we might term the "you" pairing. This occurs when the speaker pairs an individual directly ("you") with an aversive stimulus or a reinforcer. Thus, we can make the one thing a person can never escape, themselves, reinforcing or aversive to themselves.

Parents, for example, can do irreparable harm by bombarding their children with these aversive pairings: "You are such a sloppy child." "Can't you do a better job than that?" "Why are you so frightened all the time?" "You are such an ignorant child; why do you say such stupid things!" Even adult children are often inundated with these pairings by parents who fear being insignificant to their now independent offspring. "You never call anymore." "You have no idea of the hardships we had to go through for you." "Don't you have any concern for anyone but yourself?" The recipient of these pairings will pay a heavy toll in their confidence level.

As mentioned, one of the major goals of a manager (and everyone) should be to alleviate a person's fear of liking and respecting themselves. Few experiences are more destructive and work against this goal than being subjected to frequent "you-aversive" pairings, especially from a manager (or an institution: "You are original sin.").

Depressingly few managers are reinforced by confidence and competence in their subordinates. The defensive salesman says to his manager, "I'm a good salesman." The manager replies, "Maybe, but you've got a lot of growing up to do. Believe me, you have a long way to go before you stop making mistakes like that time at Tech Corp. last year." The manager might have said, "You really are! And I appreciate and admire your dependability with customers, and so do they."

A machinist was so skilled at his trade that he started his own business. It grew and he was soon managing 20 other machinists. He would periodically walk into his plant, pick out his best machinist, literally push him aside, and "show him how a good machinist really works". These episodes always involved a number of "you aren't nearly as good as you think" pairings. Competence in a subordinate was intensely aversive to this highly competitive entrepreneur who feared being looked down on by others, despite the fact that he could increase his personal income on the basis of that competence in others.

Managers who use "you-aversive stimuli" pairings are not only usurping the confidence of their subordinates, they are also hurting profits. Conversely, the manager who tells his subordinate, "You are certainly adept at that," when a good job has been done, is helping both the individual and his company. These "you-reinforcer" pairings are an all too rare phenomenon in private industry, although the opportunities to use them are abundant.

If a bad job was done on a report, the manager must react accordingly. But the pairing should involve the report, not the person. "This report is lousy" is far better than "You really did a lousy job on this report." Conversely, when the job was well done, it is far more productive to say, "You did an excellent job on this report" rather than "This report is excellent." An unusually competent manager might even say, "You did an excellent job on this report. Frankly, you did a better job than I could have done." Will the person hearing this feel good about themselves? Will they be more confident? What's wrong with that? There must be something wrong since it happens so infrequently.

[It is hoped that every reader will now try some "you-reinforcer" pairings on people in their work or personal inner circle. It is a most crucial response to have in our repertoire, one that should be emitted when appropriate, and far more frequently than most of us do use them. Again, because of the "shock" such pairings cause in the recipient, a quick change of topics is necessary.]

Liking and Respecting Ourselves

Let us state six related principles, then elaborate on them more fully in subsequent paragraphs:

1. Fear is the cause of most problems in the workplace (and in personal relations).
2. Most fears center on the behavior of other people.
3. If we truly and sincerely like and respect ourselves, then the behavior of other people becomes much less important to us, thus diminishing many of our fears.
4. Other people do not want their behavior to be less important to us and often feel threatened and frustrated when they sense this is happening.
5. These fears and frustrations lead people to engage in excessive behaviors that often have the effect of compromising and undermining our liking and respect for ourselves.
6. These conflicting forces are continually present throughout our lives.

Now, let us elaborate:

1. Fear (ours or those of others) causes most of our problems. Fear leads people to engage in excessive behaviors and to excessively avoid behaviors that should be periodically engaged in. The very definition of excessive indicates the person's behavior is straying from what is appropriate and realistic. Thus do problems in interactions with others arise.

2. Virtually all common fears center on the potential behavior of other people, be it our fear of criticism, rejection, being disliked, intimacy, confrontation, being controlled, and so forth. Indeed, the question of why a person "does that" is not truly answered until we determine what potential behavior in others is involved. The person who bogs down in details does it to avoid mistakes. But why are they so intent on avoiding

49

mistakes? Because mistakes might lead people to criticize them. The intensely ambitious person does not fear failure; the intensely ambitious person fears *being seen by others* as a failure.

Business consists essentially of interpersonal interactions. While technology can be terribly frustrating, the frequency and consequences of people-interactions trump the importance of any other workplace problem. Indeed, 90% of firings are caused by personality factors; apparently it is easier to teach someone how to carry out a technical operation than it is to teach an overly negative, critical employee to be positive and enthusiastic in their dealings with others.

3. If we don't like and respect ourselves, other people's behavior takes on much more importance to us. How can we depend on ourselves, someone we don't like and respect? Not liking ourselves, consequently, leads us to depend on others to help us with the myriad of problems encountered in this world. This means the behavior of others takes on much more importance to us. Thus do we learn to anticipate with fear what others think of us and how they might react to us.

Because so few people truly like and respect themselves, one of the most pervasive fears in our society is the fear of "being alone"; apparently many of us don't like the company we're keeping when we're alone.

4. People don't want to be less important to others. Who wants to be less important to someone in their inner circle? Every time we mouth these things we call words, we are intent upon influencing others. If we feel our efforts with others have minimal impact, we can't reach our goal of making others think and feel what we want them to think and feel, we can't make them behave the way we know they should behave. This is frustrating.

5. So people who truly like and respect themselves can elicit frustration and anger from those in their inner circle. And this anger almost always leads to behaviors from others that teach us frequently, but subtly, to fear liking and respecting ourselves (through "you-aversive"

50

pairings and other common and frequent experiences to be discussed later).

For example, my subordinate, because she doesn't like and respect herself, leans heavily on me for guidance and direction. Since I don't like and respect myself, I enjoy her dependence and my dominant position. As she learns to respect herself, however, her need for my guidance diminishes. This is threatening to me, hence I start becoming more critical of her work (using more "you-aversive" pairings in the process). Am I conscious of my desire to diminish her new-found confidence? No.

6. This is a lifelong process, not a one-time situation. Whether we do or do not like and respect ourselves will not deter people in our inner circle, let alone our boss, from wanting to be important and influential in our lives and becoming frustrated when their influence is diminished. Even the withdrawn manager who "hides" in his office is intent upon influencing his subordinates – to stay away from him.

Learning to like and respect oneself is a never-ending process, consequently, because there are *always* people with whom one must interact who are threatened by such confidence. To think one will not be influenced by such interactions is naive and self-destructive; this is why we must accept the law of inertia and be aware of the impact others can and do have on us.

The Law of Inertia

The law of inertia, arguably the most proven law in all of science, says that any object in the universe remains in its present state unless acted upon by EXTERNAL forces. If we apply this principle to human behavior, we would conclude that the external forces influencing our thinking stem primarily from the behavior of other people (a manager being an unusually important external force in our lives).

People's influence on us, especially those in our inner circle, is quite pervasive. This is difficult for many people to accept. We all want to feel we control our own thinking, feelings, and behavior. But accepting the fact that the people with whom we interact frequently and repetitively influence our thinking and feelings is merely accepting reality. Accepting the influence of others also makes us more effective in changing our focus from, "What does this person think of me" to a much more constructive, "What do I think of this person and the kind of influence they're having on me?"

But we must also remember that we are an external force acting on those within our inner circle. Thus we must especially focus on the impact they'll have on us in the critical area of enhancing or diminishing our ability to like and respect ourselves (e.g., "you" pairings). Our never-ending task is to increase the frequency with which those in our inner circle increase our confidence through their constructive behaviors with us. (The specifics of how to do so will be discussed later).

But shouldn't we focus first on helping others develop confidence? If you are flying with a small child and the oxygen masks drop in front of you, every authority will caution you to put yours on first, before you help your child. This seemingly self-centered orientation is appropriate for obvious reasons. Similarly, it would be very difficult for someone who is not confident in a given area to increase the confidence of others in that area. Fear plays an overwhelming role in the lives of those who lack confidence, a role that often prevents them from being helpful. The reader's first obligation, consequently, is to build and ensure their own confidence before assuming responsibility for the confidence of others.

The few people who truly are comfortable with themselves are reasonable people who think objectively, calmly, have reasonable expectations, are not overly concerned with the reactions of people, and sincerely treat others with respect and equality. We should always strive to be one of those people, not only for ourselves, but also for the welfare of those around us.

Dealing effectively with the individual fears of people directly is too formidable a task for anyone, including a manager. But all fears in an individual could be greatly alleviated, although not eliminated, if the manager created an atmosphere in which liking and respecting oneself was not only acceptable, but encouraged and reinforced. No managerial responsibility is more important than this.

Readers are encouraged to consider those in their inner circle in relation to who really wants others, especially the reader, to like and respect themselves and who does not. This can frequently be determined by the frequency of the "you" reinforcer or "you" aversive pairings they give out. Often, however, it's those closest to us who are most easily threatened by our confidence.]

Reinforcers or Aversives?

An important question must be asked, however: What is potentially more influential in increasing a person's confidence, a reinforcer pairing or an aversive one? Consider the two following construcing pairings:

> "If you like and respect yourself, other people will like and respect you."
> "If you don't like and respect yourself, other people won't like and respect you."

Most people prefer the first pairing because it uses a reinforcer and, by definition, we all like those. But if we fear liking and respecting ourselves, then the second pairing probably has a greater impact (even if it does pair the speaker with the aversive).

Aversives are generally more powerful than reinforcers in influencing people; that's probably the reason they're used more frequently and the reason fear is so prevalent. (Indeed, as we shall see, a reinforcer can best be defined as a stimulus that alleviates a person's fear, albeit, temporarily. This will be covered in more detail later.)

It should be recognized, however, that the use of aversives, as is true of any principle, can be appropriate on occasion, especially if the behavior targeted is itself fear-driven. The fear of respecting ourselves is fear-driven and solidified by the frequent use of aversives in this area. Hence, powerful aversives may be needed to counteract those original destructive forces. So an effective pairing may well be, "If you don't like and respect yourself, you're a fool and you'll be giving everyone else a lot of control over your life." (This pairing is especially effective, because it is so true.)

So the use of aversives is important in this area; like all aversives, it may help diminish a person's likelihood of doing what they do (not liking and respecting themselves). But, as mentioned previously, the use of aversives doesn't increase the likelihood of any specific behaviors. So both aversives and reinforcers should be used, aversives to lessen the person's destructive behavior, reinforcers to guide them to, and strengthen, constructive behaviors.

[Readers might try some of these "like and respect" yourself pairings, especially with people they admire. Both reinforcer and aversive pairings should be tried. Which are you most comfortable using? Which do you feel is more effective in building the person's confidence?

These pairings are crucial and are in the reader's best interest to learn and use frequently, since those in their inner circle who fear liking and respecting themselves probably account for most of the problems in the reader's life. After all, the fears of those in your inner circle, even if you don't share them, will eventually be visited upon you.]

I'm inhibited when trying to be emotionally expressive; is this a
problem?

If someone won't cooperate with me, what does that indicate?

If sales drop in a given territory, what should I look at first?

What should one be most concerned about in a new job?

CHAPTER 6

DEVELOPING EFFECTIVE PAIRINGS: Part 2

Emotional Reactions as Reinforcers and Aversives

Some of the strongest reinforcers and aversive stimuli involve tone of
voice and facial and body gestures. Tone of voice, the music of
interpersonal interactions, and body language reflect the feelings of the
speaker and are often far more intense reinforcers and aversive stimuli
than are in the actual words being used. The phrase, "That's pretty good",
enthusiastically spoken, has quite a different impact than the same phrase
spoken in an unenthusiastic monotone. To return to an earlier example: A
compliment on a man's tie will be enthusiastic when the tie is truly a
reinforcer to the speaker. If, on the other hand, the real reinforcer
controlling the speaker is "being liked by the other person", then the
compliment will not be genuinely enthusiastic – a difference the listener
will quickly notice in the speaker's tone of voice. This is the primary
reason "sincerity" is so important and manipulation is so difficult for most
of us. People are quite perceptive in responding to slight nuances, and the
same words may be reinforcing or aversive, depending on the inflection
and the gestures accompanying them.

By the very nature of their responsibilities, managers are required to
periodically pair themselves with aversive stimuli. They have to, for
example, refuse pay raises or bonuses, point out mistakes, give critical
feedback, and see that employees conform to the rules and regulations of

the organization. To overcome and counteract this inherent disadvantage, it is necessary for managers to periodically pair themselves with stimuli that are reinforcing to subordinates. The alternative is that the manager will become an intense aversive stimulus to his/her subordinates. Lack of communication (the subordinate avoids his superior) and time wasted in bickering, backbiting, complaining, sabotage, and strikes are sometimes the consequence of such a situation. If managers were as quick to use reinforcers when dealing with subordinates as they are to use aversive stimuli (because of their own fears), many of these problems would not occur.

Positive emotional responses are probably one of the strongest reinforcers to the greatest number of people (partially because positive emotional responses temporarily alleviate so many fears, e.g., being disliked, confrontation, being criticized, being seen as insignificant, and so forth). If managers are not emotionally expressive, if they are overly monotone, it is unlikely they are capable of really reinforcing anyone. And if a manager does not reinforce people, they must rely on aversives to impact others. This means their influence will be minimal at best and chaotic at worst. While it is true that the use of aversives by managers can decrease the strength of some behaviors, we rarely know what behaviors will take their place; frequently they're worse.

When a manager becomes a strong reinforcer to his subordinates (by using and thus pairing himself with reinforcers), the manager's goals soon become their goals; after all, by definition, they're being paired with a reinforcer, the manager. Conscientiousness, dependability, open communication, as well as other constructive behaviors increase in frequency. But many managers, especially males, have difficulty expressing emotion; hence, this crucial managerial tool is missing from their repertoire (a fact that is often confirmed by their frustrated wives).

This lack of expressiveness is often accompanied by a lack of enthusiasm, an enthusiasm that, if present, could constructively influence the attitudes of those around them, especially their subordinates. Apparently, expressing positive feelings leads to a sense of vulnerability by some people, possibly because such behavior was ridiculed as naïve, Pollyannaish, and sissified, especially in a male's teen years, when criticizing everything was considered cool and sophisticated.

[Readers are encouraged to tape some of their conversations and note whether or not their tone of voice conveys emotion through its inflection. If not, some acting classes or speech courses emphasizing emotional expressiveness may be helpful. The ability to be emotionally expressive is a crucial asset in any person's repertoire.]

Communicating Likes and Dislikes

Managers, through their behavior, should be encouraging constructive behaviors by pairing such behaviors and profit producing goals with reinforcers. Managers must also, however, pair destructive behaviors and undesirable goals with aversive stimuli. These pairings can have an immediate and critical impact on subordinates.

Consider the following statement by a manager in the presence of his subordinates. "The indecisiveness in this department is driving me up the wall!" The manager has paired indecisiveness with an aversive stimulus (especially his negative tone of voice). Several pairings like this will lower the likelihood of his subordinates engaging in indecisive behavior. But, by using aversive stimuli, the manager has also paired himself – and his department as well – with the aversive stimuli. This, too, will influence the behavior of his subordinates. Also, as we've seen, merely because the probability of indecisiveness is decreased doesn't tell us what will take its place. It may well be an excessive avoidance of the manager, thus leading to communication problems.

Most subordinates, in attempting to please their immediate superior, will (often subconsciously) try to find out what is reinforcing to her and engage in that type of behavior. If, for example, their manager constantly complains about various people in the organization, her subordinates will also engage in that type of complaining behavior, especially when they are in her immediate superior's presence. If the manager promotes or makes favorable comments about detail-oriented people (pairing), there will be a strong shift toward details on the part of most of her other subordinates. (Promotions are one of the strongest reinforcers available to managers. When an individual is promoted, his/her attitudes and style of work are being associated with strong reinforcers, and others in the department will soon start to emulate that behavior.)

On the other hand, if a subordinate has a strong dislike for her manager, she may well engage in behavior patterns that are aversive to her manager. Consider the case of a micro-managing superior who delegates no authority downward and blocks all communications upward. He gives no credit to his subordinates but is quick to blame them for all mistakes. He has, however, a highly independent subordinate who, to no one's surprise, dislikes him intensely. The subordinate knows that her manager becomes uneasy when a subordinate goes around him and interacts with his superior; consequently, she may well go out of her way to do just that! If this behavior were not aversive to the manager, the subordinate might be much less inclined to engage in it. Managers must use reinforcers and pair themselves with them in the process; the alternative has little to recommend it.

[Readers may wish to ask themselves whether they are reinforcers or aversives to those around them (as determined, for example, by the degree of cooperation they elicit from others). Having a "feel" for this will go a long way in determining what they have been using to influence people and in evaluating how best to respond to each person in the future. This is another reason we should not try to influence groups of people; each person must be treated individually if we are to be effective.]

So, like all of us, managers, without being aware of it, often pair behavior patterns and stimuli that they like with reinforcers, and behavior patterns and stimuli that they dislike with aversive stimuli in the presence of their subordinates. Consider a highly cautious, conservative sales manager whose only goal is to live out his few remaining years in the organization without some subordinate causing trouble and jeopardizing his position and retirement plans. A new subordinate enters his office and the following exchange takes place:

> <u>Subordinate</u> (in a quiet but excited tone): Hey, Jim, I just got an order for two hundred units from the Tough Corporation.
>
> <u>Manager</u> (in a quiet monotone): That's good (looks down at his desk and picks up a piece of paper, then speaks more loudly and with more emotional inflection): While you're here, John, there's some question about the expense report you turned in last Friday. I noticed you stayed in the same motel on Wednesday and Thursday nights but you charged almost twice as much for dinner on Thursday night. Someone upstairs is going to call me on it unless we give them a reasonable explanation.

What happened? The manager did not pair the sale with any strong reinforcers; he did, however, pair "inconsistencies on the expense account" with aversive stimuli. His reaction has decreased the probability that the subordinate will focus his attention on sales, while it has increased the probability that the subordinate will focus on avoiding discrepancies on his expense account. A better response might have been, "I can't believe it! You've been trying to get them for ages. Congratulations! What a coup! You know, it's your perseverance that did it. You never gave up. I sure wish I had that much determination!" Then, after a break in the interaction (to prevent pairing this positive interaction with an aversive; no more than one minute is required), bring up the expense account in a monotone, perfunctory manner (unless expense discrepancies are a frequent, repetitive occurrence).

Is Our Company Reinforcing to Our employees?

Since people pair those things that are reinforcing to themselves with reinforcers, it is absolutely essential that senior management makes certain the company product or service is reinforcing to its salespeople. When this is not true, sales calls can be destructive.

To illustrate: New senior management had been brought into a large company and numerous firings and demotions in the sales force resulted. One disgruntled salesperson introduced himself to a prospective customer by saying, "I'm Jim Smith from Micro-Data Company. As you may know, we've had a lot of personnel changes at our company, but hopefully things will settle down soon." Another smoldering salesperson replied to a complaining customer, "Well, that product is always getting fouled up by our plant people." These salespeople were pairing their company and product with aversive stimuli, a procedure that seems unlikely to increase sales. Periodic surveys that tap into the feelings of the sales force concerning their managers, the company, and its products may be of some benefit.

The frequency with which salespeople engage in these pairings would probably astound many managers. It is the manager's responsibility to make certain the company and its product or service are reinforcing to her/his salespeople. The alternative is, at best, a salesperson that will discuss baseball, fishing, or family with his customers – anything that builds a personal rapport with the customer. That is, the salesperson pairs himself with reinforcers to the customer so that, like Willy Loman, he is liked and well received. He does not, however, pair what he's being paid to pair with reinforcers, his company and its product (aversive stimuli, after all, are avoided).

[Readers might want to list five behaviors they feel are essential for anyone in their position, then ask their manager to do the same. A comparison of what each feels is needed (reinforcing) should prove enlightening to everyone.]

Putting the Aversives (Blame) on Others

One of the most disruptive pairings of this sort occurs when a manager pairs his own immediate superior with aversive stimuli in his subordinate's presence. Suppose, for example, a new young manager (Randall) is hired to head up a plant operation. In the presence of several foremen, the old-line plant superintendent, who wanted but didn't get the job, pairs his new boss with aversive stimuli, "That guy Randall doesn't know how to open a door, let alone run a plant," and, "Randall is going to get us all fired with his screwball ideas." The new plant manager will soon find the foremen implementing his policies in a halfhearted, uncooperative manner; communication between the manager and the foremen will be superficial at best; productivity in the plant will slide downhill.

It's always wise when you're promoted or start a new job, to determine who "lost out", who wanted the job but didn't get it. The likelihood of that person pairing you with aversives to others, subtly or not, is high. These pairings can be quite powerful and quite destructive. Frank discussions with the aggrieved party, especially concerning their feelings, are in order. The appropriate use of reinforcers with this person can be beneficial, especially if the issues are confronted immediately, before damage to your reputation is done with aversive pairings and the use of reinforcers by you becomes emotionally impossible.

[This is another good reason the reader may wish to periodically ask people in their inner circle, especially subordinates, "What's my greatest shortcoming?" and note both the words and emotional reactions.]

These situations occur quite frequently in life. If a close friend becomes hostile for no apparent reason, it is almost certain that a third party has been providing the friend with "other people-aversive stimuli" pairings that include and possibly center on you. The reasons for these attacks are frequently unfathomable, but can be overcome with the judicious use of reinforcers.

Accepting Limitations

Emotional involvement represents a major difficulty in implementing pairings effectively. Consider this interaction between a father and his seven-year-old daughter. The young girl is shy and gentle; she would never hurt anyone. Her father loves her deeply and finds anything that hurts her intensely aversive. She has refused to go outside and play for three days. Finally the father questions her reasons for staying in. She responds, "Mrs. Sampson (a next-door neighbor) said I was bad to her son. She said I was a mean girl and she doesn't want me around her children." The daughter has just paired Mrs. Sampson with what to the father are intense aversive stimuli. His natural reaction is to have a "talk" with Mrs. Sampson or, at least, turn to his wife and say, "Who the hell does Mrs. Sampson think she is?" The fact is, however, that his daughter will not go outside because Mrs. Sampson is an aversive stimulus to her. The father's natural reaction will increase his daughter's withdrawal because he is also pairing Mrs. Sampson with aversive stimuli.

If the father's goal is to have his daughter go outside, he would do well to pair Mrs. Sampson with stimuli reinforcing to the girl. He might make comments like, "Mrs. Sampson is really a very nice person. I know Mrs. Sampson likes you very much. If you go outside, you will see that Mrs. Sampson is happy to see you." The father was able, in this instance, to make these comments with successful results.

It is asking a great deal of an individual, however, to engage in this type of behavior under such emotionally difficult circumstances. Readers, consequently, should not be concerned with these principles every waking moment of their lives. When we encounter stimuli that are intensely aversive or reinforcing to us, we will and should respond the way we feel to them. Any other approach is often doomed to failure and will only increase one's frustrations and sense of failure (the opposite goal of this book).

If subsequent reflection indicates we could have done a better job, so be it. Guilt and self-recriminations will do us little good but could do us much harm. All of us say the wrong thing at the wrong time to the wrong people at times. That gives our personalities texture. Besides, we can always do constructive pairings at some future date, when our feelings are not running so high.

In many managerial interactions, however, stimuli are not intensely emotional. Nor is the manager being paid "to do his own thing".

Managers are being paid to elicit and strengthen the most effective behavior patterns possible from their subordinates as judged by a profit criterion.

Summary To Date

We have seen that any stimulus can become a reinforcer if it is paired with reinforcers and that any stimulus can become aversive if it is paired with aversive stimuli. These pairings go on constantly throughout our lives and account, in large measure, for our attitudes, opinions, and feelings about people, events, ideas, situations and, most important, ourselves. That our attitudes often remain stable reflects that fact that we tend to pick out the same types of people for our inner circle. (More specifically, we tend to pick as friends those who share our fears, which make them poor candidates to help us overcome ours. We tend to pick as lovers those who we hope will alleviate our fears.)

Managers are a potent source of influential pairings. Whether or not they are effective sources depends on a host of factors, including their ability to determine stimuli that are reinforcing or aversive to themselves and to their subordinates. Managerial effectiveness is also dependent upon emotional maturity and the ability to look at one's own behavior objectively. The manager who has a strong need to impress others may pair himself frequently with comments such as the following to his subordinates:

> "I set a production record last month."
> "I am submitting the production figures to accounting sooner than anyone else ever did."
> "I have developed better quality control systems than this company ever had."

These pairings may be reinforcing to the speaker but quite aversive to his subordinates, especially if they feel he is taking credit for their work. Unless the manager grasps the consequences of his behavior, he will always wonder why people avoid him and give him minimal effort and cooperation, especially since he is "obviously" so competent. Managers are being paid to focus outside themselves, specifically on other people, their strengths and their needs. (That so few of us do so is surprising in view of the fact that virtually all the joys and pains of life come from forces outside ourselves.)

Managers may not believe nor even like the thought that they have so much influence over the behavior of subordinates, but ignoring the fact does not decrease their impact; it merely makes that impact less effective. No orientation a manager has, however, will make them more effective than a sincere comfort with, and respect for, themselves. And the easiest way to determine if managers have this orientation is to see if they promote a liking and respect for themselves among their colleagues and/or subordinates.

Should we promote best performers into managerial positions?

How can I stop someone from always trying to be the center of
attention?

What should I focus on first if I'm given a new managerial position?

Shouldn't I just focus on a person's behavior, not its consequence?

CHAPTER 7

CHANGING ATTITUDES, BELIEFS, AND BEHAVIOR: Part 1

Managing people is an unnatural act. Managers are responsible for the
behavior of their subordinates, but their subordinates are adults who have
been, and continue to be, influenced by other people, people over whom
the manager has little, if any, control. (A spouse and boss sometimes
compete with each other over the same person, each subtly pairing the
other with aversives.)

Indeed, managing people is often a frustrating, frightening, grossly under-
appreciated responsibility. It is hoped that those who assume a managerial
role realize what they are getting into. It is also hoped that those who
assign managerial roles do not do so as a reward for performance, but
rather, because they feel the person so anointed will have a constructive
impact on others (especially in the area of increasing their liking and
respect for themselves).

It must be admitted that an individual's immediate superior is extremely
influential in their life, comparable to that of a spouse (and sometimes
more so). Thus, the manager's potential for changing people is
substantial.

Up to this point, we have been discussing people as they are and what has
made them that way. It is to the subject of changing people and their
behavior that we now turn.

Principle I

To weaken behavior that is controlled by a reinforcer, pair the reinforcer with aversive stimuli.

The word "weaken" is used in principle I to indicate that one or two pairings are not going to change behavior dramatically. We are dealing with people who have adopted certain attitudes after years of experience; we will not change them during a two-minute interchange (we shall see later that a quick change in behavior is quite possible, but dangerous). We can, on the other hand, with concentrated effort, alleviate the intensity and power of a given reinforcer or aversive stimulus quite effectively over a two or three-week period.

The word "behavior" signifies overt (observable) behavior. Although behavior also encompasses such unobservable elements as thoughts, feelings, attitudes, opinions, and ideas, all anyone can really "know" about a person is her overt behavior; the rest is inference.

The phrase "controlled by a reinforcer" means that the behavior is being immediately influenced by a rewarding stimulus (see Chapter XI). As indicated in the previous chapter, identifying this reinforcer can be a difficult proposition. Nevertheless, managers must always make their best guess as to what is reinforcing and what is aversive to subordinates. They must "know their people", and they do not know them until they have made this determination. We would do well to remember, however, that the most powerful reinforcers and aversive stimuli usually stem from the behavior of other people. What a person says to us has far more impact on our behavior than the same words in a written report.

The phrase "pair the reinforcer with aversive stimuli" means pairing the reinforcer controlling the behavior with a stimulus aversive to the subordinate, not necessarily aversive to the person (manager) doing the pairings.

In other words, our principle might read, "To decrease the likelihood of behavior that is being influenced by a reinforcer, associate the reinforcer with stimuli aversive to the listener."

Suppose, for example, that attention from other people is an overly strong reinforcer to a subordinate. Indeed, it is so reinforcing that he constantly interrupts people to tell them jokes, disrupts meetings by giving long-winded speeches on irrelevant matters, and is forever disagreeing with people so that they must look at him when discussing a point. Almost every statement by his manager in the following developmental session will pair "attention from others" with an aversive stimulus.

> Manager (in a disparaging, but soft, concerned tone of voice): Jim, I feel attention is a little too important to you at times. How do you feel about that?
>
> Subordinate: I suppose it is at times.
>
> Manager: Why? Why do you think attention would be so important to you?
>
> Subordinate: I really don't know.
>
> Manager: I wonder if you would consider the idea that people have their own problems. So when people are giving you attention, often they may not really care that much about you. Most people are mainly concerned about whether or not their car will start, what they will have for dinner tonight, who won the football game. So when people are looking at you, they're not usually that concerned about you. As a matter of fact, they may be focused on you because you have made them angry.

The manager's remarks have decreased the likelihood that the subordinate will find attention as reinforcing as he did before the remarks were made. As a result, they have decreased somewhat the strength of the subordinate's attention-seeking behavior. It is important to note that the subordinate's attention-seeking behavior is excessive, hence it must be fear-driven. What fear does attention from others alleviate? The fear of being insignificant to them. (Does this indicate that the individual is having problems in the area of liking and respecting himself? Probably.)

67

Yet periodic pairings along the above lines by the manager will gradually lessen the frequency and intensity of attention-seeking behavior by his subordinate (but not the fear of being insignificant to others).

[Readers are encouraged here to think of someone in their inner circle who engages in a specific excessive response pattern. How do people react when the person does so? This is likely the reinforcer strengthening the excessive behavior by temporarily lessening the fear driving it. That is, since experiencing a reinforcer so often decreases a person's fears, albeit momentarily, one might ask what fear the reinforcer is alleviating?

For example, I excessively make comments such as, "What a bunch of wimps those guys are!" My fellow "macho" cohorts agree that we are not and could never be such sissies, as we constantly prove by our common love (mutually reinforcing each other) of violent, tough-guy actions in sports. What fear does their reinforcing "bonding, macho" behavior alleviate in me (even if it's only temporary)? Being seen by other people as weak and frightened. But that may be who I truly am as evidenced by my excessive (fear-driven) love of violent sports.]

The New Manager

Surprises are often in store for new managers who assume authority over people they have not previously known. Stimuli thought to be reinforcing to virtually everyone may have a negative impact on some. Most managers assume, for example, that money is a reinforcer to all employees. To many people it is not. Some people pair the acquisition of money with "crass materialism and a "gross distortion of values." Some religions pair money with the "root of all evil."

Indeed, managing people is often a frustrating, frightening, experience. It can be made much easier, however, if the new manager evaluates her subordinates as quickly and as accurately as possible. Most managers extol the cliché, "Every subordinate is an individual and must be treated differently"; few actually practice it, however. To really know a person in the work setting one must be aware of her/his effective and ineffective behavior patterns and which types of stimuli are reinforcing and aversive to them. Without this knowledge, the manager will make numerous mistakes.

A new sales manager may assume, for example, that one of her subordinates, who is 140% over quota, is happy with his quota and his own performance. The manager is surprised to find the salesman actually hostile toward his quota and generally displaying an "I don't give a damn" attitude. What the new manager does not know is that the previous manager had, for several months, been pairing the salesman's outstanding performance and his quota with aversive stimuli, using such comments as:

"Jim, I just got your sales figure for last month. They're really good, but do you think your quota is too soft?"
"Jim, you're really beating hell out of your quota. We'll have to raise your quota by 100% next year to give you humility."
"Say, Jim, I noticed that while your sales are over your quota, your expenses are starting to go up."

The new manager, therefore, can make numerous mistakes by logically – and wrongly – assuming that the quota and recognition are reinforcing to a salesman who is far ahead of his peers in this performance area.

"Rational" assumptions concerning behavior can lead to a distortion of reality. To say that profits are the primary goal of a chief executive officer is, as we have mentioned, often untrue and misleading. The placating behavior of incompetent subordinates may well take precedence over increased profits as a reinforcer for a company president. The managerial assessment of subordinates, consequently, should focus less on rational assumptions and more on observed behaviors and the interpersonal reinforcers and aversive stimuli that are seen to influence that behavior.

The Need to be Liked

One of the most common, but debilitating reinforcers to an individual is a "need to be liked by others". Such a reinforcer often prevents people from speaking up for their ideas in the face of opposition, from making decisions that might hurt others, and from carrying out their responsibilities independently without frequent reassurance they're doing the right thing. (If the desire to be liked is excessive, it is fear-driven; that is, "being liked" is a reinforcer because the fear of being disliked is what is truly driving the person.) A strong desire to be liked or approved of is a difficult reinforcer for most managers to deal with because the subservient, compliant, cooperative behavior stemming from it is so often reinforcing to the manager (why try to change some behavior in a subordinate that makes my life so much easier?).

It is the outstanding manager who pairs this reinforcer with aversive stimuli by saying to the subordinate, for example, "Your need to be liked by people is a weakness on your part," and, "When people like you, they often do not respect you." Toning down this deadly reinforcer by pairing it with aversive stimuli (weakness, no respect) helps an individual contribute his fullest to his company and to society. To so influence behavior is the manager's responsibility; if he doesn't do it, who will?

[Can you think of some excessive, fear-driven behavior engaged in by someone in your inner circle that you shouldn't like, but really do (e.g., they're excessively complimentary)? What is your typical reaction to their behavior? Can you pair that reaction with an aversive or would you feel too deprived if it worked?]

Behavior Versus Consequences

Dealing with behavior effectively often means recognizing and dealing effectively with the consequences (e.g., reinforcers) controlling the behavior, rather than the behavior itself. This can be difficult because it is usually the person's behavior that irritates us; thus, it is that behavior that is most readily focused on and attacked.

A psychologist was treating an alcoholic manager who, when dealing with close friends and relatives, was consistently late, hypercritical, and generally obnoxious. It was pointed out to him that seeing significant people in his life emotionally upset was reinforcing to him. He accepted this diagnosis as accurate. It was then suggested that he refrain from criticizing anyone during the following week. He agreed. This directive focused specifically on his critical behavior patterns; it did not pair the reinforcer of seeing people upset with any aversive stimuli.

At his next appointment, the patient stated that he had experienced one of the most rewarding moments of his life over the weekend. He had spent the day with his children and had "not criticized them all day." What was the rewarding moment? When he returned the children to his ex-wife's apartment, "They cried because I was leaving." The rational discussion on emotionally upsetting significant people apparently had little impact on him, since his "most rewarding moment" consisted in seeing his children weep! In effect, focusing directly on the behavior (being critical) and stopping it, even temporarily, did nothing to lessen the reinforcing value of seeing people upset to this person. As a result, he may become less critical, but readily engage in other behaviors that achieve the same destructive result.

This is why focusing on the reinforcer (usually a particular behavior of others) that controls a response is sometimes more important that focusing on the behavior itself. Even eliminating the response itself will usually lead the person to find other behaviors that enable them to get the reinforcer. If the reinforcer is destructive to others, eliminating the obnoxious behavior will do little good. In the above example, the father may stifle his own criticalness, but put his children in frightening and/or frustrating situations that successfully elicit crying.

A manager may find dependency in his subordinates quite reinforcing, as attested to by the fact that he punishes any independent initiative on their part. But suppose we threaten him with being fired if he continues to do so. He may well stop, but only give bonuses, perks, and raises to those who continue to seek out his advice and approval.

Indeed, two very different personalities may find the same thing reinforcing but achieve their goal in markedly different ways. Two intensely ambitious fellows, for example, share the same goal of attaining higher-level positions. One, however, may try to get promotions by back-biting competitors while being quite subservient with his superiors. The other may try to reach the same goal by aggressively, but constructively attacking relevant problems. They are very different people, but have much in common. (Which one successfully achieves his goals by being promoted will have enormous consequences for these two people, for the organization, and for other employees who "get the message" as to what top management wants.) That two people have a common insatiable thirst for attention makes them quite alike; a dramatic difference between them, however, would lie in the one reaching that goal by constantly criticizing people, the other by always being humorous.

[The reader is encouraged here to again determine an excessive behavior pattern on the part of someone in their inner circle. Then think about people's typical reaction to the excessive behavior; that's the reinforcer. Try pairing that reinforcing behavior with aversives to the person.

For example, say that I am excessively self-deprecating, as shown by my frequent comments, such as, "I really didn't do well on that. Other people are so much better at it than I am." People, of course, respond with reassurance, "Hey, everything will be fine!" Rather, the effective manager might say something like, "You know, when people reassure you, they really are showing very little respect for you. People often reassure someone because they like people who lack confidence and who they can then control."]

Do our emotions have an impact on the pairings we use?

How should I handle two people who won't talk to each other?

What is the most destructive pairing that can be made in a company?

Why is it important to note the pairings of employees?

Are pairings important in performance reviews?

CHAPTER 8

CHANGING ATTITUDES, BELIEFS, AND BEHAVIOR: Part 2

Principal II

To weaken behavior controlled by an aversive stimulus, pair the aversive stimulus with reinforcers.

People As Aversives

To illustrate: Suppose two subordinates are not communicating; in fact, they are avoiding each other. Since we don't like aversives and try to avoid them, the obvious conclusion is that they are aversive to each other. If communication between the two is important, it is the manager's job to pair one subordinate with reinforcers to the other.

If, for example, Jack Smith and Jim Rolin do not get along, the manager might go to Jack and ask him what he feels Jim Rolin's greatest asset is in the work setting. After Jack has finished complaining about Jim, he will usually admit to one or two positive points in Jim. The manager can then convey these positive elements to Jim: "You know, Jack Smith feels you are one of the best report writers in our company." After Jim's incredulous reaction, the manager should repeat the pairing: "Really, I was talking to Jack last Thursday, and he feels you write excellent reports." These pairings will increase the likelihood that Jack will be less aversive to Jim in subsequent interactions.

73

It is not being suggested, however, that one or two pairings of this type will have the two subordinates embracing each other. The pairings are but an example of what the manager should be doing to establish a productive interpersonal climate. The manager, incidentally, is not being asked to lie. She/he must elicit positive statements from the one subordinate before conveying them to the other subordinate. If they are not true, the manager's altered tone of voice and other subtle cues will be aversive rather than reinforcing. Sincerity is therefore appropriate, for pragmatic as well as ethical and moral reasons.

It is important to remember that managers will be paired with what they use, reinforcers or aversive stimuli. The manager in the foregoing example will be liked more by Jim when she tells him, "Jack thinks you write excellent reports." She is pairing both Jack and herself with a reinforcer. On the other hand, she will not be liked by Jack if she says, "Jim is the best report writer in the company." She is pairing both Jim and herself with stimuli aversive to Jack.

The opportunities to pair one person (and oneself) with reinforcers to another individual are ample indeed. That these opportunities are so rarely used is indicative of our pervasive fear of people liking others (rather than us). Nowhere in an organization, however, is this more crucial than in the relationship between the salesperson and the customer. Customers can be frustrating to deal with! If, in the process, they have paired themselves with too many aversives to the salesperson, the effectiveness of that salesperson with that account will be greatly compromised. It is the manager's responsibility to know how their salespeople feel about each customer. More important, it is the manager's responsibility to pair the customer with realistic reinforcers to the salesperson whenever and however possible.

[The reader is urged to elicit a positive comment from one individual about a person they dislike ("What do you think A's greatest strength is?"). Now go to A and tell her/him about the glowing comment the first individual made. Is this so hard to do? Does the idea of other people liking each other bother you? Pairing one person with a realistic and sincere reinforcer to another should be part of anyone's repertoire, easily and readily emitted. After all, most of us have little hesitation pairing others with aversives.]

Pairings: The Precursors to Problems

Managers would do well to watch the pairings verbalized by their subordinates. They are often a quick and certain cue to impending trouble. Consider this exchange between a sales manager and one of his salespeople in the presence of the manager's vice president:

> VP of Sales: Instead of making all the salespeople memorize this canned sales pitch, why don't we just list some basic points and let them present the points any way they want?
>
> Sales Manager: Because half of the salespeople don't know which side of our product is up or down, and the other half couldn't care less.

The sales manager has paired his own subordinates with aversive stimuli. His immediate superior must start to look for other negative indices. She must find out if this attitude is temporary or permanent. Does the sales manager find increased sales reinforcing or aversive? How aversive is the sales manager to his subordinates. Most important, how aversive are the salespeople to the manager? This will readily tell her how he is treating them. Pairings such as these are the precursor to a drop in sales and profits. Managers who do not focus on these precursors – who focus on profits only, rather than the controllable *causes* (the behavior of subordinates) of profits – will always be caught off guard, react too late, and be forever putting out fires.

Many sales managers find customers aversive, whatever they may say to the contrary. Their conversations with subordinates often pair customers with ridicule or outright animosity. Oddly enough, this is especially true in organizations that have a dominant market share, that are the "leaders" in their field. Too often managers in these leading companies dislike their continued dependence on others, such as customers, and their customer-aversive pairings (the most destructive pairings in a company) show it. The same managers then wonder why their salespeople avoid making sales calls or are so easily dissuaded from pursuing an account.

The manager who says, "The people at AIC Corporation are the biggest jerks I've ever run into," decreases the probability that his salespeople will even call on AIC Corporation, let alone do an effective job on the call. This manager should instead be saying to his salespeople, things like, "The people at AIC Corporation called; they think you're one of the most conscientious salespersons they've ever seen."   By pairing AIC Corporation with a reinforcer, this statement increases the likelihood that the salesperson will indeed call on AIC Corporation and say the right thing at the right time. When we like people, we tend to do that! Of course, the statement must be true.   But there are ample opportunities for these realistic and true reinforcer pairings; many managers do not see them because they do not want to see them. And even when they do, too many don't tell the salesperson, because, "It'll go to their head." (What they mean is, "I don't want my salespeople getting too confident because I'll become less important and less influential in their lives.")

[The reader is urged to find something about a customer that is reinforcing to the salesperson calling on them. Say it to the salesperson! Please make this an integral part of your behavioral repertoire.]

Destructive Pairings

Self-destructive behavior by managers is all too common. Consider this not unusual comment by a manager to his subordinate at salary review time: "I want to give you the raise, but Jack (the controller) says our profits are off so much that nobody will get a raise." The manager is obviously attempting to pair himself with what to his subordinate is a reinforcer, and to pair "Jack" with an aversive stimulus. Such a remark not only reflects excuse-making or avoidance of responsibility, it also indicates negative attitudes toward other managers and a desire to have those negative attitudes shared by subordinates. It is not merely a reflection of a *weak* manager; it is a reflection of a *destructive* manager.

76

Companies, in their house organs, sometimes take realistic reinforcers to employees and make them aversive with destructive pairings. It is well known that few people are inspired by fringe benefits, despite their cost to the organization. This is due, in part, to the fact that many organizations do a poor job of communicating these benefits to the employees. The simple statement, "Our company has a pension plan that is second to none and will provide some real financial security when you need it," pairs both the company and the pension plan with a reinforcer. Consider the following, however:

> Our company pension plan will pay you, at age sixty-five, sixty percent of your highest salary averaged over five years, conditioned upon the five years being continuous with the company, or it will pay you forty percent of your highest salary averaged over the previous five year period, if employment was maintained in this organization for the five years, and the employee declares retirement at age sixty.

The complexities involved in this statement are so aversive to most people that the pension plan, after these pairings, is hardly considered worthwhile. Worse yet is the following:

> The pension plan does not cover nonexempt employees unless they have been with the company a minimum of four years. Pension Plan participation is not available to employees with more than three reprimands in their personnel folder. The pension plan payments will be decreased by the amount of social security benefits the employee receives.

Each of these statements tells the reader what the pension plan will not do, that is, the statements pair the pension plan with aversive stimuli.

[The reader is asked to look at organizational documents (e.g., Company Policies" or "Personnel Manual") for statements that pair organizational rules and/or benefits with aversives. Could they be made more positive? Analyses of memos or emails can also be interesting to dissect from a pairings point of view. A word of caution: Don't offer your insights to the writers of these missives; such insights can be quite aversive and, since the messages are in "black and white," there is little that can be argued and/or defended.]

Emotional Involvement and Effective Pairings

Managers, like all of us, often find effective pairings difficult to make because of their emotional involvement in a given situation. This emotional difficulty, as we have seen, can prevent a manager from doing the right thing at the right time. It is, for example, sometimes in the best interest of everyone concerned for an individual to pair himself with *what to the other person* is a reinforcer, even though that same stimulus is aversive to the speaker.

A father and son were running their jointly-owned company. The father was aversive to his son because of his frequent "interference"; the son was aversive to the father because of his "ridiculous, new-fangled ideas". Their animosity and lack of constructive communication was pulling the company apart and hurting its seventy employees.

It was suggested to the son that he pair himself with stimuli reinforcing to his father. The son was asked to say to his father, for example, "Dad, based on all your years of experience, what do you think I should be concentrating on to develop myself?" The son's reply to this request was, "No way could I ever say that! I would choke on it!" However the son did eventually bring himself to admit mistakes to his father when he made them, to ask his father's advice, and to praise his father's strengths to others in front of his father. These statements, although emotionally difficult, were true. The result was more tolerance for change by the father and a more positive relationship between the two, which benefited everyone.

The manager's task is not an easy one. But managers are being paid to elicit the best efforts of subordinates. Sometimes this may require them to make statements which, while true, are highly aversive to them. It might be highly effective for the sales manager to say to a subordinate, "You did an outstanding job on that sales call. Frankly, you handled that fellow better than I could have." Few managers, however, have the confidence to engage in behavior they feel will be self-deprecating and lead others to feel "above" them, even when it is true in specific situations and will result in increased confidence, hence competence, on the part of a subordinate. (Again, excessive self-deprecation would be fear-driven and potentially destructive.)

Many managers, on the other hand, inadvertently pair themselves needlessly with aversive stimuli in subtle ways. Consider the following managerial memo:

> I have noticed a recent trend toward using the phone for personal calls; this is permissible only during emergencies.

The manager could have toned down the subtle impact of pairing herself with aversive stimuli by changing the memo slightly:

> There seems to be a trend toward using the phone for personal calls; confining such calls to emergencies would be greatly appreciated.

Managerial responsibilities require managers to pair themselves with aversive stimuli; some thought can minimize the frequency and intensity of these pairings. Managers should try reinforcing pairings first; they might work. If they do not, more aversive associations can always be a subsequent alternative.

[Readers are encouraged to look up the "rules of conduct" manuals of their organization and make a few attempts to put them in more positive, reinforcing, less aversive terms.]

Developing Others with Effective Pairings

Developing a subordinate by pairing aversive stimuli with reinforcers is a topic we will examine in greater detail later in the book. It might be beneficial, however, to look at one example of this type of interaction.

Suppose a manager is having a developmental session with a meek, passive subordinate. The manager in this instance is attempting to elicit more decisive behavior on the part of the subordinate. The manager knows that interpersonal interactions have a greater impact on people than do any other stimuli. He has, therefore, reasoned that this subordinate is indecisive because the subordinate fears she might encounter dissension or an argument if she commits herself to a judgment in front of other people. The manager, therefore, must pair "dissension and arguments with others" with reinforcers.

> Manager: Lisa, I feel at times you're not quite as decisive as you could be. How do you feel about that?
> Subordinate: Well, I suppose you might be right.
> Manager: Why do you think you're a bit indecisive at times?
> Subordinate: I don't really know.
> Manager: I wonder if it's because you think someone might argue with you if you committed yourself to a judgment.
> Subordinate: That might be part of it.
> Manager: I wonder if, when someone argues with you, he's really telling you that your views have had an impact on him. When someone says to you, "No, Lisa, I disagree with you," he's really telling you he respects your views enough to try to sway you to his point of view. When someone gets angry with you and starts shouting, he's really saying that you and what you're telling him is important to him, that he cares about you and your point of view. "You know, if someone just accepts my ideas, I don't have much respect for him. But when he comes at me hot and heavy and really argues vehemently with me, I know that what I have said is important to him and that I'm important to him."

Here the manager is attempting to pair the aversive stimulus (dissension) with reinforcers (they care about you). The manager is, of course, judging which stimuli are actually aversive and which are actually reinforcing to the subordinate. A person is often the worst judge of themselves, and to ask the subordinate to determine which stimuli she finds reinforcing and aversive can be quite misleading.

[The reader might wish to think about some reaction from others that is, but shouldn't be, aversive to a person they know well. Can you make this reaction less aversive, and the person less sensitive to it, with some reinforcer pairings? For example: "Criticism from others can be quite enlightening. Criticism tells you what the other person is thinking and can prevent surprises in a relationship."]

Summary

We have now discussed two critical principles which can have an impact on an individual's behavior. While the principles are two sides of the same coin, choosing which one to use (that is, whether to pair a reinforcer with an aversive stimulus or vice versa) can be crucial in impact and diagnosis.

If the leaders of a women's organization pair equal treatment toward everyone, including females, with reinforcers, it may have one kind of effect on people. If, however, they pair males with aversive stimuli, it may have quite another impact.

If the black person says, "Black is beautiful," it means one thing; "Whitey is a honky," means quite another. The liberal may pair the poor with reinforcers or the rich with aversive stimuli.

An analysis of pairings sometimes indicates that the crusader may find it more reinforcing to hurt his unjust enemy than to make his enemy more just.

History teaches us that people in government often ensure their political survival, not by pairing themselves with reinforcers, but rather, by pairing people in another country with threatening (aversive) stimuli; this approach certainly increases the probability of war.

[Readers are encouraged here to think of someone with whom they must interact periodically, but who is somewhat irritating (not hateful) to them. What might be reinforcing to this person, a compliment, attention, admiration? Can you try to give them what they are seeking, even if it's aversive to you? Be strong. Be brave. But pick something you feel is true of the person (everyone has some assets), despite your doubts.]

How do I encourage behavior in a person who never engages in that behavior?

How do I weaken behavior in others?

What's the most effective way to handle groups of people in meetings?

Do the questions people ask me tell me anything about them?

CHAPTER 9
CHANGING ATTITUDES, BELIEFS, AND BEHAVIOR: Part 3

Principle III

To strengthen a certain behavior, pair a description of the behavior with a reinforcer.

Consider this comment about a third party from a manager to his subordinate: "Jim sure is decisive. I like to see that in a man." Assuming that what his manager likes to see in a person is a reinforcer to the subordinate, this statement has increased the likelihood of decisiveness in the subordinate. It has paired the verbal equivalent of decisive behavior with a reinforcer.

Giving Advice

This principle is frequently involved when managers attempt to offer advice to subordinates. Its use is not always effective, however, because people generally use stimuli that are reinforcers or aversive to themselves rather than to their listener. Worse, we often describe behavior without pairing it with anything ("Jim sure is decisive. Say, how are things going with that X project?"). This accounts, in large part, for the frustrating fact that much of what we say goes unheeded or has the opposite impact of that intended. Inhibitions over expressing sincere reinforcers probably account for more personal problems than all other factors combined (as we shall

83

see even more dramatically later). It cannot be stressed enough: The ability and confidence to express sincere reinforcers with other people is one of the most essential skills necessary for living a full and productive life.

A consultant hoped to tone down the aggressive, abrasive behavior of a plant manager who had lost rapport with his subordinates. To do this, the consultant attempted to pair the verbal equivalent of the plant manager's behavior with aversive stimuli. He commented, for example, "When you yell at your people, you scare them half to death. You're so abrasive in the plant that people are frightened of you. You come on so strong that your subordinates back away from you." Subsequent reports indicated the plant manager had become even more aggressive with people below him. "People being afraid" may have been aversive to the consultant, but it was a strong reinforcer to the plant manager, thus increasing the frequency and intensity of his abusive behavior.

The same problem occurs when a "mass audience" approach is used, whether it be in a textbook on management, the Bible, or the writings of Confucius:

- The meek shall inherit the earth.
- If you vote for John O'Reilly, you'll be voting to lower your taxes.
- Selecting good people is the first step to increased profits.
- Positive attitudes make for positive results.

The purpose of all these statements is, of course, to effect behavioral change in others by pairing the desired behavior with reinforcers. However, the same stimulus may be neutral, reinforcing, or aversive to different people. "Increased profits" may be quite reinforcing to a chief executive officer, of little concern (neutral) to many people in the company, and even aversive to some disgruntled employees. Employment ads stressing the idea that the employer is an "aggressive company" may turn away people who are truly competent, but in whose experience aggressiveness has been paired with aversive stimuli, such as hostile or overly critical people.

[Readers are encouraged to think of some behavior they would like to see in someone in their inner circle. This is the easy part. Now determine what would be truly reinforcing to that person.

Examples: No pairing: "Could you loan me some money?" Bad pairing: "If you loan me some money, I'll be able to buy the couch I always wanted." Good pairing: "If you loan me the money, I'll be eternally grateful and help you with that computer problem."]

Dealing with More than One Person

Managers must be careful with their use of reinforcers and aversive stimuli in general meetings. It is all too easy for the manager to pair a desired response pattern with a stimulus reinforcing to one subordinate but quite aversive to many others. The manager might, for instance, say to a highly ambitious subordinate in a group meeting, "Jack, you are always so well organized. Why don't you make the presentation of our report to the president next week." There is little doubt that Jack's efforts to organize his personal work habits will be increased in the future because of this "organized-reinforcer" pairing.

To other ambitious people at the meeting, however, an organized approach has just been paired with the aversive stimulus of Jack making the presentation to the president. Some of these people may subsequently complain about the "undue emphasis placed on organization in this department". To less ambitious people at the meeting, Jack's opportunity to make a presentation to the president may well be a neutral stimulus of little consequence; little change in their behavior can be expected.

It should again be emphasized that if managers use reinforcers to influence the behavior or others, they will themselves become more reinforcing. If they use aversive stimuli, they pair themselves with those stimuli and will become aversive. In the above example, the manager is now a little more

85

reinforcing to Jack, more aversive to the other ambitious people, and unchanged to the less ambitious people.

Managers are paid to treat subordinates as individuals, as people with different fears, likes, dislikes, frustrations, hopes, etc. To think that a stimulus is reinforcing to everyone is naive; it usually reflects our belief that it *should* be reinforcing to everyone. Praising people in public for their accomplishments can be quite damaging, as we saw when discussing the effects of sales contests. Yet most people will vehemently protest that they are pleased as hell that a colleague is being singled out for honors. Such protests sometimes become excessive because they are driven by the fear of being seen as petty or as a "sore loser".

[Readers are asked to determine something that they think might be reinforcing to more than one person at the same time. Try it and watch reactions. Experience has shown that people usually think of "reinforcers" that are so mild or weak that, while not aversive to anyone, they also have little impact on anyone.]

Principle IV

To weaken some behavior, pair a description of the behavior with an aversive stimulus.

This is, of course, the obverse of Principle III. It is, unfortunately, more important since aversive stimuli are used much more frequently than reinforcers to influence behavior in our society.

Almost all rules, regulations, and laws are a pairing of the verbal equivalent of a response pattern with aversive stimuli:

- Anyone smoking in this area will be subject to a three-day suspension.
- Anyone not wearing safety goggles on the plant floor will be terminated immediately.

- Failure to yield the right-of-way to a pedestrian is punishable by one to six months in prison.
- The divulging of information marked 'top secret' shall be punishable by five to ten years in prison and a fine of not more than $5,000, or both.

Three pairings are actually taking place in these examples. First, the behavior specified in the rule, regulation, or law is being paired with the aversive stimuli used as potential punishment. Second, rules, regulations, and laws in general start to become aversive, since they are almost always being paired (enforced) with aversive stimuli. Third, the organization issuing the rules, regulations, and laws is becoming aversive to its people because it is pairing itself with both the rules and regulations, and the same aversive stimuli used to enforce its standards. The company that relies heavily on rules and regulations, consequently, is likely to be aversive to many of its employees.

At an individual level, managers constantly pair response patterns with aversive stimuli with comments like the following: "You know, Jim, if you keep talking with your hand in front of your mouth, no one will hear you and people won't listen to you." "If you can't get that job done by Friday, you'll have to come in over the weekend and do it." "All that guy does all day long is play up to the boss; some day he'll catch his."

[Readers are asked to think of a behavior pattern they dislike in someone and pair it with an aversive stimulus. If, for example, you feel your boss is too frequently critical, you might say, "You know, I was reading the other day that people who criticize others a lot are critical because they're afraid of people, especially of people getting too close to them. It said that if someone's criticizing you, look to see what's frightening them." Remember, of course, that you're pairing yourself with the same aversive.]

Evaluating Your Manager

Managers' questions tend to pair response patterns with aversive stimuli because they often are followed by reprimands.

> Manager: Did you write up that report?
> Subordinate: No.
> Manager: Why the hell not? I told you I needed it today. Don't you ever do anything I ask of you? I want to see you in my office at three today.

The questions managers ask subordinates convey a great deal about the manager's concerns and fears. They can set the tone of the entire department because they are so often paired with aversive stimuli if the "wrong" answer is given and reinforcers if the "right" answer is given. Indeed, a manager's questions, followed by reinforcers and aversive stimuli, constitute a primary vehicle by which his/her attitudes and philosophies come to permeate their department.

The sales manager who constantly questions her people about their sales calls will increase the probability that the salespeople will be outside selling. The sales manager who repeatedly questions expense account discrepancies will soon find her salespeople spending an inordinate amount of time poring over their expense reports.

A consultant was called into an unprofitable plant operation. He spent two hours walking around the plant with the plant manager watching the latter interact with the superintendents and foremen. He ventured the opinion that the rejection rate by the inspection department must be very low. The plant manager, surprised the consultant knew this, said it was near zero. Indeed, the plant's high reputation for quality was acknowledged by both customers and competition. It was then pointed out that every question the plant manager had asked his subordinates during the previous two hours had centered on accuracy and quality. Mistakes revealed by the manager's questions ("Is that piece within tolerance limits?" "Are the corners there rounded off enough?" "Is that angle perpendicular to this side piece?") were punished with reprimands. As a result, the pace of the plant was slow and cautious but certain. Quality was very high; productivity was very low.

The plant manager was asked not to hire more help, but to start asking productivity questions ("When will this job be finished?" "How much longer do you have to go on this job? Can't we get it out sooner?"). The initial reaction was negative. One worker stated that he could run the machine at a faster r.p.m. rate, but complained that it put stress on a washer and the washer would periodically break. The washer cost five cents, however, while the profit from an increased r.p.m. rate was in the thousands of dollars. After six weeks, productivity had taken a marked upswing in the plant. After six months, productivity had increased over 40% without an appreciable drop in quality.

Managers, when they dislike a response, frequently pair the verbal equivalent of the response with aversive stimuli. A manager was ostensibly attempting to tone down the emotional frustrations of a subordinate. He said, "You're the kind of guy who aggressively seeks change in an organization, and you have to realize that you're bound to have more failures than successes." The manager was not pairing emotional reactions with aversive stimuli, but rather, the response of aggressively seeking change. This particular manager was close to retirement and "seeking change" was aversive to him. It is difficult for people to avoid pairing response patterns which are aversive to them with aversive stimuli.

[Readers would do well to determine where their manager focuses his/her questions. Again, this will often reflect the concerns and even the fears of the manager. A little thought can then indicate what reinforcers we should pair ourselves with to alleviate the manager's concerns and get that raise.

If, for example, your manager frequently asks detailed questions about "who said what" concerning an interaction you had with his boss, it probably indicates he's too concerned with what his boss thinks of him. Reinforcing your manager for his unusual skills in front of his boss would probably be a good career move. (No one said this would be easy!)]

Which is more powerful, a reinforcer pairing or an aversive pairing?

Are backward pairings one of the reasons no one pays attention to me?

Can "selling" something, by pairing it with too many reinforcers,
   backfire?

CHAPTER 10

CHANGING ATTITUDES, BELIEFS, AND BEHAVIOR: Part 4

Reinforcer vs. Aversive Pairings

Most managers use aversive stimuli so frequently that the use of reinforcers is all but forgotten. Because we are to others (reinforcing or aversive) what we use most often to influence them, it makes sense to use reinforcers to influence behavior whenever possible. Unfortunately, the negative approach is more typical, often because intimidating subordinates is too reinforcing to many managers.

Suppose a manager is attempting to inspire his subordinates to give more feedback to their subordinates. He will probably make comments like the following:

> "If anyone here has not given their people their annual performance review by the end of next week, I want to know about it, and the reasons better be good."
> "Most of you people aren't giving feedback to your subordinates because you're afraid to."
> "If you're not going to give your people more feedback, maybe you guys shouldn't be managers."

The speaker, in this case, is becoming aversive to his audience because he is so often using aversive stimuli to "motivate" them. He is also pairing what they should <u>not</u> do with aversive stimuli. As a result, he has not

91

made "giving feedback" more reinforcing; he has made "not giving feedback" more aversive! Now it is true that aversives probably have a more immediate impact on behavior than reinforcers, but the side effects of using a constant dose of aversives can be quite destructive and should always be counterbalanced by an ample use of reinforcers on other occasions.

Contrast that approach with the following:

> "You know, if you give Jack some personal feedback, I think his work will improve dramatically and he'll probably respect you more for it."
> "I noticed you gave Jim some feedback yesterday. Beautiful! I think he could become an excellent employee because of your help."
> "The manager who gives her/his people frequent, constructive feedback is almost always considered for promotion."

The speaker, in this case, is making both himself and "giving feedback" more reinforcing. He will reap many benefits from this approach. "If you have the report in by Thursday, I'll worship the ground you walk on," is far more constructive than, "If you don't have the report in by Thursday, I guarantee that you'll regret it."

It might also be noted that pairing behavior with aversives does indeed weaken the behavior, but it strengthens nothing (except frustration, hence anger). Worse, we have no idea what behavior will take the place of the behavior we've weakened. It may well be behavior that is even more destructive. The manager who constantly paired not giving feedback with aversives may end up with some subordinates who merely avoid communicating with him, while others may start lying about their feedback actions.

[Readers are asked to try pairing some behavior with a reinforcer on one occasion and its opposite with an aversive on another occasion, but to the same individual. What are you most comfortable using? If you are comfortable using both, you are confident indeed.

At the risk of being labeled a sexist, the author feels women generally have greater difficulty using aversives than men, while men generally have greater difficulty using reinforcers than women. This is unfortunate. Both are needed in one's repertoire if one is to be effective dealing with the myriad people and situations encountered throughout life.]

Backward Pairings

Much of what we say to people seems to have little impact on them. We have seen that one reason for this is our use of stimuli that are reinforcing or aversive to us, but not to the people we are trying to influence. Another reason for our lack of impact is our use of backward pairings.

The stimulus (or behavioral description) we are attempting to change must come before the reinforcer or aversive stimulus we are using in the pairing. If the reinforcer or aversive stimulus comes before the behavioral description, for example, the impact is minimized.

The reader may find this difficult to believe, but it has been proven time and again in experimental work. For example: If we want to make "Mike" aversive to our audience, we must not only pair "Mike" with aversive stimuli; we must also place the word "Mike" first in the pairing. It is much less effective to say, "There are some pretty bad rumors being spread about you by Mike," than to say, "Mike is spreading some pretty bad rumors about you."

The stimulus that is changed by the subsequent reinforcer or aversive is the one that comes first. The comment, "You did a fine job in your presentation, but you missed the whole point of the meeting," has the effect of making compliments aversive. Conversely, the comment, "You missed the point of the meeting, but you did a fine job in your presentation," has the effect of making criticism more reinforcing.

Ineffective (backward):   No one will listen to you if you keep mumbling.

Effective: If you keep mumbling, no one will listen to you.

Ineffective (backward):   You'll make quota easily if you make eight sales calls a day.

Effective: If you make eight sales calls a day, you'll make quota easily.

Damaging Backward Pairings

Not only are backward pairings ineffective, they are often destructive as well. The manager, for example who *continually* follows compliments with criticisms or criticisms with compliments (as in the above examples) sets up unrealistic reinforcers and aversive stimuli in his/her subordinates. A new manager is then bewildered by the "de-motivating" impact his compliments have on his subordinates, to whom compliments now seem "phony". Likewise, many people find affection from persons close to them aversive; the parent who frequently punishes her child by saying, "I love you, darling, but you've got to learn to be more responsible," is leading his child to develop this unrealistic attitude. The lover who continually professes his devotion, then abruptly breaks off the relationship, will make his ex-lover more suspicious to "professed devotions" in the future, a response that may certainly confuse future lovers. Many managers feel guilty using aversives, thus quickly pair them with reinforcers as a way of alleviating their guilt; this is not a constructive message.

The members of some aggressive departments may have frequent frank, but highly critical, almost insulting exchanges, yet everyone seems to like and respect everyone else and few people voluntarily leave the department. This is because hostile criticism has become a strong reinforcer. New members of the department may be appalled at the apparent "hostility", but they will never feel accepted until everyone starts openly criticizing them ("What the hell did you do that for?"). Compliments are rarely given in such a department and are even used sometimes as a punishing (sarcastic) device. Anyone leaving the department will require an "adjustment" period until criticism again becomes aversive and compliments reinforcing. If the individual lacks patience during this period, he will often become uncomfortable (with such pansies) and either requests a transfer back to his old department or leave the company.

[Readers may wish to watch TV or newspaper ads and note the numerous times backward pairings are used, e.g., "You'll get more miles with X gasoline," should be, "With X gasoline, you'll get more miles."]

Expectations

The expectations of people can be driven to *unrealistic* heights with strong reinforcer pairings. When reality is encountered, so is frustration. "You've got to see this movie; it's the best movie I've seen in five years. It was so intense! I mean, from the moment it came on the screen, people were on the edge of their seats. This movie makes you laugh, it makes you cry; by the time it's over, you're completely drained emotionally!" Few movies would have this impact and seeing it after this series of unrealistic reinforcer pairings may lead to disappointment indeed. Had these intense pairings not been made, less frustration would have been felt during the movie and a more positive reaction felt after the movie.

Managers, frustrated with the selection process, often over-react by selling job applicants with a brighter picture of the position than is true. Salespeople calling on customers and under pressure to get orders or intent upon proving their aggressiveness often engage in this hyperbole. But everyone pays a heavy price when reality sets in. How intense should reinforcers be? As intense and only as intense as reality dictates.

[The reader is asked to think about a "disappointing experience." Consider discussions with others prior to the experience. Were too many reinforcers used leading to unrealistically high expectations? Were the reinforcers used too strong?]

Summary

We have now examined four principles of classical learning. As with any science, they are simple principles in the abstract; they are extremely complex in practical application. The manager might consider observing and diagnosing pairings before attempting to use them. Printed material is a perfect medium for study because of its permanence. The manager might, for example, be sensitive to the pairings politicians use when they are quoted in the daily newspaper. "We cannot divulge that material because it would compromise national security" (a favorite pairing used by many Presidents). Readers might ask themselves why the speaker has made the pairing, whether the reinforcer is really reinforcing (or aversive) to a large number of people, and whether the speaker has used backward pairings. After developing proficiency in this area, the manager might consider attempting quick analyses of verbal behavior while observing children, watching movies, attending meetings, and, most important, when analyzing the behavior of her/his subordinates.

Implementation is the next step. It requires, above all, accurate evaluations. It requires objectivity and emotional maturity. It requires a flexible sensitivity and adaptation to the specific audience at the moment. It requires the confidence to use realistic reinforcers and aversives without inhibitions. In short, it requires managers who like and respect themselves, hence want the same for others, for it is these managers who think in objective, insightful, clear and crisp ways. In sum, it requires managers who are not afraid to think.

Effective pairings of the organization with reinforcers are different when one is talking to customers than when one is talking to financial analysts. Goal-setting by management requires the pairing of company goals with different reinforcers to different employees or employee groups by their managers. Any other approach is likely to be less than effective and possibly destructive, especially when it involves a "blanket" approach for all employees by senior management (often using reinforcers to the CEO but to few others).

These requirements are most important when managers are dealing with subordinates. Managers must be (and are in any case) a different person to different people. To be an effective manager, one must use different pairings with the subordinate who lacks sufficient confidence to make decisions than with the subordinate who is himself destructively pairing customers and/or clients with aversive stimuli.

The most important decision an organization makes is the selection of its chief executive officer. His/her attitudes and philosophy will permeate the organization, primarily because of the pairings he/she makes. If a cautious, conservative chief executive finds mistakes intensely aversive, he will frequently pair mistakes with his wrath (aversive stimuli) in the presence of his immediate subordinates, the vice presidents. This will quickly set up mistakes as an aversive stimulus to the vice presidents which they will, in turn, pair with aversive stimuli when dealing with their subordinates, and so on down the line. Promotions (reinforcers) will be paired with people whose behavior pattern reflects a lack of mistakes, that is, cautious, conservative people who take few risks. The entire atmosphere of the organization will eventually become aversive to more risk-oriented people and they will leave.

The pairings involved in human interactions can be more than effective tools in helping managers develop confidence and competence in subordinates. It is a long and arduous task to develop expertise in this area, but the rewards are well worth the effort.

SECTION 3

OPERANT LEARNING

INFLUENCING BEHAVIOR AS IT OCCURS

Is it better to use pairings or to respond directly to a person's behavior?

Is it always good to reinforce behavior?

Will ample doses of reinforcement diminish a person's fears?

Is "when" I reinforce someone important?

What is "extinction"? When should it be used?

CHAPTER 11

REINFORCEMENT AND EXTINCTION: Part 1

Responding to the Behavior of Others

Up to this point, we have discussed methods of influencing people without regard to their behavior at the moment. That is, the influence was dependent only on the pairings initiated by the speaker. In the following chapters we will consider changing behavior directly, the moment it happens. This is called operant learning. To do this, we must examine four basic principles of operant learning.

The reader should heed two warnings. First, while the principles are deceptively simple, their actual application in the "real world" is enormously complex. No one can hope to accurately diagnose and perfectly implement these principles all the time; imperfect implementation some of the time is a reasonable goal. Second, we should, in our interactions with other people, focus on their behavior and its impact on us, especially on our confidence, and on our liking and respect for ourselves. Thus, we would do well to spend less time worrying about our own behavior and what people think of us and how they will react to it and us. With these points in mind, let us turn to the first two principles of operant learning.

Principle V: Reinforcement

Any response followed immediately by a reinforcer is strengthened and has a higher probability of recurring.

Principle VI: Extinction

Any response not immediately followed by a reinforcer is weakened and has a lesser probability of recurring.

Let us begin with two examples of a subordinate speaking up in a meeting with his manager and six of his peers. In the first example, the manager's behavior will increase the probability of the subordinate speaking up subsequently in group meetings. In the second example, the manager's behavior will decrease that likelihood.

> Manager: How do you feel about our treatment of the bad debt reserve, Jim?
> Subordinate: I don't think we've allocated enough reserves here. We've averaged 25% more than this over the last three years.
> Manager (with a strong emotional expressiveness): You know, you're absolutely right! Excellent point! I think we had better discuss Jim's idea that our allocation is underestimated here. John, how do you feel about it?

(The manager has followed Jim's response with what we will assume is a reinforcer to Jim; she has thereby increased the likelihood of Jim speaking up in meetings.)

> Manager: How do you feel about our treatment of the bad debt reserve, Jim?
> Subordinate: I don't think we've allocated enough reserves here. We've averaged 25% more than this over the last three years.
> Manager (in an uninterested monotone, meanwhile looking down at papers in front of her): All right. Let's turn now to the next

102

item on our agenda; here we've got the figures on our current inventory. Michael, how do you feel about these figures?

(The manager has *not* followed Jim's response with a reinforcer; she has thereby decreased the likelihood of Jim speaking up in subsequent meetings.)

Generalized Effects

It is important to note, in the second example, that the manager has not merely *decreased* the probability of her subordinate speaking up about the bad debt reserve; she has also decreased the probability of the subordinate speaking up in meetings generally. In the first example, the manager *increased* the likelihood that her subordinate will speak up at subsequent meetings.

The manager's behavior, in a specific situation, will influence a subordinate's behavior in all situations that are *similar* to that specific situation (in this example, meetings). This accounts for the fact that people behave differently in *different* situations. The subordinate who rarely says anything in group meetings may be quite talkative in one-on-one interactions because he has been extinguished in the former instance and reinforced in the latter. Some dynamic, expressive motivational speakers can be quite shy and retiring in more personal, one-on-one interactions

[Readers may wish to consciously try reinforcing someone with a positive emotional response in reaction to a specific behavior by the other person. Two things might be noted: the speaker will be liked more by the other person because he/she has paired him/herself with a reinforcer; the reinforced behavior will start to increase in strength and frequency.]

Classical Versus Operant Learning

Operant, unlike classical, learning is directed toward affecting immediate consequences, primarily in the form of changing other people's thoughts, feelings, and behavior. And no stimulus has as strong an impact on an individual's behavior as does the behavior of another person. The effects of classical pairings may not be apparent for some time. This explains why staff members and consultants often weaken their impact on line managers and on an organization when, after completing their "objective" study, they merely submit a written report. Figures and graphs rarely have a strong impact on an individual, and such reports are likely to gather dust in someone's desk drawer.

Were the consultants or staff to take the time to interact at a personal level by successfully establishing rapport with top management, it is much less likely that their recommendations would be ignored. Likewise, sales are rarely achieved by written correspondence; they require face-to-face interactions – again, because virtually no stimulus is as potentially reinforcing or aversive to an individual as is another person's behavior, especially their emotional reactions. If personal interactions are handled badly, of course, their potential for destructive consequences is also quite high.

The immediate effect of extinction is *always* anger and an underlying uneasiness. When a manager does not respond to a subordinate's comments directly and immediately, the subordinate will experience feelings of frustration, anger, and fear. (This crucial point will be discussed in more detail later.)

[The reader may wish to ask a person some innocuous question and, after the person has responded to the question, monotonely go on to a different topic. Example: "What did you do last night?" After the person answers, especially if they did something enjoyable, say something like, "You know, I think I'll have lunch at Harvey's cafe tomorrow; I haven't been there in a long time." Note their frustration. Imagine their reaction if your question had addressed an important issue.]

The Dark Side of Reinforcement

It is important to be specific when analyzing manager-subordinate interactions. The details of a manager's behavior (minute gestures, subtle changes in tone of voice, choice of words) as well as its timing can have a crucial impact on a subordinate.

Generally accepted principles of how a "good" manager should act can lead to crucial mistakes. For instance, a general philosophy of "concern" for one's subordinates may sound like "good" management, but it can have unfortunate results.

Consider the following example: A subordinate was known to be excessively (fear-driven) self-deprecating. He often used such phrases as, "I'm all thumbs when I try to do that," or "I sure am stupid when it comes to working with numbers." The manager wanted to eliminate this behavior. One day, the subordinate was asked to role-play a performance review in the presence of a group of people that included his manager. When the review was finished, the following exchange took place:

> Subordinate: Well, I sure bombed that one.
> Manager (showing "concern"): No you didn't, John. That was a fine job. I thought it was handled very well.

The manager, as most people do, has followed his subordinate's typical (and often nonrealistic) self-deprecating response with a stimulus reinforcing (reassurance) to the subordinate. Thus, the manager *increased* the likelihood that the subordinate will engage in similar behavior in the future, behavior that is already excessive. Also,
the manager has actually decreased the subordinate's confidence and increased his dependency on others and his need for their reassurance.

Indeed, the subordinate may well have a self-deprecating view of himself precisely because so many people, but especially his manager, reinforce that type of behavior with their too frequent reassurance.

A more effective response in this situation would be silence, or merely ignoring the response and addressing oneself to another topic (extinction). This type of response, by failing to reinforce the unwanted behavior, would decrease its strength and frequency. Strangely enough, the manager would be bolstering the person's confidence because he/she did not reinforce this constant self-criticism. (For the brave of heart, an even better response to the self-deprecation might be agreement: Subordinate: "I sure bombed that one." Manager: "Well, maybe you're right.")

"Showing concern" for a subordinate often results in lengthy discussions with the subordinate about her/his problems and complaints. This is another example of a "good" management theory that is too general to be effective. If a manager's attention is reinforcing to a subordinate (as it frequently is), and if the subordinate only elicits this managerial attention when he complains about the company, then he will complain about the company whenever possible. It is also important to note that, not only his overt complaining, but also his actual feelings toward the company, will become more negative because they are being reinforced.

A large Midwest company was undergoing a complete revamping of its sales department. Numerous firings and demotions, as well as some promotions, were occurring. One of the managers asked that further changes be delayed so that the "dust could settle" because "morale was falling to a low level". Investigation showed that a typical interchange between this manager and his subordinate went as follows:

> Subordinate: What the hell is going on here? I just found out they fired Jack. Hell, he's been with this company twenty-five years.
> Concerned Manager: Well, why don't we go into my office and talk about it? (Reinforcer)
> Subordinate: All right, but I don't know what the hell there is to talk about. When a guy gives up twenty-five years of his life and then has the company put him out in the street, I don't know what you're supposed to expect next.
> Concerned Manager: Well, I think things are settling down now. (Reinforcer) How do you feel about your own position?

Subordinate: How the hell should I feel about my position! I'm scared. Everybody's scared. You've got a blood bath going on and nobody knows whom the axe will fall on next.

Concerned Manager: Now, Jim, I don't think there's anything to worry about. You're doing an excellent job. I was at corporate headquarters and all of us were talking about how well you were doing. (Strong reinforcer)

By following the subordinate's complaining behavior with reinforcers, the manager has increased the likelihood of further complaining responses by his subordinate; in fact, *he has increased the probability of low morale in his department.* The manager's attention, concern, and compliments were contingent upon his subordinate complaining; they should have been expressed when the subordinate was more positive and/or had accomplished something constructive.

A better response on the manager's part would have been a perfunctory acknowledgement of his subordinate's point, quickly followed by a change of subject:

Manager (in a quiet monotone): Oh, I don't think things are quite that bad. (Then quickly and with much more inflection): Say, how did your sales call go yesterday at Preston Corporation?

[The reader is encouraged to think of someone in their life who does a lot of complaining about other people. Then consider people's reaction to this person's complaints. Are some people reinforcing the behavior? Why? Do they like to see someone angry at others?]

The Timing of Reinforcers

A valid objection might be raised that people need reassurance and concern when their behavior indicates they are frightened, upset, or lacking in confidence. True. The crucial element is timing, however. The time to give the salesperson reassurance and compliments is when she/he says a sales call went well, not when they are complaining.

If a manager shows concern only when her assistant pouts, she will pout in the future. If the manager responds emotionally when her assistant expresses positive attitudes, her assistant will be more likely to hold positive attitudes. The time to tell one's wife she is liked and respected by many people is when she says she has had a good time at a party, not when she says nobody cares for her. The time to tell one's husband he is not overweight is when he feels good about himself, not when he is asking, in an insecure moment, if he looks fat.

In other words, it is not only the manager's concern that is important, but also, *when* the concern or reassurance is shown. To follow self-deprecatory or complaining response patterns with reassurance or a show of concern is to reinforce – and increase the strength of – these attitudes. In both instances the manager might instead have replied with a quick monotone, "Maybe so," followed by a more interested, "Say, how are you coming along with your sales call on Preston Corporation?" While this might well have been irritating to the subordinate (extinction), it would have *weakened* ineffective behavior, and *strengthened* the focus on relevant matters (sales). The road to hell is indeed paved with good intentions!

The criterion of when to stop reinforcing some behavior is determined by its frequency. If your daughter walks in the house crying, show her concern and support. If your daughter walks in the house crying three or four times a week, extinction may be in order. A manager can destroy a subordinate's confidence by giving him reassurance and concern when he is self-deprecating, especially when the ineffective behavior is frequent and repetitive.

[The reader is asked to note who is the most reinforcing person in their inner circle. That is probably the person you like the most. Then note what behavior in others, especially you, that person is reinforcing.

The reader might also try to be self-deprecating and note how many people reinforce you. Why do they? Because self-deprecating people alleviate our fear.]

Why Such Bad Timing?

In fact, there are many situations in which managers give subordinates attention and reassurance at the worst possible time. If a salesperson does not successfully make a sale, many managers rush to her side, explore the situation in depth, condemn the customer, and reassure the salesperson that she has made the best effort possible. If the salesperson successfully completes a sale, she is often given a perfunctory pat on the back and sent on her way (extinction). Success seems to have little effect on, and can even be threatening to, the manager, hence the extinction.

The time to rush to the salesperson's side, explore the intricacies of the transaction, and provide enthusiastic reassurance, of course, is when she has been successful, not when she has failed. It is her success that should be reinforcing to her manager, not her failures that frighten him. Too often, this type of fear reaction on the manager's part leads to behavior that is intensely reinforcing to the subordinate, thus reinforcing the wrong thing at the wrong time in the wrong way.

The time to reassure and appreciate the director of computer services is not when he apologizes for his inability to get reports out on time; it is when he does get the reports out on time. His failures should probably be met with silence. If the failures are too frequent, more drastic action may be called for. But if his successes are reinforced, it is less likely failures will occur in the first place.

That we are loved by someone is not nearly as important as *why* we are loved by that person. It is a relatively simple task to gather about ourselves those who love us when we are crushed by misfortune, when we feel despair, when we fail an appointed task, when we accept our inferiority, when we express our fears and self-doubts. Such "love", however, decreases our confidence, our liking and respect for ourselves. Far more difficult is the task of gathering about ourselves those rare people who truly love us when good fortune befalls us, when we successfully accomplish our goals, when we are confident about our ability to handle a given task, when we are happy and content about our life. This "love" increases our confidence, our liking and respect for ourselves.

[The reader is asked to finish this phrase with an appropriate act in their life, "You know, I think I did a pretty good job of ..." Say this to everyone in your inner circle, including your boss. Who reinforces you for liking yourself? Who extinguishes you? Who seems to like your confidence? Reinforce them for doing so!]

Are compliments a good reinforcer?

Does self-deprecating behavior increase people's liking of me?

Why are operations and sales so often at each others throat?

Is being number one in your industry dangerous for an organization?

CHAPTER 12

REINFORCEMENT AND EXTINCTION: Part 2

What Is A Reinforcer?

It is important to recognize that unusual stimuli can be, and often are, reinforcing to an individual. Suppose we turn our reinforcement principle around to read: Any stimulus which strengthens a response when it immediately follows the response is a reinforcer. When a particular type of behavior by a subordinate continually recurs, consequently, managers should note how they are reacting to the behavior; that managerial behavior may well be a reinforcer to the subordinate.

If, for example, a subordinate is hostile and frequently insulting to his manager, it may well be the manager's frightened uneasiness, and nervous, apologetic reactions that are reinforcing the insulting behavior.

> Subordinate: Did you talk to the VP about my idea?
> Manager: I really haven't had a chance yet.
> Subordinate: You're really intent on putting things off all the time, aren't you?
> Manager (becoming uneasy): I don't think that's true.
> Subordinate: Baloney. I'll bet your wife has to remind you to tie your shoes every morning.
> Manager: I may get to see the VP tomorrow.
> Subordinate: You'll find a way to duck it.

111

People who fear confrontations, like this manager, are often the target of hostile people. Why? Because their nervous, frightened reactions are so reinforcing to hostile people. How do we know when a person is hostile? When they frequently and repetitively use "you-aversive" pairings in order to elicit hurt feelings from others. Who won't hostile people attack? People who do not respond in a frightened way to their attacks.

[The reader is asked here to wait for a "you-aversive" pairing directed at him/her by a hostile person or even someone who is temporarily angry. What's your best reaction? Since your uneasiness and discomfort are so reinforcing to them at that moment, your best reaction, to weaken their hostility, is…laughter. Example:

> They: Hey, where do you get those ugly shirts you always wear?
> You (laughing): Oh, thank you for taking an interest in how I dress.

[Why not try it?]

Consider the following: A general manager of operations is talking to his subordinate, a plant manager. The general manager has always wanted his plant manager to fire the plant superintendent, Paul Wicker. The plant manager rejects this idea, partially because he is a personal friend of Wicker. The following interchange takes place:

> Manager: How's Wicker doing?
> Subordinate: Well, I know you feel he's fallen off a bit in the last few weeks, but I think it might be a personal problem. I think he's been having some trouble with his wife
> Manager (grimaces and makes a series of mildly skeptical, challenging responses): Come on, do you really think it's due to a personal problem?
> Subordinate: Yeah, I think it is.
> Manager: Oh, come on. I don't think his personal life would have that much impact on him down here at the plant.

Subordinate: Sure it could. I was over at his house several weeks ago, and I know the problem is serious.

Manager: It can't be that serious.

Subordinate: The hell it's not serious. It's very serious, and it's having a very bad effect on him.

This example would seem to contradict our basic reinforcement principle, but only because we often make wrong assumptions about what constitutes a reinforcer. The manager has emitted a series of skeptical, challenging responses which have actually solidified his subordinate's position. The subordinate started off "thinking" Wicker's behavior was a personal problem and ended up "knowing" it. If following a response with a reinforcer indeed increases its strength and likelihood of recurring, then a skeptical, challenging response by the manager is a reinforcer to this particular subordinate. Being astute, the manager accepts this fact and, on a later occasion, uses it to good advantage:

Manager: Have you made up your budget for next year?

Subordinate: Well, I've got the preliminary figures in. I'll have to wait for the final figures, but I think I might come in with a budget that is 96% of this year's. (Most of the general manager's plants are estimating a budget that exceeds the present year's, hence he wants to reinforce this subordinate's response.)

Manager: Ninety-six percent of this year's budget? I don't see how you can do it.

Subordinate: It won't be the easiest thing in the world, but I think we can do it.

Manager: I think you're making a mistake. I can't see how you could possibly go under this year's budget.

Subordinate: We run a pretty tight ship here. I'm quite sure we can hit 96% of budget.

Manager: Well, I doubt that you're going to make it.

Subordinate: Well, my own guess is that we'll not only make 96%, we might even go below it.

Can a skeptical, challenging response by the manager act as a reinforcer to the subordinate? Absolutely.

The point is that virtually any stimulus, including pain, is a reinforcer to someone. Many managers err in not being able to see and accept the fact that a stimulus which is quite aversive to them is reinforcing to several of their subordinates. In this example the subordinate initially "thought he might come in with a 96% budget", but firmly committed himself by the end of the interchange. It would now be emotionally difficult for him to come in with a higher budget. He is motivated! (We are not concerned with the appropriateness of the budget here, only with behavioral changes.)

Fear and Reinforcers

Fear is a pervasive motivator; its presence is ubiquitous. But periodically we feel free of fear. What gives us this freedom? Anything that alleviates our fear, even temporarily. We have seen that reinforcers do alleviate fear, albeit temporarily. Thus, we could define a reinforcer as anything that stops our fear, even for a short time.

Larry, for example, has a fear of being insignificant to his boss, Sandra. This is indicated by his frequent banal questions of Sandra, his inappropriate interruptions, and, in general, his excessive prolonging of conversations with her. Personal attention from Sandra is a strong reinforcer to him. This personal attention, when given, will strengthen any of Larry's behavior it follows, but it will eliminate his fear of being insignificant as only long as it is being given. When the personal attention stops, the fear reactivates and again becomes a primary motivator of Larry's behavior.

> Larry (driven by his fear of being insignificant, pops his head in Sandra's door): Sandra, have you got a second?
> Sandra: Sure Larry, what's up?
> Larry (sits down): I was just wondering if you wanted the marketing report or the sales figures first.

Sandra: The marketing report.

Larry: OK. Although you know, some people like to see the sales figures first.

Sandra: Not me, OK? (Looks down at some papers on her desk.)

Larry: OK. I just wanted to be sure how you felt about it.

Sandra (looks up): By the way, I thought you did a good job on that marketing analysis.

Larry (who has just been reinforced): Oh, did you? Thanks, thanks a lot.

Sandra: I thought your conclusions were right on target.

Larry: Well, I tried to think it through (Larry's fear is diminished; he's feeling pretty good about himself).

Sandra: Anyway, let's get the marketing report done first (looks back to the papers on her desk)

Larry (Sandra's focus has slid off him, hence his fear starts returning to drive his behavior): You know, I agree with you. I think a marketing report...

Probably few reinforcers are as powerful as those that stop a fear driving excessive behavior. Nevertheless, they do little to alleviate fear over any appreciable length of time. They do, however, direct fear-driven behavior by strengthening the responses they follow. In the above example, had Sandra waited until Larry was leaving, she would have at least reinforced the response of severing the interaction. Better, she might have waited until he was working quietly in his office to "pop-in" and reinforce him (a difficult task since most of us prefer to let "sleeping dogs lie" and not disturb them, even with reinforcers. The key point is this: If you're going to reinforce a person by temporarily alleviating their fear, try to make sure their behavior of the moment is constructive and something you want.

[The reader is asked to determine some fear-driven, hence excessive behavior on the part of someone in their inner circle. Then try to determine what would stop that fear, albeit temporarily. Try that stimulus as a reinforcer and see if the person responds to it as such (likes you more). Be sure the person is doing something you want when you use the reinforcer.

If, for example, an assistant is driven by a fear of criticism, wait until they are doing something constructive, then compliment them, preferably in the area in which they most fear being criticized, such as making travel arrangements.]

The Danger of Fear

The example of Larry and Sandra leads to a most important conclusion. Fear-driven behavior usually elicits, from confident people at least, the very behavior that is feared. If Sandra is confident, she will find Larry's constant need for attention annoying and frustrating. As a result, she will tend to avoid interacting with him whenever possible and be "in the middle of something important" when he does trap her. In short, Larry is eliciting the very behavior from Sandra (being insignificant) he dreads most.

If, on the other hand, Larry had a boss who feared "lack of control, then that boss would probably love Larry and his constant need for attention and approval. And Larry would enjoy such a boss because they would be having so many mutually reinforcing interactions. This is why, when we have a choice, we tend to pick as friends those who share our fears. Unfortunately, this ensures our fears will never be confronted nor permanently lessened. (It must be said that we tend to pick as lovers those who we think will alleviate our fears. This explains why so many men focus on superficial looks when dating; having a "trophy" on one's arm tends to diminish our fears of being looked down upon, disrespected, or ridiculed by other men.)

That we do not have the freedom to pick those with whom we must interact in the workplace accounts for the fact, in the author's experience, that most people are more effective in work environments than in personal relations. Being exposed to, and forced to interact with, different personalities, some of whom don't put up with our foolishness, may make us a better and more adaptable (wider response repertoire) person indeed.

[It is suggested that the reader determine any common fears among his/her closest friends. Do you have that fear? Are your closest friends highly independent people? Do they fear being controlled by others? Do you?]

Managing Up

Since the behavior of others has more impact on us than any other stimulus, it stands to reason that a subordinate can influence the judgments and attitudes of his/her superior. Influence depends not only on position, but also on behavior and the astute use of reinforcers and aversives.

To illustrate: A subordinate has determined that self-deprecating behavior in others is indeed reinforcing to her manager. She therefore engages in such behavior when her manager compliments her:

> Manager: Leslie, you did a fine job on the sales call.
> Subordinate (apologetically): Gee, I don't know. I think I made a few mistakes I shouldn't have made.
> Manager: Well, I think you did an outstanding job!
> Subordinate: Thank you, but I know I've got a lot to learn.

The subordinate has increased the probability that the manager will make positive comments to her. Also, by pairing herself with a stimulus reinforcing to her manager (self-deprecating behavior), she has increased the likelihood that the manager will think highly of her in future assessment and promotional situations. The behavior of a person is often reinforcing to others because that behavior alleviates their fear. The above manager probably fears confidence in others, especially his subordinates, possibly anticipating some loss of control if a person likes and respects him or herself; self-deprecating behavior by someone, consequently, alleviates his anxiety and is a reinforcer to him.

A crucial aside: Remember to never reinforce someone in another person's presence. Third parties, because they aren't the recipient of the reinforcer, usually dislike such interactions. Anyone present during the above exchange might well pair the subordinate with aversives to her manager when they are alone, "Don't you find her manipulative?"

[The reader is again asked to determine some excessive behavior patterns in a person with whom they interact frequently. What behavior in others might they be trying to prevent? This is their fear. What behavior by you would alleviate that fear? That's a reinforcer to them.

My manager is extolling his physical prowess excessively. He may well fear being seen as weak. Telling him he is certainly a powerful person at the appropriate time could be quite reinforcing to him. Please use these ideas judiciously.]

Do We Like People Liking Each Other?

Many managers consider it aversive if two or more of their subordinates interact with each other in a mutually reinforcing manner. This is especially true of chief executive officers. The "loneliness of command" often leads chief executives to feel even more alone and left out if they see two vice presidents chatting amicably, and without any apparent need for their superior's advice and direction. This in turn may lead the chief executive to reinforce negative comments by one vice president about another while giving real accomplishments short shrift.

> Vice President-Sales (walking into president's office): Say, I thought you would like to know we just sold Ford our first order of sheet rolled steel.
> President (looks up momentarily): Oh, that's good. I've got to pull these damn figures together for the board. (Extinction)
> Vice President-Sales (starts to walk out, then stops): By the way, I don't know if Jim (vice president-operations) will be able to give you those production figures by Thursday as you'd asked him to (pairs vice president-operations with aversive stimuli).

President (puts down his pen, looks up with much more emotional interest, thus reinforcing the speaker): When did you hear that?

Vice President-Sales: I heard him telling the auditors the other day he's behind on those figures (again pairs VP-operations with an aversive).

President (stronger emotional reaction, again reinforcing speaker): He always seems to be behind on figures! I don't know what the hell goes on in his mind (another VP-operations aversive pairing).

Vice President-Sales: Well, I don't think he feels they're too important (another aversive pairing).

President (more intense): There seem to be a few things he feels aren't important.

Vice President-Sales: I know. I tried to get him to go with me on an important sales call, and he said there just wasn't enough time.

President: When did that happen?

Assume that attention from the president is a reinforcer to the vice president of sales. What is this attention contingent upon? Obviously not sales, since the announcement of a new customer was met with a perfunctory response by the president (extinction). Condemnation of a colleague, on the other hand, was met with a high degree of attention, emotional reactions, and concern.

Operations and sales are often aversive to each other. This animosity is not innate. It is the result of the chief executive reinforcing mutually negative attitudes which then sweep through the two departments. Destructive internal competition is the inevitable result.

A possible solution lies in the subordinate's influence on his manager. A vice president, for example, can pair his president's reinforcement of such behavior with aversive stimuli. A subordinate can also extinguish his manager's reinforcing comments when criticism of others occurs. It is important to note in the above example that the subordinate is also reinforcing the manager with his critical remarks about a colleague; stopping this mutually reinforcing, but destructive, interaction would alter the president's behavior. How do subordinates feel when their manager

119

criticizes another subordinate? Too often, it's reinforcing. How do many managers feel when a subordinate criticizes another subordinate? Too often, it's reinforcing.

The negative attitudes of the VP-sales toward operations, reinforced by the president, in the above example will then be passed along and infect his department. The following example of a subsequent interchange between a sales manager and one of his salespeople is too often the result:

> Sales Manager: Mike, you're really not getting the sales we need out of your territory. How come?
> Salesman: Well, I don't know how you can expect me to get sales when those bloody people in the plant can't make the product right and never get it out the door on time.
> Sales Manager: Yeah, I know your problem. The plant manager is not really tough enough on his people. Well, do the best you can.

The manager's agreement has reinforced his subordinate's negative attitudes toward operations people. Notice also that both the salesperson and the manager have paired operations people with aversive stimuli—a response that is not likely to enhance positive attitudes.

Yet this sales manager would be the first to agree with higher management that attitudes between operations and sales must be "cleaned up"; and he would be sincere. This sales manager, like most of us, would be unaware of his influence in this area; it's just too hard to engage in some behavior and, at the same time, observe and evaluate your own behavior.

[The reader is asked to pair a colleague with an aversive to his/her manager, then note the manager's reaction. Are you reinforced or extinguished? This exercise should be carried out in the interests of science and learning, not in the interests of getting rid of competent competition.]

A Most Destructive Situation

Certainly one of the most destructive situations in an organization occurs when managers reinforce subordinates who pair customers or clients with aversives. This type of situation always presages a rapid decline of the organization.

Oddly enough, it most often occurs in organizations that are the leaders in their field. The arrogance that being number one can so readily breed, frequently leads employees (including the CEO) to look askance at anyone who might deign to make demands on them. Such foolish people are immediately ridiculed.

And who would be so presumptuous as to make demands on these titans? Only a customer. Thus, they must be put in their place. And what better way to do so than by pairing them with aversives. If anything leads employees to treat customers poorly, these customer-aversive pairings will. Examples of arrogant "customer-aversive pairings" by industry leaders unfortunately abound in the history of business. These pairings probably have much to do with competitors eventually taking over the coveted top spot.

[The reader is asked to try a customer-aversive pairing with some members of senior management. If you are reinforced, you might want to consider updating your resume.]

How can I reinforce (encourage) behavior that never occurs?

What is the quickest way to change someone's behavior?

What is the best criterion for judging behavior as excessive?

CHAPTER 13

REINFORCEMENT AND EXTINCTION: Part 3

Organizations rarely reinforce managers for managing the behavior of their subordinates properly. Promotions to management levels are too often based on a person's technical competence, a policy that often leads to failure. Generally speaking, the higher a person moves in an organization, the more influence they will have on the behavior of employees.

Individuals reinforced (promoted) for their technical abilities will obviously continue to focus on technical problems rather than on employees and their behavior. They can easily end up with weak, ineffective subordinates because they often do all the work themselves; after all, they have to maintain their excellent reputation in the technical area because their promotion was based on it. Eventually, the workload becomes too great, and the department functions at minimally adequate levels. If the company grows, more work is shunted to the department until a bottleneck or a collapse of the manager or the department occurs.

This sequence of events is especially true in the case of entrepreneurs who, when they start a company, must do everything themselves. If the company grows, the response of doing everything oneself is being reinforced by its success. When the company grows to the point at which delegation of authority and responsibility is essential, the entrepreneur is unable to delegate. Why should she? The company's growth has amply reinforced the entrepreneur for doing everything herself (worse, she may have delegated once and the job turned out poorly).

Hence does success often breed the seeds of failure. Behavior that is reinforced in one context may well be ineffective in different environments – and the environment is always changing ("There is no hitching post in the universe.").

Indeed, people often start their own business because of a fear of being controlled by others. Owning their own company doesn't diminish this fear. As with most micro-managers, their fear gets in the way of organizational growth and the confidence of employees (Who can develop confidence when they're not trusted?).

[The reader is asked to wait for his/her manager to delegate some responsibility to them, even if it is expected, and emotionally express appreciation (reinforcement) for the manager's trust in them.]

Changing Behavior

As mentioned, the influences over an individual's behavior are often external and stem from the behavior of the manager and, to a lesser degree, that of other people in the work environment. The quickest way to change behavior, consequently, is to change the individual's environment, especially the interpersonal environment, such as the manager.

An individual can be quite successful under one manager and cause serious problems under another, even though his/her responsibilities remain unchanged. And one of the quickest ways to change the behavior of everyone in an organization is to change the chief executive officer. Every employee joins a "new" company when a new CEO is brought in, especially if he/she is quite different from the old CEO.

It is often tempting, nevertheless, for managers to say that behavior is internally caused (by factors within the individual himself). This allows the manager to avoid blame for another person's incompetence by criticizing their faults rather than looking at themselves and the impact they are having, what behaviors they are reinforcing or extinguishing, what pairings they are making. In other words, we pair failures with our subordinates, rather than allowing others to pair us with them.

This approach leads us into a blind alley, however. Outside of performing a lobotomy, there is little anyone can do to change what goes on inside an individual. Even the behavioral changes caused by psychotherapists come about, not because of the patient's new and brilliant insights, but because of her/his interaction with the therapist. Thus, it is often our behavior, not internal factors, that leads others to behave the way they do in our presence, especially if we have interacted with them frequently, and most especially if we're their manager.

The most effective way to change an individual's behavior in the work setting, consequently, is to change the manager's behavior.

[The reader is asked to think about their own typical response to some frequent, repetitive behavior by someone they know well. Think of a behavior that would be opposite your usual response. When the person engages in their typical behavior, respond in a way opposite your normal reaction. Note their reaction and the subsequent frequency of their typical behavior.

Suppose someone you know well is typically hypercritical. When they next say, "Those guys are really jerks!", respond in an opposite manner to your usual approach. If you normally agreed ("You got that right!"), try disagreeing ("Oh baloney, those guys are great; I really like them!"). Are they startled? Do they dislike you a bit? Does their hypercriticalness become weaker? Do you sense the influence of your behavior on them?]

Shaping Behavior

Following a desirable response with a reinforcer increases its strength and probability of recurring. But suppose the desirable response never occurs in the first place. We may be ready to jump in with a strong reinforcer when our manager says, "You did a beautiful job on that report," but what if she never says it? How can we reinforce behavior that is not occurring at all?

The answer is that we must "shape" behavior. This means patiently reinforcing *successive approximations* to the desired response. The instance in which the manager gave a skeptical, challenging (reinforcing) response to his manager's budget projection was an instance of shaping. The subordinate initially "thought" he could make a 96% budget. By successively reinforcing this behavior with his skeptical challenges, the manager made the subordinate's commitment stronger and stronger until the subordinate "knew" he was going to make the budget, or better.

Consider the following example in which a salesperson is attempting to elicit a "purchase" response from a prospective customer:

> Customer: Our current supplier is really taking care of our needs.
>
> Salesperson: Do you think you might be making a mistake relying on only one supplier?
>
> Customer: Well, you may have a point there.
>
> Salesperson: I believe you're right. Having several suppliers can give you more reliable service; a little competition for your attention can't hurt.
>
> Customer: Well, I suppose I could try you on a small order.
>
> Salesperson: I believe you'd be quite happy you did. You'd have the sense of security of having a second source if anything happened to your other one.
>
> Customer: How would I go about placing an order if I wanted to?
>
> Salesperson: Your wish is my command. Just tell me what you'd like now and I'll make sure you get it.
>
> Customer: I suppose I could give you a small order for six gross of .5 nuts and bolts.
>
> Salesperson: Excellent! I think you're making a wise decision. When would you like them?

The salesperson has successfully shaped the customer into a purchase response and solidified that response with reinforcement. It is important, of course, to know what is reinforcing to a specific customer (sometimes violent arguments are). Notice also that each time the salesperson uses a reinforcer, she is pairing herself with it; in effect, she is becoming a reinforcer to the customer and increasing the probability that the customer will see her on subsequent visits.

The point of shaping is to reinforce the listener's slightest tendency toward the desired response. Had the salesperson settled for nothing but a large order, it is doubtful that she would have gotten any order at all. Setting our sights on a specific behavior often leads us to miss numerous opportunities to reinforce others when they are making some movement toward that behavior.

By aiming only for the big order, she would not have reinforced small, tentative responses on the customer's part that leaned in the direction of making a purchase—and by not reinforcing the responses, she would have, by definition, extinguished them! Indeed, it is surprising how few salespeople even reinforce a customer who says, "I'll place the order with you." Most salespeople merely pick up their order books and start writing; then they wonder why their relationship with customers is so tentative.

The ability to reinforce others, even when we sincerely like what they did, is a rare phenomenon in our society. Indeed, it is often paired with aversives, such as "phoniness", especially by people who are not the recipient of the reinforcement at that time. Nowhere is the inability to use reinforcers more destructive than in the managerial ranks, but sales is a close second.

[Think of some rarely seen behavior you would like in your manager, such as a compliment directed at you. Try to shape behavior by emotionally reinforcing your manager when he/she shows any tendency to say anything positive about anyone or anything until they eventually get around to you. Be patient. But shaping can take place quite rapidly if you truly express emotional reinforcers. And remember, each time you do, you're pairing yourself with them.]

Rational Arguments Versus Reinforcers

Behavior is not necessarily a rational, objective process. Consider the case of a somewhat contentious person who finds arguments with his manager reinforcing (probably because arguments have been paired with an emotional response on the manager's part).

> Manager: Well, the consensus seems to be that we start shipping our goods by rail instead of trucking them. Dick, we haven't heard from you about it. How do you feel?
>
> Subordinate: Well, I'm not as certain as apparently everyone else is that we should do it that way. You know, we really don't have solid figures on what it will cost us to ship by rail.
>
> Manager: Yes, but the estimates given us by the railroad people are substantially below our trucking costs.
>
> Subordinate: Maybe, but we don't know if those estimates will hold water.
>
> Manager (getting irritated): We don't know that they won't hold water.
>
> Subordinate: I've got a friend who started to use rail and found out the costs were underestimated by 50%.
>
> Manager (getting quite irritated): That doesn't mean this railroad is underestimating our cost.
>
> Subordinate: Maybe not, but you know the railroad people never have pinned down their costs too well.
>
> Manager (now fuming): I think the service they have given us in the past was quite accurate!
>
> Subordinate: Well, I think we're making a mistake. We know what the shipping costs are when we use trucks, and we are moving into an area where we don't know what's going to hit us. I think we should stay with trucking for our own good.

Unrealistic though it sounds, the subordinate's final determined option for trucking is not the result of rational, logical analysis; it is, rather, the result of reinforced shaping by the manager. The subordinate's response has been shaped from one of tentative choice (favoring trucking) to the point at which there is little doubt in his mind that trucking is the most effective alternative. Had the manager, instead of engaging in a debate, greeted his subordinate's initial tentative response with mild acceptance, he would have decreased the probability of the subordinate's firm dissenting opinion.

Feelings Are the Fathers of Thoughts. Virtually all management decisions involve subjective judgments. An individual's perceptions of an issue can result from his feelings toward the people holding a given position on the issue as much as from rational analysis. In the above example, had the consensus favored trucking, that particular subordinate might well have opted for shipping by rail—and would have supplied excellent reasons for using the railroad, because there are two sides to any management issue. Which one a person chooses too often depends on their feelings toward the other people involved in the decision or their need for attention rather than on their analyses of the issue itself. Any expressed idea has to come from (be paired with) a person. If that person is disliked (an aversive stimulus to an individual), the probability is increased that the individual will disagree with the idea.

This is a much more common phenomenon than most people believe. In the example just mentioned, the manager—and possibly the group as a whole—constituted aversive stimuli to the subordinate, hence his frequent oppositional response. Suppose, however, a manager had just given this subordinate a large, unexpected raise. By pairing himself with this strong reinforcer, the manager has increased the probability that the subordinate will agree with any position the manager takes on a given matter. Both would probably be shocked if the subordinate were to oppose the manager in a meeting taking place a day after the raise was given.

Individuals assume the position that is paired with the strongest reinforcers for them. This explains why management is for management, labor is for labor, and neither stands up for a rational, just analysis of the issues.

[The reader is asked to think of two rational reasons why smoking is destructive to men (e.g., it may cause cancer). Now think of two emotional aversives (it may make men impotent and lead to embarrassing sexual encounters). Which is more influential? We would all do well to remember this when we're trying to sell our proposal to management or customers.]

Frequency

Shaping is an important concept for the manager. Wisely used, it can overcome a subordinate's resistance to the manager's views. Lest managers fear developing a group of subordinates in their own image, however, they might remember that they should also reinforce reasonable dissension.

Determining what is reasonable and what is not is the manager's responsibility and, in making this decision, the frequency of the behavior is the best criterion. (For example, repetitious contrariness by a subordinate is not reasonable.) Complaints should be given minimal attention (extinguished) when they come from a subordinate who frequently complains; they should be thoroughly explored when they come from a subordinate who rarely complains. Overly positive assessments of problem situations by a subordinate should be given short shrift when such assessments have been frequent, repetitive, and unrealistic (excessive) in the past. Positive assessments should be amply reinforced, however, when given by a subordinate who has been constantly complaining in the past.

How important is money as a motivator?

Would it help a new manager to know what kind of a person his predecessor was?

What can I expect if I extinguish hostile behavior?

Is extinction ever appropriate to use?

CHAPTER 14

REINFORCEMENT AND EXTINCTION: Part 4

The Reinforcing Value of Money

We should note two problems connected with the use of money as a reinforcer in industry. First, as mentioned previously, money is not a reinforcer to some people. In fact, the reinforcers and aversive stimuli found in other people's behavior have far more influence on most people. Those who strive to accumulate great sums of money often do so only because being wealthy has elicited (been paired with) admiration, awe, subservience, and even respect from other people in their past experiences. Seeing people stop and stare at a man getting out of a chauffeur-driven car is but one example of this pairing.

The second problem with money, as used by most organizations, is that its presentation is not contingent upon any particular behavior. Money is generally given at certain time intervals, not immediately after a specific response by an individual.

Even without this response contingency, an organization obviously pairs itself with the money it gives people. Thus, high paying organizations will generally elicit favorable responses concerning the organization from employees to whom money is a reinforcer. This may have little impact on their day-to-day work behavior, however, especially if their manager is an

131

aversive stimulus to them. Managers often rely on money to motivate people because they don't want the responsibility themselves.

Extinction

We have stated (Principle VI) that any response not immediately followed by a reinforcer is weakened and has less probability of recurring and that this is called extinction. Unfortunately, the situation is not quite as simple as it first appears.

It is true that when a particular response has been reinforced *every time* it has occurred, if the reinforcement is suddenly stopped, the response will quickly cease to occur. Every time we drop something and look down for it (response), it is *always* there (reinforcement) because of the force of gravity. This does not hold true in outer space, however, and our astronauts have easily adapted to looking around and up, rather than down, for dropped objects; the response of looking down was quickly extinguished, partially because it had been reinforced every time in the astronaut's past experiences.

Suppose, however, we don't follow every response with a reinforcer; rather, we reinforce every tenth response, on average. That is, we might reinforce the eighth response of a given behavior, then the twenty-second response, the thirty-first response, and so on. We reinforce the response at a rate which averages every tenth occurrence of the behavior, but the reinforcement is given randomly. Extinction in this case takes much longer. *A response will have to be emitted many more times during extinction before it stops occurring if it has previously had periodic rather than constant reinforcement.* Gambling behavior illustrates this situation. If a gambler who places bets on horses wins *every* time, he will soon stop wagering on horses if he suddenly begins losing every time. If he wins *periodically*, however, he will have to lose consistently many more times before he stops gambling completely. Such consistent losing is unlikely, which accounts for the tenacity and persistence of gambling behavior.

Classical Extinction. In operant learning, we are concerned with specific behavior and the responses of others to that behavior. In classical learning, on the other hand, we are concerned with the pairings which occur in an individual's experience, regardless of his behavior at the moment. A situation similar to operant extinction occurs in classical learning. Suppose a mother *always* spanks her child after shouting the word "no". If she continues shouting "no" but suddenly stops spanking her child, the word "no" will soon lose its effectiveness (extinction). If she had *periodically* paired the word "no" with a spanking, it would have remained effective much longer.

The manager who continually shouts at his subordinates, but always gives them appropriate raises and promotions, soon finds subordinates smiling at his shouting. New subordinates are initially terrified of him, but are consoled by peers with the admonition that "his bark is worse than his bite". Far worse is the manager who, in his frantic desire to be liked by his subordinates, constantly praises them for everything they do. The mere frequency of these comments, spoken without periodic pairing with other reinforcers, leads them to be extinguished quickly as reinforcers. New subordinates love this manager initially, but soon label him a "phony". A manager can only tell a subordinate he "will soon get a raise" so many times; if the comment is not periodically paired with an actual raise, it will become meaningless (extinguished) to the subordinate.

Extinction is a pervasive factor in our lives. Its influence is often subtle but, in the long run, dramatic. The first operation by a surgeon, the first flight by a pilot, can be emotionally inspiring events. After hundreds of operations and flights, however, emotional reactions and the stimuli they involve are extinguished, and boredom sets in. The first sales call by the sales trainee, the first interview by the new personnel assistant, also mark the beginning of the process by which enthusiasm, conscientiousness, and attention to detail are gradually extinguished.

The negative effects of extinction counterbalance the positive effects of experience. Thus, ten years in the same position not only means one year's experience ten times over, it also means ten years of undergoing the deadening effects of extinction. It is the manager's responsibility to overcome these effects by frequently and creatively pairing the responsibilities of his subordinates with reinforcers and by periodically, not continuously, reinforcing high levels of performance.

[The reader is asked to think of some behavior they are always expected to reinforce (e.g., returning a friendly "hello" when passing someone in the hallway). Try periodic reinforcement of the behavior by using extinction occasionally.]

Timed Reinforcement

In some instances, an individual is reinforced on a time schedule. If we reinforce an individual for a particular response every half hour, we will elicit a short burst of the response immediately after the half hour (reinforcement), followed by very little response for 15-20 minutes, and then a gradual build-up preceding the time of reinforcement (the half hour).

Suppose a report card is reinforcing to a child and he receives it every five weeks. He will normally devote a good deal of time and energy to homework for two or three days after he has received the report card. His devotion to homework then falls off rapidly. After three weeks, his attention starts slowly to drift back to his homework. After four weeks, he is spending still more time on his homework. After four and a half weeks have elapsed he will again be devoting much time and energy to his homework, and this behavior will continue for two or three days after he receives his report card, at which time the cycle will repeat itself.

In industry, subordinates' performance reviews are normally arranged on a similar schedule. If a performance review is given every six months, it will normally have some impact on the subordinate's behavior for a few days after the review and its greatest impact for a few days prior to the next review. It will have little impact during interim periods. The same is true of such regularly scheduled reinforcers as salary adjustments and sales and expenditure reports. To the extent that a monthly sales performance report is a reinforcer to an employee, it will affect his behavior immediately prior to and subsequent to its issuance; it will have little impact during the long interim periods.

To be effective, therefore, performance reviews, reports, compensation, and other reinforcers should be given at random intervals as much as possible, rather than on a rigid time-contingency schedule with long interim periods.

[The reader is asked to note any fixed time schedules under her/his control. Try to make the schedule more random, e.g., give subordinates randomly spaced performance reviews. The impact will be greater...after the protests have quieted down.]

The Fear and Anger Borne of Extinction

There is one exception to our rule that extinguishing a response weakens it. This exception occurs when the behavior being extinguished consists of a hostile, aggressive response. We often engage in certain behaviors because they have been followed by something we like; they have been reinforced, hence our expectations are high. Experiencing extinction when we engage in the same behavior, consequently, is a frustrating situation. Frustration always leads to anger. Hence hostile behavior will be strengthened initially if it is extinguished.

Consider the following interchange. The manager in this case is normally a cheerful, emotionally expressive person who readily compliments his subordinates.

> Subordinate (somewhat excited): We just got the figures in our plant efficiencies for last month. We ran the plant at 98.7% efficiency, our best month ever!
> Manager (in a monotone voice): Fine. Have you got the scrappage rates yet?

This is a frustrating experience for the subordinate. It has decreased both the likelihood of his feeling good about constructive results and his desire to tell his manager about them. It has also, however, increased irritation and anxiety on his part. He is likely to wonder why his manager is in such a "lousy mood."

Aggressive behavior can be extinguished, but it shows an initial increase in intensity before weakening. Again, managers must always be alert to what is really reinforcing and/or aversive to their subordinates.

Suppose an indecisive manager is an aversive stimulus to her faster paced, impatient subordinate. Seeing his manager uncomfortable or uneasy may then be a strong reinforcer to the subordinate, especially in front of others:

> Manager: Is there anything else we should be discussing here?
> Subordinate: Yeah, when are we going to get an answer on whether or not we bring in that new personal computer?
> Manager (feeling uneasy): Well, we're going to be discussing that in the finance committee next Friday.
> Subordinate: Well, that decision's been hanging in the air for over two months now. Don't you think management has had enough time?
> Manager (shifts in chair and tries to avoid eye contact with anyone): Well, you know it's a complex issue and it takes time to pin everything down.
> Subordinate: Good grief, it doesn't take that much time!
> Manager (quite uncomfortable now): Well, I should probably have some news for you by Friday.
> Subordinate: I certainly hope so. We can't go anywhere without some decisions around here.

In this example, the manager has reinforced her subordinate's aggressive responses by exhibiting uncomfortable feelings in the presence of others. Suppose we now tell the manager to "toughen up" and extinguish those responses by her subordinate. The manager can accomplish this by responding in a relaxed manner to the subordinate's questions. This will at first increase the probability and intensity of the subordinate's aggressive responses because the manager will no longer be reinforcing them; the subordinate will find his manager's nonchalance frustrating and, oddly enough, frightening (we fear, for example, lack of influence over others). However, extinction of the subordinate's challenging, hostile behavior will eventually occur.

[The reader is asked to note a habitual, destructive behavior by someone in their work environment, someone with whom they interact frequently. Consider your typical response. Are you, for example, reinforcing negative attitudes by always agreeing with the expression of them? React with absolute silence the next time they occur. How do you feel? How do you think the other person feels? Extinction is a powerful tool.]

The New Manager

Extinction often plays a role in the animosity new managers encounter in their subordinates. All managers reinforce various behavior patterns they enjoy in different subordinates. Hence, Manager A may reinforce (with his laughter) a good sense of humor in one subordinate and (with his admiration) quick decisiveness in another subordinate. After six months under Manager A, the two subordinates "know what to expect"; their behavior has been shaped, and they engage in it with subconscious satisfaction because it is periodically reinforced by their manager.

After five years under Manager A, their behavior is quite stable. Now, however, Manager B arrives to assume A's position. She will almost always reinforce different types of behavior in the two subordinates than did her predecessor. More important, she <u>will not</u> reinforce behavior that was previously reinforced by Manager A. Manager B, for example, may find the one subordinate's sense of humor a "time waster" and the other subordinate's quick decisiveness a cause of too many mistakes. Even if Manager B does not express disapproval of these types of behavior, she will certainly not reinforce them. The extinction that results almost invariably leads to animosity toward the new manager.

Extinction, in fact, is unavoidable when a manager assumes a new position, because she/he will always extinguish some behaviors previously reinforced. This will be a frustrating/fear inducing experience for subordinates.

The problem is intensified because most managers "pull back" from responding when they are given authority and responsibility in new and unfamiliar areas. Their immediate goal is to find out what is happening and get their feet on firm ground before giving guidance, direction, praise, and reprimands. If their predecessor was quite liberal in reinforcing subordinates, there will be a sudden drop in the *frequency* of reinforcement. This partly explains the behind-the-back, hostile remarks subordinates often direct at new managers, although if the previous manager was an aversive stimulus to the subordinates and rarely gave out reinforcers, "extinction anger" will be minimized when the new manager takes over. Knowing who your predecessor was, consequently, can help minimize a difficult adjustment period for everyone.

If the typical manager could be justly accused of any one failing, it would be that she/he misses far too many opportunities to reinforce subordinates. This may be due to their uneasiness at having authority over others, their lack of emotional expressiveness, or the fact that they do not like to see subordinates enjoy their work. Whatever the reason, extinction is an all too common phenomenon in manager-subordinate interactions (probably the most common in the workplace and in personal relations).

[Readers who wish to experience the fear that extinction causes might start a speech, tell two jokes, and note their feelings when no one laughs. Indeed, giving speeches is often avoided like the plague because the speaker is expected to talk for some length of time with no feedback or audience reaction, the very definition of extinction.]

Managerial Failures Caused by Extinction

Extinction also accounts, in large part, for the frequent lack of communication and understanding that occurs between managers and the people below them, as the following example illustrates:

> Subordinate (enthusiastically): I think the merger possibilities are excellent, and I think we ought to buy this company; I know a lot of people here don't feel that way, but I think our profits per share would increase 30% if we bought this company.
>
> Manager (looking at his watch): I've got to get into a management committee meeting in a few minutes. Maybe we can discuss this some other time.

The subordinate will leave this meeting not knowing where he stands, and he may not pursue his analysis of the merger because his enthusiasm was so effectively extinguished. At a subsequent meeting, however, the manager may reprimand him for this neglect of duty; the manager may want the merger desperately, but he has failed to communicate his feelings.

Managerial guidance is a vital reinforcer. If a subordinate states, "We just got AIC as a customer, but we lost DOT," the manager should try to at least quietly mutter "Excellent" in the middle of the statement and frown at the end of it. The subordinate will then be more likely to focus on getting customers than he will if the manager remains silent.

Even trite exchanges have a subtle influence. Managers frequently ask their subordinates, "How's it going?" before going on to the topic they want to discuss. This often elicits a positive response, "Good," reflecting a positive attitude. The manager should quickly reinforce this attitude ("Excellent" or "I'm glad to hear that") before moving to his topic. Most managers, however, fire back another question ('How are the sales figures?"). Subordinates soon stop responding with "Good" or do so in a perfunctory manner. The manager has extinguished the response, and more important, he has missed an opportunity to reinforce constructive behavior and pair himself with a mild reinforcer in the process. This is how an atmosphere is created.

[We're often asked "how we're doing" in a non-interested, habitual manner. The reader, as an experiment, might want to respond with an enthusiastic, "Great! And how nice of you to ask! I really appreciate your interest!" While this may be a bit embarrassing to the reader and confusing to the other party, it will probably increase the frequency of people's interest in you (unless the other party is fearful of emotional reactions and thinks you're nuts).]

Extinction as a Constructive Tool

It is important to note that extinction can be used constructively. Allowing subordinates to air their negative views or holding group gripe sessions is of little consequence in and of itself. The important factor is whether the negative views or gripes are reinforced or extinguished. Indeed, such sessions can be destructive if the manager or others in the group start reinforcing complaining behavior with their uneasiness, sympathies and/or concerns. Negative feelings, if amply reinforced, can easily grow beyond the bounds of reality. In such instances, extinction could be relied upon to stop the intensity of the destructive behavior. After all, extinction doesn't mean not acknowledging or not responding at all to someone's views; it means not responding emotionally. (It is sometimes recommended that people get rid of their aggressive feelings by expressing them in a socially acceptable manner, such as at a football game. This could easily increase aggressiveness if the reaction of colleagues at the game reinforces such expressions.)

Yet the effect of managerial extinction is paradoxically dependent upon the manager's history of reinforcing subordinates. If she has rarely reinforced her subordinates, withholding reinforcement at an appropriate time will have minimal impact. The superior who has never told her subordinate he is doing an excellent job will have little influence on her subordinate's gripes by **not** telling the subordinate he is doing an excellent job when his subordinate is complaining.

A primary reason managers should use reinforcers frequently, consequently, is that it gives the manager the added tool of extinction as a means of influencing behavior. Using reinforcers infrequently blunts the impact of a deliberate use of extinction since the manager is always extinguishing behavior anyway. The parent who rarely gives his child love has minimal impact if he withholds his love deliberately when his child is behaving badly. The manager who rarely reinforces his subordinates will eventually end up with a lethargic or frustrated department and any deliberate, even constructive, use of extinction will have minimal impact.

Extinction increases fear, frustration, and anger. When should it be used by the manager? When destructive behavior by subordinates is frequent and repetitive, especially if it's excessive. When should it not be used? When behavior, even destructive behavior, is not frequent and repetitive, but realistic. Who judges when behavior is excessive and when it's realistic? The manager, just as she/he is being paid for their judgments in other areas of the work setting.

[Pick someone in your inner circle who frequently complains or is generally negative. When they next complain, respond in a bland, non-emotional manner, and then ask them a question about something else. Can you sense their feelings, especially toward you? Does this mean you've been reinforcing their complaining, negative behavior in the past? Why?]

Summary

Managers are required to pair themselves with aversive stimuli. They have to say "no" periodically, to reprimand, to demote, and to fire. They should therefore take every opportunity to pair themselves with reinforcers by reinforcing constructive behavior. The counterbalancing effects will increase their subordinates' effectiveness and motivation, minimize misunderstandings, and enormously enhance the manager-subordinate relationship.

The initial reaction by most people to extinction of a response that has previously been reinforced is an aggressive response. If an aggressive response itself is going through extinction, it will increase in strength for a short time before it starts to weaken and diminish.

It is hoped that it is becoming increasingly clear to the readers of this book that managers must always be alert to frequent, repetitive and especially excessive behavior in interactions with subordinates. For, like it or not, the manager's behavior selectively reinforces some of her/his subordinates' response patterns and extinguishes others. Unless these interactions are analyzed appropriately, the manager is in danger of reinforcing destructive responses and extinguishing constructive ones.

What are the effects of "punishing" someone?

What are the long-term effects of the frequent use of aversives?

How can I get people to "open up" with me?

Shouldn't a manager be highly competitive?

Why is someone always negative and critical?

CHAPTER 15

PUNISHMENT

Let us now look at the effects that aversive stimuli have on our behavior, especially our fears.

Principle VII: Punishment

Any behavior immediately followed by an aversive stimulus is weakened and less likely to recur.

Responding to some behavior with an aversive stimulus is known as punishment. Again, the principle is quite simple; however, there are two considerations one must bear in mind. One is the intensity of the aversive stimulus. If the stimulus is intensely aversive, it will quickly and dramatically lower the likelihood of the behavior it follows from recurring. If the stimulus is only mildly aversive, however, the behavior may recur, albeit at a weaker level. The history of the behavior is also a factor here. If it has a long history of reinforcement, following it with an aversive stimulus has special outcomes, which will be discussed later.

Responding to a behavior with a stimulus intensely aversive *to the other person* can potentially stop the response from ever recurring. For example: A spontaneous, aggressive line manager was complaining that a highly competent, but somewhat sensitive, staff person was no longer taking the initiative in communicating with him. Subsequently, a meeting brought together both men and a psychologist.

> Psychologist (to staff man): Jim, how do you feel about Mike here? Is there anything about him that might bother you a little bit?
>
> Staff Man (somewhat hesitatingly): Well ... I sometimes think Mike says things he doesn't really mean, I think ...
>
> Line Manager (interrupting staff man and pounding hand on desk): Oh, not true! Dammit, that's just not true!
>
> Psychologist (to staff man after quieting Mike down): Are there any other feelings you have toward Mike that you would like to explore?
>
> Staff Man: No ... no, I think that about covers it.

Two things have occurred here. First, the line manager has obviously responded to the staff person's attempts to communicate openly with a stimulus intensely aversive to the sensitive staff person. The line manager's behavior has, consequently, decreased even more the probability of the staff person taking the initiative to communicate openly with him in the future. This is not an atypical situation in industry. Managers often complain about the "lack of something" in a subordinate's behavior, yet closer examination reveals that when that "something" did occur, the manager responded in a manner that was aversive to the subordinate, in effect, punishing the behavior and weakening it even further. Managers, for example, frequently complain about the lack of people who will "*really* tell me what they think"; when subordinates do just that, however, they often find themselves meeting a barrage of criticism or an emotional self-justification (aversive stimuli) from their manager.

The second thing that has occurred in the foregoing example is that the line manager has also paired *himself* with behavior intensely aversive to the staff person. The manager, consequently, will become more aversive to the staff person, and this will further decrease the probability of the staff person communicating with him. Aversive stimuli, as we have seen, are avoided.

The critical point to remember here is that the use of aversive stimuli pairs the person using them with those aversive stimuli. The frequent use of aversives by a person is what that person then becomes to others – aversive. And aversive stimuli elicit fear! And fear elicits aberrant behavior! Hence people will often behave in strange, atypical ways when they are around those who use aversives frequently.

[Readers are asked here to think of a person in their inner circle who uses aversives frequently. Consider people's behavior in the presence of that person. Do they react somewhat differently than they do when they interact with others? How? Why?]

The Constructive Use of Punishment

Every principle in this book is appropriate to use at one time or another. It is important to have a wide response repertoire, to be able to use reinforcers and aversives, each when it is appropriate.

Let us look at a slightly more constructive use of aversive stimuli to weaken a deleterious behavior. A general sales manager has been having difficulty getting one of his regional sales managers to give feedback to the regional manager's subordinates. The general manager knows that "interference from people over her" is an intense aversive stimulus to this highly independent regional manager.

> General Manager: How's Dick (a salesperson) coming along?
> Regional Manager: He's doing all right.
> General Manager: Is he taking more initiative in getting out to see his customers?
> Regional Manager: Frankly, I haven't seen much change in him.
> General Manager: Have you talked to him about it recently?

Regional Manager: Well, I've been at meetings for the last two or three weeks and I've been working with Jack a good deal of the time on those financial reports. I haven't really had a chance to talk to Dick.

General Manager (grimaces): Well, why don't I talk to him about it while I'm here? (The threat of interference, an aversive stimulus to the regional manager)

Regional Manager (quickly and spontaneously): No, that's all right, I'll set up a meeting to see him tomorrow morning and make sure we go over it.

General Manager: Excellent! (Reinforcer)

This manager has decreased the probability of his regional manager avoiding a discussion of Dick's lack of initiative with Dick himself. By using aversive stimuli, however, the manager has taken two risks. First, he has paired himself with an aversive stimulus. Second, by following an "admission of guilt" with an aversive stimulus, the general manager has decreased the probability that the regional manager will again tell him about things she has not done.

[Readers are asked to note some frequent, repetitive, but deleterious behavior in a person with whom they interact frequently. When the behavior next occurs, punish it with some aversive stimulus. Suppose, for example, someone excessively (fearfully) worries:

They: I'm worried about my upcoming performance review; I think my boss may rake me over the coals.

You: Well, maybe you're right. (Instead of reassuring, hence reinforcing, their excessive worrying.)

Those who have difficulty using aversives will have difficulty in life. Their response repertoire will be narrow, reflecting a lack of confidence. The use of aversives is appropriate and important at times!]

Communication Problems

The overly frequent use of aversives is often a cause of the "breakdown in communications" so often discussed in industry. The subordinate may not want to "admit" his mistakes to his manager for fear of encountering aversive stimuli from the manager. His reluctance is often justified, since telling his immediate superior about something he did which he should not have done (or vice versa) frequently does elicit anger (aversive stimuli).

What is the appropriate managerial response to admissions of mistakes? Extinction. If possible, reinforce the honesty, extinguish the mistake. If the aversive stimuli used by the manager are intense enough, subordinates will be reluctant to pass on <u>any</u> bad news to their superior, even news concerning matters for which the subordinate has no responsibility. This situation is not uncommon in departments headed up by emotional managers who go into a tirade at the slightest opportunity.

What is the best criterion for determining when to use aversives and when to avoid them? The frequency of the behavior in question. If a subordinate frequently (or excessively) avoids interactions with her/his manager, the use of aversives should be avoided whenever possible. More importantly, interactions should involve reinforcers for the subordinate when they do occur. On the other hand, if a subordinate needs too much attention and excessively interrupts the manager with picayune issues, the use of punishment may be appropriate.

A Balanced View

The shortcomings of using aversives can be minimized somewhat if managers pair themselves with reinforcers whenever possible.

Despite protests to the contrary, managers have a good deal of influence over subordinates. Subtle changes in a manager's behavior can have dramatic effects on the attitudes, feelings, and behavior of people who report to them. Hence managers should use only mild aversive stimuli. These may not have as noticeable an impact on the behavior of their subordinates as will the use of intense aversive stimuli, but, as we have seen and shall see, certain undesirable side effects will not occur. (Of course, if the manager's interactions with subordinates consist *only* of mild aversive stimuli, but no reinforcers, the manager will still become an aversive stimulus to her/his subordinates.)

Each Person is Different

It must be remembered that what constitutes an intense aversive stimulus to an individual is a highly personal matter, contingent upon their past experiences. It does not necessarily involve shouting and screaming.

For example: A sensitive young man had recently been evaluated and reviewed by a management psychologist. The psychologist had told him to be less subservient with authority figures, to speak up for his ideas more forcefully, and to be less awed by people in high positions. (The young man was four levels below the president.) Several days after the review, the young man ran into the president and told him some of the things he had discussed with the psychologist. He concluded by saying, "And frankly, I'm not going to treat you like Jesus Christ any more" – to which the president quietly, but indignantly, responded, "Well, I am the president after all."

The president's quiet remark virtually eliminated any gains the psychologist may have made in this area. Despite the lack of shouting, it was an intense aversive stimulus to the young man, an aversive stimulus which immediately followed the response of "speaking up more forcefully to authority figures".

A competent psychologist or consultant can probably change almost any behavior in an individual temporarily, but only the manager can maintain the changes. And if the manager does not like the changes, she/he can and will eliminate them in short order. Organizations that use consultants, consequently, should always make certain the consultant's goals are consistent with senior management, especially the CEO. If they are not, time and money will be spent on "fixes" that are short-lived at best and disruptive and destructive at worst.

[Readers are asked here to think of the most sensitive person in their inner circle. When that person says something you feel is detrimental to them, merely grimace. Is this aversive to them? Did they acknowledge or say anything about your behavior?]

The Destructive Use of Punishment

Just as managers might reinforce destructive behavior (giving rapt attention to the subordinate who downgrades others), so too can they sometimes punish constructive behavior. Hourly workers who exceed their piece-rate suddenly find the rate increased. The sales person who exceeds her quota by a wide margin is "rewarded" by having her quota increased an inordinate amount or her commission lowered the next year. If such changes must be made, they should be made gradually and paired with effective incentives (reinforcers).

Intensely competitive managers often put themselves into direct competition with their own subordinates. As a consequence, the subordinates' practical achievements (which increase profits) may well be threatening to, and punished by, their managers. Consider the following examples:

> Salesman: I just sold ten carloads of tires to BIM Corporation.
> Sales Manager (who should have reinforced): That's good, but you still haven't gotten into Tad Corporation; when are we going to get an order from them? (Punishment)
> Manager: Jim, how come you never call on TDI Corp?
> Subordinate: I do. Actually, I just called on them last Tuesday.
> Manager (who should reinforce): What happened? (Extinction)
> Subordinate: I'm supposed to get together with them on Friday. They said they would place a small order with me in order to try out our product.

> Manager (who should have reinforced): God, don't blow it!
> (Punishment)

Clearly, another person's achievements are not necessarily reinforcing to the manager. A company that promotes its best salesperson into a managerial position because she/he excels in sales often runs into this difficulty. An individual may be the best salesperson precisely because he is so competitive that contests motivate him to put forth a good deal of effort, hence he usually wins the contests. He may be a poor manager for the same reason; he is so competitive that he punishes success in others, even his own subordinates.

[Readers are asked to think of the most competitive manager they know. If it is your own boss, tell him/her about a success you recently had. If it's another manager, express admiration for a recent success of one of their subordinates. In either case, note the manager's reaction.]

Punishment and Confidence

Punishment often diminishes a person's confidence. Now, confident people tend to do the right thing at the right time in the right way. Yet too many managers seem intent on destroying their subordinates' confidence. Why? Because, as we've seen, confident people, people who truly like and respect themselves, find the behavior of others less important; this can easily threaten the manager's sense of importance and his/her actual influence. Managers should ask themselves, "Is confidence in a subordinate really reinforcing to me?" In the following examples, the answer apparently is "No".

> Subordinate: I think the management committee is really going to be impressed with this report on inventory – I think we really did a good job.
> Manager: Don't be so naïve. There are a couple of guys on that management committee who never are satisfied. (Punishment; the manager might have said, "Excellent! I'm looking forward to reading it.")

Subordinate (in the middle of a defensive argument with the manager): I'm a good salesperson.
Manager: Yeah, but you've got a lot to learn. I used to think I was good at your age too, but you'll find there's a lot going on you don't know about. (Punishment; also, the manager's last sentence paired the verbal equivalent of confidence with an aversive stimulus; the manager might have said, "I agree, I think you're an excellent salesperson," with no 'buts' or 'howevers')

When we speak of confidence, we are not speaking of arrogance or conceit. The truly confident individual treats other people with respect and consideration. He/she is realistic enough to know that everyone does something better than they do or knows something they do not. People who are arrogant and conceited, on the other hand, actually lack confidence. They act superior because they feel inferior; if they were truly confident, they would have no need to impress others with their confidence via their arrogance.

[Readers are encouraged to engage in some self-deprecating behavior (I don't think I'm too good at that.") Then note if anyone has the confidence to punish or extinguish you rather than reinforcing you with reassurance. If someone does have the confidence to punish or extinguish you for being self-deprecating, ask yourself whether or not you have the confidence to reinforce them for doing so.]

Punishing to Whom?

Effective managerial behavior requires, in one sense, the most selfless, altruistic orientation possible; one must focus entirely on what is reinforcing or aversive *to the other person*, not to oneself. This is a very difficult orientation for most people to achieve. All too often we assume that what is reinforcing and/or aversive to us must be reinforcing and/or aversive to others – and then we wonder why we are failing to have an impact on others. If one person is having an intense argument with someone who is pouting, for example, any irritation shown by the "poutee" may well be reinforcing to the pouter; the person's anger at the pouter does not allow him to see that he could weaken the pouting behavior by being happy (to an angry person, happiness shown by their "target" is aversive, hence punishing). Or, consider the following:

> Subordinate: Jim is just not doing his job; I've got to let him go.
> Manager: I think a lot of people are going to be upset if we let Jim go.
> Subordinate: I don't think so. I think many of the competent people will be happy.

In the above example, the weak manager has attempted to block the firing by punishing his subordinate's response. The punishing vehicle (other people getting upset) may be aversive to the manager, but it is apparently not to the subordinate. We know this because the strength of the subordinate's response pattern has not diminished; she is as adamant as before about firing the person.

Questions as Aversives

As previously mentioned, questions readily become aversive stimuli because of their frequent pairing with other aversive stimuli. Denials to the contrary, questions are often used to punish unwanted behavior in others. A manager may bemoan the fact that Paul Smith is indecisive, but he never mentions this to Paul Smith. Yet he may punish actual decisions by Paul Smith with harsh questioning. Married people may relate to more homespun examples:

> Husband: Darling, we'll go to dinner anywhere you'd like.
> Wife: Well, why don't we go to Bistro Francais?
> Husband: Why would you want to go to that place?

***

Husband: I may not be home Saturday morning; I told Jim I'd play golf with him.
Wife: Why didn't you tell me sooner?

In both instances, the person asking the questions would certainly contend that they were merely seeking more information. Being sensitive to the impact our behavior is having on others, however, would diminish the likelihood of such questions if this contention were indeed true.

[Readers are encouraged to use a question as a mild punishing tool merely to get a feel for its effectiveness.

They: I really enjoyed that presentation.
You: Didn't you find it a bit trite?

Confident people may well respond, "No, not at all." Less confident people may admit to some negatives in order to avoid a confrontation.]

Fear from Extinction and Punishment

Experiencing extinction and punishment weakens the behavior we're engaged in at the moment. But it does something far worse: it leads us to *fear* engaging in that behavior. Consider the following common examples as being indicative of some typical experiences throughout this child's life:

Child (excited): Daddy, Daddy, I got a 94 on my arithmetic test.
Father: Let's see. But why did you miss six times seven; we just practiced that yesterday!

Child (excited): Mommy, Mommy, I got a 94 on my arithmetic test.
Mother: Not now dear, I've got to finish this report.

Child: Mommy, Mommy, I was just picked to be in the school play!
Mother: Does this mean I have to make you a costume?

Child: Daddy, Daddy, I was just picked to be in the school play!
Father: Oh, I'll probably be out of town.

In these all too typical examples, the child is proud, using "I-reinforcer" pairings that reflect a liking and respect for herself because of what she has accomplished. The child, however, is both extinguished and punished for doing so. This diminishes the child's feelings of being proud of who she is and of their accomplishments.

But extinction and punishment also instill in the person a fear of engaging in the behavior that was followed by extinction and/or punishment. Hence the child is not only less likely to be proud of who they are and what they've done, they are also developing a fear of liking and respecting themselves (the consequence being an increased sensitivity to, and fear of, the behavior of others).

Our exhortations encouraging them to like and respect themselves years later would seem to be a simple matter, but it is not. Why? Because reaching this goal is not merely pointing out the need to be confident, to like and respect oneself, but the far more difficult task of first overcoming their fear of doing so. Indeed, how can we reinforce confidence in someone who fears showing it? (Punishing lack of confidence or self-critical behavior won't accomplish anything because punishing lack of confidence doesn't necessarily increase confidence.)

[Brave readers may again try finishing this embarrassing, but constructive, phrase with an appropriate ending: "You know, I really think I did a pretty good job of ..." Then say this to those in your inner circle. Who responds with reinforcement, who extinguishes you, and who punishes you? Now you might have a better idea of who will increase and who will decrease your liking and respect for yourself if you interact with them.]

We Are Who We Are Not (A Narrow Response Repertoire)

The more diverse the genetic pool of a species, the more likely is that species to survive in this world of ever changing environments. Similarly, the more diverse the response repertoire of an individual, the more successfully will that person negotiate the myriad types of people and events all of us encounter throughout our lives. But extinction and punishment weaken behavior; they make it less likely we will engage in the behaviors they follow. In effect, extinction and punishment narrow our response repertoire, making us more rigid, less able to adapt effectively to the different situations and people we will be confronting.

People who are *always* indecisive have a narrow response repertoire; they are fear driven. People who are *always* decisive have a narrow response repertoire; they are fear driven. Confident people are mostly decisive, but can be indecisive when appropriate. They are able to say, "I don't know the answer to that question," rather than merely guessing because they're afraid of appearing stupid.

People who are *always* dependent have a narrow response repertoire; they are fear driven. People who are *always* independent *also* have a narrow response repertoire; they are fear driven. Confident people have a wide response repertoire. They are mostly independent (comfortable relying on themselves) but can be dependent when appropriate. They are able to ask for advice and/or help when necessary, rather than having an inappropriate fear of appearing weak or dependent by expressing a need for the aid of others periodically.

People who are always negative and critical have a narrow response repertoire; they are fear driven. Their manager usually makes the mistake (as does everyone else) of focusing on their negativism; good managers will even confront it. But that is not the problem. The problem is that negative people have a fear of being positive and enthusiastic. They have been punished and/or extinguished for doing so, hence they feel vulnerable if they are so. That is the problem that must be confronted. In effect, their negative responses are not the crux of the problem; their fear

155

of being positive and enthusiastic is, and that is the fear that must be addressed. In effect, their response repertoire must be broadened.

We focus on what a person does to excess because that's what affects us, causes us trouble. We might, however, better ask what behaviors are appropriate that are too difficult for the person to engage in. Often, the behaviors avoided are the opposite of those engaged in excessively. Hence, the excessively indecisive person fears being decisive, the excessively independent person fears appearing dependent, the excessively negative person fears being enthused, the excessively macho person fears intimacy, the excessively attention-seeking person fears being ignored (insignificant to others), and so forth.

[Readers are asked here to consider some behaviors they have difficulty engaging in. Have you been punished or extinguished for doing so? List some basic behaviors required in managerial positions. Which do you have difficulty engaging in? These reflect your fears. And these fears narrow your response repertoire, rendering you less effective.

Try to engage in those behaviors with someone who won't punish or extinguish you for doing so. You might pick some gentle soul who wouldn't punish or extinguish anyone for doing anything. If, for example, you fear intimacy, pick someone who isn't hesitant in intimate situations and tell them about some of your fears.]

What is the quickest way to change someone's behavior?

Is it difficult to use aversives when someone is doing something you
   like, such as criticizing someone who hurt you?

What are the dangers of using aversives?

Can I merely extinguish avoidance behavior?

CHAPTER 16

AVOIDANCE LEARNING: STOPPING THE AVERSIVE

What do we do when we're punished for engaging in some behavior? We avoid engaging in that behavior; indeed, a desire to do so will trigger fear in us. We spoke up as a child and our parents punished us. Now, there are too many occasions when we later wish we had made the brilliant remark in a confrontation.

When we are actually encountering aversives, however, we do something that has a dramatic impact on our personality, on who we become. We engage in "trial and error" behaviors in an attempt to stop the aversives. That is, experiencing aversives leads us to try to find a behavior that will stop the aversives directed at us. The behavior that we find, which successfully stops the aversive, is called, appropriately enough, *avoidance behavior*. It will quickly become an integral part of our personality, of who we are.

Stopping an aversive when the individual engages in a specific response is a quick and certain way of changing the person's behavior. It also accounts for many problems people experience when dealing with each other. It is subtle and frequently difficult to diagnose while it is happening, which is often in the business setting. Let us take a look at this crucial and extremely influential principle and attempt to break it down into recognizable parts.

157

Principle VIII: Avoidance Behavior

Following a response with the cessation of an aversive stimulus strengthens the response and greatly increases the likelihood of the response recurring.

Implicit in the principle is the idea that aversive stimuli are almost always avoided. The proverbial breakdown in communications in any organization is, as we've seen, usually the result of managers pairing themselves with aversive stimuli; hence, the managers are avoided (as are all stimuli aversive to us), and people "just don't get around" to telling them what they should.

In many situations, however, an aversive stimulus suddenly arises while two people are interacting. It can come in the form of a request, a question, an order, a directive, a suggestion. It is at this moment that avoidance learning takes place. Any response that successfully stops the aversive stimulus, that shuts it off, will have a *much greater* probability of recurring in the future.

Consider the salesman to whom making out sales call reports is aversive; he avoids the task merely by not doing it, a response that's aversive to his manager.

> <u>Manager</u>: Bob, I didn't get your sales call report last Friday. Do you have it?
> <u>Salesman</u>: Gee, I just haven't had time to get around to it.
> <u>Manager</u> (angry): Oh, for God's sake! I want that sales report in here and I want it in on time! Maybe we should start looking at whether or not you need a company car since we don't know if you're making sales calls! (Punishment)

The manager has paired a question on sales call reports with aversive stimuli. He has also followed his subordinate's response with a strong aversive stimulus (punishment) and decreased its probability of recurring. Hence, on subsequent occasions, the salesman is unlikely to use the excuse of "not having enough time". Notice that the manager has not done anything to decrease the aversiveness of making out a sales call report by, for example, pairing the act of doing so with reinforcers. The probability of the salesman not making out his report, therefore, remains as high as it ever was.

Two weeks later the following conversation takes place:
Manager (angrily): Bob, where the hell is your sales call report? (Manager has started an aversive stimulus)
Subordinate: Remember you wanted me to work with Ed on that sales call to Ram Corporation? Well, Ed really wasn't prepared for the call, and I had to spend a lot of time working with him on it. I'm awfully sorry, but I thought helping Ed on this call was more important. (Trying to stop the aversive)
Manager (much more gently): Why wasn't Ed prepared? (The subordinate was able to change the topic; blaming someone else successfully stopped the aversive stimulus from his manager.)

This subtle interaction occurs quite frequently in private industry (and in life). *Excuse-making, rationalization, placing blame on other people, denial, lying, as well as absences, illnesses, and other more dramatic and deleterious forms of behavior, are often the result of such responses having been followed by the successful stopping or cessation of aversive stimuli, most of which emanate from the manager.* In the above example, because the salesman successfully stopped the aversive stimuli from his manager by placing blame on another person, he will be much more likely to blame others when he again encounters aversive stimuli, especially from his manager.

Now consider the following example: An aggressive personnel manager has been attempting to get a management development program started in his organization through his subordinate, the training facilitator. The training facilitator is a meek, passive person who finds it aversive to "impose on" various vice presidents and attempt to sell them the training program.

Manager: How's the training program coming? (Aversive

stimulus to the subordinate has just started)

Subordinate: Well, all right.

Manager: Have you held any management development sessions yet? (Aversive stimulus still "on")

Subordinate: No, not yet.

Manager (his anger starting to show): Why not? (Aversive stimulus still "on" and increasing in intensity)

Subordinate: Well, I don't think we really have the budget to bring in the speakers we need.

Manager: Oh, for God's sake! I don't ever want to hear that excuse used again. If you need the money, I'll get it for you! I've told you and everyone else on my staff that before! (The manager has just knocked "budgetary excuse-making" out of his subordinate's repertoire by punishing the response severely. Thus, the aversive stimulus is still "on" and the subordinate tries again to stop it.)

Subordinate: Well, I did try to get to the V.P.'s of operations and sales, but they're always out of town. And when they are in town, their secretaries tell me they're all tied up.

Manager (anger subsiding somewhat as his attention is shifted to the V.P.'s): How many times have you tried to get them?

Subordinate: At least three times. I don't think they feel this management training program is very important. (The subordinate has paired the vice presidents of operations and sales with what to the personnel manager is an aversive stimulus – their resistance to management development.)

Manager: Well, we'll see whether they want management development or not. Let me give them a call and we'll both go up and talk to them. (The subordinate succeeded in stopping the aversive stimulus by pairing others with aversives.)

Again, blaming other people has been followed by the cessation of aversive stimuli (the manager's anger). This interaction has greatly increased the likelihood that the training facilitator will blame others when faced with aversive stimuli (and "blaming others" may well become an integral part of his personality). At the same time, it has diminished the

160

likelihood that the training director will blame the budget, because this response did not stop his superior's harsh manner.

[Readers might wish to think of their boss' worst enemy in the organization. When you are next reprimanded by your boss, blame his/her "worst enemy" by criticizing them (i.e., pair them with an aversive). Did that stop the reprimand?]

Understanding Avoidance Learning

Because of its pervasiveness in industry, it is important that the manager grasp the principle of avoidance learning. Most crucial is the idea that once you start an aversive when dealing with someone, *you must not stop the aversive stimulus until the person is making a constructive response.* The behavior that is occurring when the aversive stops is strengthened a great deal.

Consider the following ineffective and effective examples of dealing with an employee who excessively makes excuses:

Manager: Why didn't you get that order completed and shipped out yesterday?
Subordinate: I wasn't feeling too well yesterday.
Manager (sympathetically): Why? What was wrong? (The manager stopped the aversive stimulus after the subordinate made a typical "excuse".)

Manager: Why didn't you get that order completed and shipped out yesterday?
Subordinate: I wasn't feeling too well yesterday.
Manager: Why didn't you tell one of your people to get it out? (The manager appropriately keeps the aversive stimulus going; hence he is unlikely to encounter more excuse-making in subsequent dealings with his subordinate.)
Subordinate: I'll check with John now to see why it didn't go out. (Constructive response)

Manager: Good. Are you feeling better today? (Appropriately "turns off" the aversive stimulus because his subordinate is indicating he will take effective action)

The manager correctly asks about the employee's health, but waits until the employee is showing constructive behavioral tendencies. The person who excessively worries may indeed need reassurance. The key is to reassure them when they are showing some confidence, not when they're worried. The person who is excessively attention seeking should be given attention, but not when they are engaged in non-constructive, attention seeking behavior (e.g., interrupting others with trivialities), but when they are quietly focused on some relevant project.

[This may be an emotionally difficult exercise for some people, but it is important. Readers are asked to start an aversive stimulus with someone, e.g., criticize them. Now the difficult part; maintain the aversive stimulus until the recipient is doing something that is constructive. Example:

You: Jim, I feel you're too indecisive at times.
Jim: Well, your insights are so good that I guess maybe I do rely on you too much.
Bad You: Well, thank you very much. That's very kind of you to say.
Good You: Well, if you're going to rely on me so much, maybe I should get some of your pay.
Jim: That's OK; I'll be more decisive in the future.
You: Excellent! You're wonderful.]

The Liabilities of Using Aversives

There are three major liabilities managers encounter when they use aversive stimuli to influence the behavior of subordinates. First, they pair themselves with the aversive stimuli used and, to that extent, become aversive to their subordinates. Second, while they may eliminate (punish) some ineffective response patterns, they do nothing to increase the probability of any effective behavior. Third, they too often stop the aversive after a subordinate's deleterious response. Thus, they often increase the strength, hence the likelihood of behavior (such as lying and blaming others) more harmful than that which they are trying to eliminate. (A fourth liability will be discussed later in this chapter.)

The complications and side effects involved in the use of aversive stimuli should make the manager quite hesitant to employ them. When they must be used, they should be kept at a mild level. The only area in which mild aversive stimuli may not be used frequently enough is, oddly enough, sales calls on potential customers. Most salespeople go to such lengths to pair themselves with reinforcers and not antagonize a potential customer that they inadvertently reinforce rejection responses by the customer. The customer who says, "I'll call you when I think it's necessary," often encounters much acquiescence, even in good salespeople. Highly competent salespeople, however, mildly punish such a response by saying, for example, "I think you're making a mistake," then pair immediate action with reinforcers.

Sales and operations are inextricably linked to profits. If profits drop, sales blames operations and operations blames sales. The president reinforces both for blaming each other so no one will blame him. Within a short time, the vice president of sales and the vice president of operations are intensely aversive to each other. Anyone who pairs the one vice president with aversive stimuli to the other vice president will be reinforced. The subordinates of both vice presidents soon learn this and use the knowledge to good advantage:

> V.P. of Sales: Why the hell aren't we getting more sales out of your region? (Aversive stimulus "on")
> Regional Sales Manager: Well, it's pretty difficult to get sales when the operations people make such shoddy stuff and ship it late on top of that.
> V.P. of Sales: You've got a point, and I know you've been hurt more than the other regions. Considering the circumstances, I guess you're doing pretty well.

Not only did the regional manager successfully stop the aversive stimuli by blaming the operations people, he was reinforced as well. We can be certain he will be trying, through his subordinates, to find as many operations mistakes as possible. After all, this is the behavior for which he is being reinforced; worse, it is the behavior that successfully stops aversive stimuli. The V.P. of Sales should have said, "If we made a perfect product and always got it out on time, what the hell would we need you for?"

[Readers are asked to think of a person they dislike in their organization. Does anyone know that you dislike that person? Ask several people what they think of that person. Can you reinforce someone who makes positive comments about that person? Can you argue with (punish) someone who says something negative about the person with which you disagree?]

Cessation of Aversives through Collusion

One of the most aversive situations for both manager and subordinate is the performance review. Each contributes his share toward making the situation less aversive, but also less productive. The manager tones down his criticisms, and the subordinate placidly agrees with all of them. That way no one gets hurt and both successfully avoid aversive stimuli (although no one learns anything and/or becomes more adept, either).

One of the most self-destructive avoidance patterns occurs with the meek, placating, highly sensitive subordinate who exists only to say "yes" to anything her superior suggests. The most abrasive, demanding manager has his limits; few managers want to destroy anyone. As a result, most "tough" managers become quite gentle when dealing with the meek and sensitive subordinate, and that is exactly why the subordinate remains meek and sensitive. She has frequently seen her manager "chew out" a confident subordinate, and she successfully avoids (albeit, not consciously) this aversive stimulus by remaining subservient.

A more subtle avoidance pattern occurs when both the salesman and his customer are aversive to each other. The following phone conversation might take place:

> Salesman: I'll be in your area Wednesday, and I was wondering if I could see you.
> Customer (hesitant): Well, I have a meeting with the management committee at ten in the morning.
> Salesman: That will probably tie you up for a good part of the day. Why don't I try to catch you on my next trip?
> Customer: I wish you would.
> Salesman: Good. I will.

We might call this avoidance of aversive stimuli through mutual reinforcement. Note that, if asked, the salesman will tell his manager quite sincerely that he has been trying to get to this company, but they are always busy.

[Think of the most sensitive person in your inner circle. Gently tell them they're too sensitive to criticism. Do they become upset? Do you then stop the aversive feedback and reassure them, listing their many strengths? Are they controlling you (and everyone else) by becoming upset? Try pointing that out to them and not stopping the aversive feedback until they're reacting more constructively.]

Stopping Aversives in Your Presence

Earlier we discussed three disadvantages managers encounter in using intense aversive stimuli; let us now consider a fourth disadvantage. If some behavior has been reinforced in the past, then punishing it with severe aversive stimuli will stop the behavior immediately, *but only in the presence of the punishing agent.* Suppose a four-year-old boy has played in the street and enjoyed it (reinforcement) for several days. On this particular day, however, the boy is seen in the street by his father and severely spanked. The boy will not play in the street any more when his father is around; he may when his father is absent, however. The street has been paired with reinforcers for several days; hence one aversive pairing or punishing the behavior itself once or twice will probably not overcome that. Also, it is the father, more than the street, who is being paired with aversive stimuli. Moreover, the father never really reinforced the boy for <u>not</u> playing in the street.

By using severe aversive stimuli, managers may stop an undesirable response pattern immediately, but only in their own presence, especially when the response pattern has previously been followed by reinforcement.

For example: Imagine a young man joining a software company as a salesperson. The young man is "highly independent" (doing things his own way has been reinforced in the past), and he dislikes being told how to reach his goals; indeed, he joined the company precisely because it gives him so much leeway when he's out making calls. After a short training program, his systematic, methodical manager gives him a "canned sales pitch" and orders him to memorize it word for word and use it on his sales calls. Because of his independence, this procedure is aversive to the young salesman, and he does not memorize the talk. A week later, both the salesman and his manager go out on their first sales call together. The salesman does not use the "canned" approach. The manager and his salesman leave, and the following interaction takes place:

> <u>Manager</u> (angrily): I thought I told you to memorize that sales speech I gave you.
> <u>Salesman</u>: I didn't feel it fit my personality.
> <u>Manager</u> (in a low, quiet voice, very angrily): I told you to memorize that sales pitch. I don't care about you or your personality. I'm going out with you on a sales call next week and if you don't present it word for word, I'll have you out of this company so quick, you won't know what hit you.

One week later both the manager and the salesman go out on a sales call together. Lo and behold, the salesman presents the canned sales pitch, word for word. And he continues to do so as long as he remains with the company – but only when his sales manager is with him! The sales manager has become a discriminative stimulus in the presence of which the canned sales pitch is made. In the absence of the sales manager, however, the salesman reverts to his old style of doing things his own way.

Few response patterns change overnight. If an individual suddenly engages in behavior that is virtually incompatible with his particular personality, it is almost invariably the result of severe aversive learning that has led to the establishment of a discriminative stimulus in the presence of which the new behavior will occur, in the absence of which, it will not.

Consider the case of a large Midwest steel company. The previous chief executive officer had found it aversive to delegate authority and responsibility to other people. As a result, he had surrounded himself with cheerful, but highly dependent personalities who were adept at following orders and doing little else. The predictable drop in profits had occurred. The board of directors then brought in a highly aggressive, hypercritical president from outside the industry. In his first meeting with his vice presidents, the president turned to the first man on his left and asked what problems he saw in the company. The vice president, as he had for the past five years, cheerfully responded, "I think we're doing pretty well." The new president quietly said, "This company's profits have dropped 40% in the past three years. If you don't see anything wrong, maybe you don't belong in this company." Almost overnight, a number of weak personalities began engaging in highly critical, aggressive behavior patterns – but only in the presence of the president.

[Readers are asked to avoid using strong aversive stimuli, for many reasons. Consider a manager in your organization who is pervasively disliked. This is probably the result of that person using, and pairing themselves with, intense aversive stimuli. Do people behave differently in that manager's presence than they normally would in their day-to-day activities? What behaviors are different? What are the types of aversives the manager probably used?]

It has previously been noted that many salespeople do not use mild aversive stimuli frequently enough when a potential customer is rejecting the idea of placing an order. The opposite extreme is also quite possible. If a customer agrees to an order in the salesperson's presence, then cancels the order by telephone several days later, the salesperson may have been using overly intense aversive stimuli to get the order. If customer cancellations are a frequent occurrence with a specific salesperson, this is almost certainly the case; hence customers "buy" in his/her presence to stop the aversive, but cancel in his/her absence.

This type of behavior is best described as "sham behavior"; it generally occurs when a new manager joins a company and starts to follow his/her subordinates' undesirable response patterns with strong aversive stimuli. This is a difficult and dangerous technique for managers to use because it requires managers to perceive that a subordinate is behaving quite differently in their presence than in their absence. It changes behavior very quickly, but the negative side effects almost always outweigh the advantages. If a manager sees quick, dramatic changes in a subordinate when the subordinate is in the manager's presence, it is almost certain that the manager has punished the subordinate's previous responses too strongly.

Which behavior is more adaptable, reinforced behavior or avoidance learned behavior?

When is the most important time to stop an aversive?

Which behavior is stronger, reinforced behavior or avoidance learned behavior?

What are the consequences of using aversives?

When does the use of aversives have the most impact?

CHAPTER 17

REINFORCED VERSUS AVOIDANCE BEHAVIOR

Let's now consider the two major reasons why specific behaviors occur and give each and every individual their unique personality characteristics. The first is that certain behaviors have been reinforced by others (external forces). The second is that the individual has learned that specific behaviors stop and seem to prevent aversive stimuli from others (avoidance behavior). Reinforced behavior is flexible, adaptable. Avoidance behavior is rigid, excessive, and often inappropriate, reflecting the fear driving it. (To repeat: the behavior we fear from others could occur at any time, hence we have to be on guard all the time; thus is fear-driven behavior marked by excessiveness.)

Extinction of Avoidance Behavior

To extinguish a response that occurs because it has been followed by reinforcers is relatively simple – merely remove the reinforcer. A young person may have been amply reinforced in their school years for their athletic abilities. Despite some initial problems involving extinction, most can usually make a good adjustment in their work life when entirely different behavior patterns are reinforced and the accolades for their athletic abilities no longer occur (extinction).

Behavior that is learned because of avoidance contingencies, on the other hand, is generally non-adaptive because there isn't any stimulus to remove to extinguish the behavior; in fact, it continually recurs precisely because nothing follows it.

Take, for example, the case of Terry Smith. Terry was raised by hypercritical parents, including an obsessive-compulsive mother who criticized anything and everything Terry did that was not up to her criteria for perfection. Terry, as a result, developed into a cautious, conservative thinker. His basic goal in life was to avoid mistakes, which had become an intense aversive stimulus to him because they had been paired with, and punished by, severe parental criticism.

Terry is now fifty-eight years old and he has spent his entire work life desperately avoiding mistakes. Because he has succeeded in this, nothing harmful (such as criticism) has happened to him. He will never know that taking a few risks and making some mistakes would also lead to nothing really harmful happening to him (after all, his parents died twenty years ago). He continues to excessively engage in cautious, conservative behavior precisely because nothing aversive has happened to him. He will never know that aversive stimuli (criticism) would probably not have occurred had he adopted a different, more risk-oriented, or more diverse set of behavior patterns. Thus, his fear has given him a "narrow response repertoire".

[Readers are asked here to determine some behaviors they find difficult to engage in, e.g., confrontation, asking for help, talking about their deeper feelings to someone, meeting new people, admitting to mistakes. What fear would you feel if you did engage in that behavior; that is, what behavior from others would you fear if you did engage in that behavior?

Now go out of your way to elicit that behavior from others! Be brave. Be strong.

Do you fear confrontations? Go to someone who holds strong views on an issue and express opposing opinions, openly and forthrightly. If doing so is easy, then you probably don't fear confrontations. But if it is difficult to express opposing views and you do it anyway, you'll find their reaction is probably not nearly as bad as you feared. Then you won't be so inhibited expressing your views in the future. The goal? To widen your response repertoire and make you more effective and more comfortable in this world.

Do you fear intimacy? Tell someone about your fear of intimacy or about another deep fear. If talking about one of your fears is easy for you, then you probably don't fear intimacy.]

Desensitizing a Person to the Aversives

There is a way out of this trap of excessively avoiding behavior that continually recurs because nothing follows it. But it requires a perceptive manager who is willing to take a risk. We have seen that an aversive stimulus that is experienced, but that is not periodically paired with other aversive stimuli, will extinguish in effectiveness. If the manager can determine what stimuli (i.e., what behavior by others) her subordinate is trying to avoid, and can discuss these stimuli openly with the employee, the manager will start a constructive extinction process.

The statement, "You know, you seem to be a bit afraid that people may dislike you," is a case in point. Some people have spent their lives obsessively avoiding the dislike of others. Because they were successful in avoiding this feared stimulus, they have never learned that the dislike of others is not always harmful. It is one of those unspoken fears which, if spoken by someone, becomes less aversive.

Had someone said to Terry Smith in the above example, "You seem to be frightened of criticism from people in positions of authority," she would have started to extinguish a stimulus Terry feared (and always would fear because he so assiduously avoided the stimulus).

171

It would have been better still to try pairing the aversive stimulus with reinforcers. For example, "When people in high positions of authority criticize you, it's because they feel you and your work is important to them." The manager should not hesitate to take chances in this area. If the manager doesn't, who will? (Certainly not all the people who are made to feel comfortable or even somewhat superior because of Terry's cautiousness and certainly not those who can more easily influence him because of his fears. Again, we tend to feel more threatened by those who don't have any major fears because the importance of our behavior is, to them, minimized.)

Can a person's friends help him overcome his fears? Not likely. Why? Because we tend to pick as friends those who share our fears. Why? Because our friends are unlikely to address and confront us about those fears. If they did, they probably wouldn't be our friends very long.

But a manager is not so easy to dismiss. And if the manager fails to act in such cases, his subordinate might well spend his life engaging in self-destructive behavior patterns because of "irrational fears". If the manager is accused of playing psychologist, the simple answer is, "Yes, just as I'm asked to play accountant at times and lawyer at other times."

[The reader is asked here to determine which behavior is feared by someone the reader likes in the organization, e.g., being seen as a failure, being controlled, and so forth. Can you pair this feared behavior with reinforcers to the person? "When people see you make mistakes and fail once in a while, they see you as human, they warm up to you more, and they're more likely to defend you to others."]

The Crucial Timing of Aversives

Managers must be extremely careful when using aversive stimuli with subordinates. The critical point occurs not only when the manager initiates an aversive stimulus (punishment), but also when she stops it (avoidance learning). "What behavior on the subordinate's part immediately preceded the cessation of the manager's aversive stimulus?"

172

is the key question. Why? Because the behavior that successfully stops the aversive is the behavior that is fear driven, hence the behavior that becomes excessive and defines, to such a great extent, who we become. Let us look at the following example:

> Manager: When do you think you'll have that report finished? (Aversive stimulus)
> Subordinate: In about two weeks.
> Manager: Oh, come on. You've got to get it in by next Wednesday. (Maintains the aversive stimulus)
> Subordinate: Well, I hate to make promises I can't keep. You know, my wife hasn't been feeling too well lately, and I've had to help out around the house. (Critical point: excuse-making response)
> Manager: Oh, I didn't know that. Well, two weeks will be all right. (Cessation of aversive stimuli)

As cold and inhuman as it sounds, this manager may be seriously harming her subordinate. By stopping the aversive stimulus at this point, she has greatly increased the likelihood of the subordinate's excuse-making, blaming others, behavior. At the least, she should have explored the extent of the wife's illness. She should probably have also used a mild aversive stimulus after the subordinate's plea for sympathy, "Well, you know we do have to get this work out."

But suppose the subordinate's wife really is sick? In sum, when should the manager keep the aversive going in order to punish ineffective responses? When the ineffective behavior is frequent and repetitive, when it's excessive, when it goes beyond the bounds of reality. This decision is the manager's responsibility; no one else can or will make it. If more managers punished meek, passive behavior and reinforced confident, adventuresome behavior, we would have far fewer meek, passive people in private industry (but then we might have less control over these more confident, adventuresome people, a frightening prospect to many managers).

[Because of the pervasive, intense, almost overwhelming strength of avoidance behavior, readers are again asked to start an aversive stimulus (e.g., criticism) with someone and keep it going until the person is doing something constructive.

> You: Why are you always so late?
> They (a normally, frightened, passive person): I'm sorry. My car broke down.
> You: Well, get the thing fixed.
> They: But it costs so much.
> You: Oh, don't give me that crap!
> They (finally frustrated with you): Well, you know I'm not really late that often.
> You: Actually, you're probably right. Sorry. I shouldn't even have brought it up. (Thus stopping the aversive when she/he more aggressively speaks up – this makes you an excellent manager and a wonderful person to be around.]

Long-Term Problems with Aversive Stimuli

Many organizations have paid a heavy price for the overuse of aversive stimuli and the minimal use of reinforcers to control their employees' behavior. Avoidance learning and aversive pairings are probably the quickest way to influence behavior. Firing a few people who are not producing can have an immediate, dramatic impact on the remaining employees. To avoid being fired, they work harder.

This quick change is short-lived, however, for two reasons. First, management has done nothing to make the work itself more reinforcing. As a result, new forms of avoidance behavior will arise. (These might include anything from employee agreements to "cover for one another" to subtle sabotage of computer equipment or leaving the company.) Second, by using aversive stimuli to control behavior, management is constantly pairing itself with these stimuli and quickly becomes an aversive stimulus itself. Likewise, the goals of management, since they are now paired with the new aversive stimulus (management), soon become aversive stimuli to the employees – stimuli to be avoided or stopped.

Many people (employees) have learned to successfully stop aversive stimuli by adopting overly aggressive, almost hostile behavior patterns. Consider the following:

> Manager: Jim, I'd like you to stay late tonight and help Ed out on that project.
> Subordinate: Why the hell am I always being picked? I stayed late twice last month.
> Manager: Well, let me see if I can find someone else.

The manager who initiates a demand (aversive stimulus) and then backs down (stops it) in the face of hostile opposition is clearly headed for much more hostile opposition.

In good economic times, there is always a sharp swing away from the managerial use of aversive stimuli to influence the behavior of employees due to the tight labor supply. To avoid the aversive stimuli of a person or a company, a subordinate can simply resign. Resignation by employees is an aversive stimulus the company will thus try to avoid (consider the late 90s).

Rapidly expanding economies lead to a sudden increase in theories of worker motivation that oppose the managerial use of aversive stimuli as a controlling device. These theories suggest that the use of such external controls is non-constructive and even unnatural. They favor instead a new emphasis on empowerment, self-control, and self-direction. (It is not surprising that the impact on industry of these theories of management generally drop dramatically in periods of high unemployment.)

Before one allows empowerment and "self-control" to assume dominance as a management tool, however, one had better be certain that the right employees have been hired and that organizational goals are reinforcers to them. (The employee to whom "upsetting people in positions of power" is reinforcing could prove disastrous to a company when left to "self-control".) This is not to say that such concepts are not useful and effective. It is to say, however, that management has a critical task before it, that of pairing organizational goals with stimuli that are reinforcing to the competent individual employee.

There is a further complication in using self-control as a management tool. As we have seen, people are largely controlled (influenced) by the people around them (managers, peers, subordinates). This control is implicit in interpersonal interactions; an individual could achieve total self-control only if he were to function in a vacuum or as a hermit.

[Since "good" and "bad" economies so often elicit different management styles, the reader is asked to assume a strategic view of their environment. Is the economy expanding or contracting? What management philosophies are now in vogue? Are they appropriate for present economic conditions?]

Stimulus Generalization

Stimulus generalization refers to the fact that the more similar one stimulus (environment) is to another, the more likely it is to evoke a similar response. The more intense the original reinforcer or aversive stimulus, the more inclusive is the generalized response.

Generalizations will only take place in situations that involve reinforcers or aversive stimuli to the individual. Suppose a new chief executive officer joins a company. If he fires and/or retires a number of employees and also brings in a number of new people, cliques will normally form. These cliques will consist of people who consider themselves pre-new-president employees on the one hand and post-new-president employees on the other.

Stimulus generalization accounts for the fact that a specific stimulus does not have to be repeated *precisely* the same way to be a reinforcer. The words, "You did a fine job and you're going to get a bonus for it," set up the phrase, "You did a fine job," as a reinforcer. Similar complimentary phrases will also be reinforcers because of stimulus generalization. The more similar a phrase is to the original phrase, the more reinforcing it will be.

The Authority Problem

One of the most important and destructive generalizations in private industry is the "authority problem". The individual with an authority problem has often experienced numerous and intense aversive stimuli paired with authority figures, the first of which is normally the individual's parent(s). These aversive pairings have been so severe that they generalize to include all authorities, including policemen, government officials, senior management within an organization, and especially the individual's immediate superior. Uncomfortable feelings in authority figures are reinforcing to such persons, and they are frequently quite aggressive and hostile in order to elicit these feelings. They often quite openly pair authority figures with aversive stimuli.

These hostile response patterns are often misinterpreted. Such individuals are frequently hired because their aggressive behavior appears to reflect an ability to get the job done. To the dismay of the organization that hires them, however, these people are far more intent on hurting authority figures than on getting the job done; indeed, their presence in an organization can be quite disruptive.

[Readers are asked to consider people in their inner circle. Do any of them frequently (excessively) pair authorities with aversives? If they do, they can have a detrimental influence on your attitudes. Try extinguishing or using aversives when they next express some negative comments about someone in authority.]

Summary

The use of aversive stimuli involves far more complexities and ramifications than does the use of reinforcers. Yet the use of both is intrinsic to managerial responsibilities. To suppose that a manager can function effectively using only one or the other is unrealistic. Generally, however, too much behavioral impact is gained through the use of aversive stimuli and too little through the use of reinforcers.

Using aversive stimuli is a quick and effective way to influence behavioral change. The negative long-term complications, however, are often not readily apparent to the manager. Fear and the resulting excessive intensity and frequency in behavior is one such complication. A superior may chafe because one of his subordinates is too dependent. If the manager were to reinforce and shape independent behavior patterns, he would gradually develop an effective, adjusted employee. By instead severely punishing dependent behavior, he will quickly develop an overly independent subordinate (hence fanaticism). He will not develop a subordinate who loves independence, but rather one who hates being seen as dependent. This avoidance drive almost always leads to excessive behavioral intensity.

In operant learning (when we're responding directly to behavior as it occurs), the use of reinforcers involves only one basic question for the manager: What behavior was my subordinate engaged in when I used that reinforcer? The use of aversive stimuli involves two basic questions at once: What behavior was my subordinate engaged in when I started the aversive stimulus? (punishment); and, What behavior was my subordinate engaged in when I stopped the aversive stimulus? (avoidance learning).

The answers to these questions are critical if managers are to gain insight into the impact they are having on their subordinates. Yet it is difficult to engage in behavior and, at the same time, objectively observe and analyze that behavior. The answers, therefore, must come from others, and the most important source of this crucial feedback are those people in your inner circle who are confident and competent.

Please remember the key question, "Hey, right off the top of your head, what's my greatest shortcoming?"

SECTION 4

EVALUATING PEOPLE

AND

THEIR INFLUENCE ON OTHERS

How can I tell what people really like in others?

Why is it important to know what others like in me?

Can't we just ignore people who have a destructive influence on us?

How can I determine who should be my friends?

What will I encounter most frequently: reinforcement, extinction, or
punishment?

CHAPTER 18

EVALUATING THE INFLUENCE OF OTHERS

Evaluating the behavior of another person is an extremely complex task.
Behavior occurs very quickly. Those things that are reinforcing or
aversive to someone are often subtle and difficult to determine when we
are constantly being bombarded with a mass of stimuli. Our own
emotional involvement sometimes precludes us from analyzing a situation
objectively. Indeed, an objective analysis of another person's behavior
can be a depressing, even frightening, experience. For example, it is
difficult to accept the fact that someone who "loves us very much" is
actually reinforcing dependent attitudes and feelings on our part.

Yet, behavior can be evaluated with a surprising degree of accuracy.
Objectively observed, it provides us with clear and useful insights about
other people. And, while some diagnoses may lead to depressing
conclusions, the principles we have learned may allow us to constructively
change the behavior of another person. We need not focus only on
behavior as it is, but also on behavior as it could be. We should also
remember that frequent, repetitive behavior is the only criterion of
accuracy; one or two instances of a behavior mean little, and focusing on
that may be quite misleading and even destructive. If a spouse expresses
his/her love for their mate frequently, occasional instances of anger and
hostile remarks should be ignored. Responding emotionally and in kind to

the anger could quickly escalate the frequency of negative interchanges (even to the point at which they define the relationship).

Whom Are We Evaluating?

In evaluating behavior, the reader should also remember that the other person's behavior is contingent upon his own. In a real sense, as we've seen, we should be held accountable not for our own behavior, but for the behavior of those with whom we interact frequently.

This standard requires us to focus our attention on the manner in which we influence others; it can quickly lead to changes in our own behavior. If a man determines that his wife has been punishing his decisiveness, he should not react by "hurting" her. If his decisiveness is aversive to her, it may well be because he made it so, possibly by making arbitrary (aversive) decisions involving demands on her. In any case, he can make his decisiveness and their relationship more reinforcing to her by constructively changing his own behavior e.g., asking for her advice or input. A person cannot change their own behavior (and is rarely motivated to do so) as quickly and effectively as can someone in their inner circle. Retaliation for someone's aversive behavior is rarely an effective, constructive change vehicle.

Our Confidence

One of the primary goals of evaluating others should be to determine what influence, constructive or destructive, those in our inner circle are having on our confidence, on our liking and respect for ourselves. More specifically, we should learn what areas we can, and what areas we cannot, broach safely with each individual. Discussing "customers" or mutual friends with those who fear people and who, consequently, pair people with aversives can only have a deleterious impact on our effectiveness with those people. Indeed, such negative people-pairings will diminish our confidence since people and interpersonal interactions are such an integral part of everyone's life. (Einstein immersed himself in physics in order to escape the "tumultuous emotions of personal relationships").

Knowing the fears of those with whom we interact is important because those fears will be visited upon us in one form or another. Even accurately analyzing the fears of others, however, does not prevent those fears from influencing us, but it does help diminish that impact somewhat. Knowing that our boss dislikes (fears) confidence in others minimizes a bit the destructive influence of his many "you-aversive" pairings, but they will still have some influence on our confidence. More direct action, including minimizing or even avoiding interaction with the person, may be most appropriate when possible. Knowing the fears of those in our inner circle at least will lower our expectations to a more realistic level.

Limitations

We may wish to try to change a person and their fears, but we must remember that we are not the only ones interacting and influencing them. Managers may dislike a subordinate's constant complaints about their salary. Punishing or extinguishing such complaints may have little impact, however, if the subordinate is frequently subjected to intense negative conversations on the topic by a spouse or colleague who feels the subordinate is being taken advantage of. Accepting our limitations is important and will help prevent confidence-shattering frustrations in our endeavors.

(Is it being suggested that the reader leave a good paying job if his/her manager is having an excessively negative influence on their confidence? Yes. Is it being suggested that the reader avoid or minimize interactions with one's own mother if "Mom" is having an excessively negative influence on his/her confidence? Yes.)

Let us now consider several diagnostic principles and tools.

Diagnostic Principles

Principle I

People generally reinforce behavior in others that is reinforcing to them.
Hence, the reader must dispassionately observe the individual in his
interactions with other people and note which behavior in others the
individual is immediately following with reinforcers.

> Subordinate (who is known to worry excessively): You know, I'm
> really nervous over making this presentation to the management
> committee.
> Manager: I'm sure everything will go very well. Some
> nervousness probably helps you do an even better job.

Is "lack of confidence" in this subordinate reinforcing to the manager?
Despite our protests that the manager is merely reassuring his subordinate,
the answer is probably yes. Not only has the manager followed the
subordinate's statement of fear with a reinforcer; he has also paired the
verbal equivalent of fear with a reinforcer ("your nervousness = doing a
better job").

Does this employee need reassurance? Yes. Should we give them
reassurance when they're feeling (and expressing) fear? No. When
should we reassure them? When they're expressing some confident
tendencies, e.g., "I suppose it'll go alright," or "It probably won't be so
bad." When are people most likely to respond more confidently? When
we stop reinforcing their fears with our reassurances.

We are reminded again that logic and rationality are not strong detriments
of behavior. We often attack the person who speaks ill of us to other
people; yet it is the other people, those who listen to gossip and subtly
reinforce the speaker with their rapt attention, who might also be more
appropriately disliked and punished.

184

Principle II

People generally punish behavior (follow the behavior with an aversive stimulus) in others that is aversive to them. If it is difficult to believe that "lack of confidence" is reinforcing to the manager in the above example, consider the following interchange between the same manager and another subordinate:

> Subordinate (excited): The purchasing agent for B. M. I. Corporation just called in an order. I knew it! I knew I sold them! I told you we'd get them as a customer.
> Manager: Don't be so sure you sold them. It's a small order and they may have called it in only because their regular source couldn't handle it. We may never hear from them again.

Despite all the possible justifications for this behavior, it is safe to assume this manager does not like success and confidence in others. Before the reader rebels at this diagnosis, he should ask himself how many people take real pleasure in the good fortune of others. The man who inherits a large sum of money is not usually looked upon with favor by his neighbors; indeed, he is often subjected to a good deal of subtle criticism. The salesperson that wins the contest and the accolades of management may be subjected to many subtle aversives (including "friendly" sarcasm) from peers. If a diagnosis reached through the above two principles conflicts with our sense of reality or appropriateness, it is most likely the principles which come closest to the truth, and not our own prejudices about what should or should not be true.

Consider this more personal example: A mother is well known to "love" her five-year-old daughter; she would do anything for her child's happiness. The girl is frightened by interactions with strangers. She is about to be driven by her mother to a birthday party at a playmate's house.

> Daughter: I don't want to go.
> Mother: Why?
> Daughter: I don't know the other children. I'm afraid.

Mother: Everything will be fine, honey. You'll enjoy it. You'll have a good time.

The mother has reinforced her child's "fear with strangers" response. But, you protest, she's just reassuring her daughter. Two hours later, the daughter returns home.

Daughter: Oh, Mommy, I had such a good time. We played games and I won prizes. I had so much fun.
Mother: See! Didn't I tell you it was foolish to carry on so about going to the party? Aren't you sorry you didn't want to go?

The mother has punished her daughter for "having fun with strangers". No one doubts the fact that the mother "loves" her child – but "love" involves very complex behavior. Is the child's happiness really a reinforcer to the mother? That's too broad a question. More specifically, is the child's happiness with others a reinforcer to her mother?

Let us consider the previous managerial examples from a more effective frame of reference:

Subordinate (the worrier): You know, I'm really nervous over making this presentation to the management committee.
Manager: I think that's a bit foolish. Besides, being nervous can only hurt you in your presentation. (Punishment and appropriate aversive pairing)

Subordinate: The purchasing agent for B. M. I. Corporation just called in an order. I knew it! I knew I sold them! I told you we'd get them as a customer.
Manager: Beautiful! I must admit I didn't think we'd get them. You must have done a hellava job out there. Come on, I'll buy you lunch and you can tell me how you did it. (Reinforcement)

Lack of confidence in subordinates is aversive to this manager; practical achievements by subordinates, on the other hand, are reinforcing to him.

[It has been suggested that we pick as friends those who share our fears. Readers are asked to engage in some responses that are opposite their normal behaviors; e.g., highly critical people are being asked to exude strong enthusiasm (or vice versa). Do your friends reinforce or punish your "atypical" behavior? Can you broaden your response repertoire if you always confine yourself to the same kinds of friends?]

Principle III

People extinguish behavior by others they find aversive or behavior to which they are indifferent. They do so by responding in a bland, monotone manner, by not responding at all, or by changing the topic.

> Husband: My boss said he is sending my report to the president because it was so well done.
> Wife: That's good; say, did you want peas or corn for dinner tonight? (Extinction)

> Subordinate: I just sold eight carloads of steel to D. T. O. Corporation.
> Manager: Fine. Say, you'll be able to make the sales meeting Thursday, won't you? (Extinction)

> Subordinate: I finished the financial analysis. I think I've put in some pretty good ideas.
> Manager: Good; hey, I heard you flew in from New York with the president yesterday. What did you talk about? (Extinction)

> Wife (excited): I won the tennis tournament at the club today!
> Husband: How many people were in it?

[The reader is again asked to indicate some accomplishment on his/her part, pairing it with pride and joy to several people in your inner circle. "I thought I really did a good job on that report. I have to admit I'm really quite proud of it." Who reinforces you? Who punishes you? Most important, who extinguishes you?]

Effects of Extinction

This type of extinction can be quite harmful. Not only does it decrease the probability of constructive feelings and behavior in many instances, it also leads to fear, frustration, and aggressive behavior. Managers (or spouses) who use extinction frequently will normally elicit a good deal of negative emotional behavior from subordinates (or spouses) over the long run.

Unfortunately, the fear, frustration, and angry responses may well be reinforcing to those who extinguish others. Thus, their tendency to extinguish others is strengthened. For example, although a husband may find his wife's emotional reactions (enthusiasm) over her work-related accomplishments aversive, he may at the same time find her emotional reactions related to him quite reinforcing. He increases the probability of his wife's emotional reactions toward himself if he extinguishes (does not respond to) her emotional reactions (enthusiasm) to situations which do not involve him (a double benefit).

Indeed, some spouses can develop a high degree of hostility toward their shy, withdrawn mates, even though the latter have never said a harsh word. While outsiders may wonder about the cruel hostility expressed by a spouse toward such a "nice, quiet, gentle" person, they may not be aware of the devastating effects that constant extinction is having on the angry spouse.

[Readers are asked to objectively watch interactions between people in their inner circle (including themselves) and note the frequency of extinction. Is it not surprising?]

Self-Development

It is the author's conviction that people cannot change themselves. Many would disagree. Few would disagree, however, that the behavior of others has a strong influence on our own thoughts and feelings. If we cannot change ourselves, we can change our interpersonal environment; more specifically, we can change the people with whom we interact.

How do we most effectively evaluate people with whom we should or should not interact frequently and with whom we should be open regarding ourselves, our opinions, and our feelings? We do it by engaging in behavior we would like to develop and strengthen in ourselves in the presence of other people and note whether the other person reinforces, punishes, or extinguishes the behavior.

Suppose we make the following comment to three individuals on separate occasions: "You know, I think I did a pretty good job on that report." We then note their reaction, including their emotional expressions:

> First Person: That's great! You always do good reports. What did you cover in it? (Reinforces)
> Second Person: Don't be too sure of that. I don't want you to be disappointed if the boss doesn't like it and you know how critical he can be. (Punishes)
> Third Person: That's good. Say, what time does that play start tonight? (Extinction)

Clearly, we should seek out the first person and interact with him openly and frequently. His behavior will have a beneficial impact on our behavior. We should avoid or at least minimize our interactions and openness with the second and third persons; they will diminish our confidence.

To verify our diagnosis, it might then be helpful to make a self-deprecatory statement and note the same people's reactions: "You know, I'm not sure I did a very good job on that report."

> First Person: Oh, hell, that's just stupid. (Punishes) Say, are we going to play golf Saturday? (then Extinguishes)
> Second Person: Well, I'd be happy to help you with it. I think we'll be able to do it together. (Reinforces)

<u>Third Person</u>: I'm sure its fine! I'm sure it's a great job! Anyway, it's not that important a project. (Reinforces)

Again, we should seek out the first person and avoid the other two.

A Real Danger

We must recognize that many people find self-destructive behavior in others reinforcing. The highly emotional person who gushes with sympathy when we complain about our mistreatment at the hands of our boss is not a good person to be around. We may relish her emotional sympathy but we will soon find ourselves getting more and more sensitive to mistreatment by our boss, since we are being reinforced so amply for doing so.

This can be compounded by the dearth of reinforcement in our lives. We may seek out the sympathetic people because they are the only ones truly reinforcing us for anything. But if they are reinforcing us for self-deprecation or hostility or fear or dependency, then we have real problems. We like them and seek them out, but we're worse off after each interaction with them.

We like those who reinforce us (so few people do); after all, they are pairing themselves with reinforcers. But we must ask ourselves what those we like are reinforcing in us because that's what they're strengthening in us and, to a large extent, that's what we'll become. If John reinforces us frequently, we will certainly like him and seek him out. But if he continuously reinforces our anger toward others, we will feel that anger more and more intensely, more and more frequently, and toward more and more people.

[Readers are asked to consider those in their inner circle whom they like the most. Who reinforces you most often and most effectively? This is who you'll truly like. But the more important question is: What feelings, attitudes, and/or behaviors are you engaged in when they're most inclined toward reinforcing you? Are these the feelings, attitudes, and behaviors you want as part of your repertoire, your personality?]

Signs of Personal Growth

It is quite difficult to respond to situations and people and, at the same time, analyze our own behavior. How, then, does an individual know when she/he is growing and changing constructively? By noting changes in the people around them.

The best criterion of change in an individual is a change in the behavior of the people with whom she/he interacts frequently.

If confidence in others has become a reinforcer to a manager, people around her (especially her subordinates) will become more confident, because she will be punishing and extinguishing lack of confidence and reinforcing confident behavior on their part.

Even if old friends are not changing, an individual who is growing personally will find they are making new friends that have different personalities than the old ones. If a person has developed a more enthusiastic orientation, the people they will be attracted to and who will be attracted to them will reflect a stronger enthusiastic bent. Old friends who are negative will be subtly punished or, more likely, extinguished by the person; interactions with these old friends will become fewer and fewer because, almost everyone will agree, "We just don't have the same interests anymore". A good criterion for judging people, consequently, is by looking at the types of people with whom they like to interact. An excellent criterion for judging managers is by looking at the types of people with whom they like to interact, who they always seek out to share ideas with, and especially who they select to join their team.

[Readers are encouraged to gauge the confidence of their best friends in a number of important areas in their lives because the fears of those friends "will be visited upon you". Where are they most (least) confident? How could you increase their overall confidence? In what areas do you feel comfortable (uncomfortable) interacting with them? What do you or they fear in those areas in which you feel uncomfortable?]

How do I know what is reinforcing and what is aversive to a person?

Is asking someone what they like a good indicator of what is reinforcing to them?

What is the difference between reinforced behavior and fear-driven behavior?

CHAPTER 19

EVALUATING PEOPLE THROUGH THEIR PAIRINGS

Another evaluation tool consists of noting which stimuli people pair with reinforcers and aversive stimuli.

Principle I

People generally pair what they like and what they want others to like with reinforcers.

The individual who says, "Most people are really interesting when you take the time to talk to them," is usually outgoing and comfortable with others. People are generally reinforcing to her, and her behavior will reflect this fact.

Similarly, comments such as "His sense of humor sure breaks me up" indicate that humor is reinforcing to the speaker, while "His ability to fire incompetent people quickly has probably increased our profits threefold" is a comment we would expect from a tough line manager.

It is difficult, if not impossible, for people to avoid pairing stimuli they find reinforcing with reinforcers. Moreover, the mere fact that they can use reinforcers is to their credit; many people cannot.

Aversive Pairings

Pairing things we don't like with aversive stimuli is far more common than is pairing things we like with reinforcers, reflecting, in large part, the pervasiveness of our fears. How often do we hear statements like the following: "This company sure is cheap when it comes to giving raises." "Mike's impulsivity is going to get him in trouble one of these days."

Principle II

People generally pair what they dislike and want others to dislike with aversive stimuli.

In order to diagnose behavior properly, one must focus not on the aversive stimulus used but, rather, on the stimuli being paired with it. This is a critical point. Many analyses are incorrect because the individual focuses on the aversive stimulus used rather than on the stimuli being paired with it. In the forgoing statements, for example, greater insight is gained when one realizes it is the company that is aversive to the person, not its cheapness. It is Mike's impulsivity (and Mike himself) that is aversive to the speaker, not Mike's getting into trouble. Again, frequent, repetitive pairings are the criterion for accurate analyses. Does the person frequently pair the company with aversives? Does the person frequently pair Mike or impulsivity with aversives?

Asking ourselves two questions would help us evaluate a person's pairings effectively. One, what is the person using, a reinforcer or an aversive stimulus? Two, what is the person pairing with it – that which is truly reinforcing or truly aversive to them?

Consider the following statements of an angry husband to his wife: "You never give any thought to anyone but yourself. You live in your own little world. You never ask me about my work and you never show any appreciation for everything I do for you. You never show me any attention or affection. You are really a selfish, self-centered person."

Do these statements indicate that his wife's lack of attention and affection are truly aversive to this person? Not necessarily. They indicate that, at the moment, his wife is an aversive stimulus to him because he is pairing "her" with aversive stimuli.

In order to elicit hurt feelings from his wife, he pairs her subconsciously with what he has learned are aversive stimuli to her, not necessarily to himself. If his wife were sensitive about being accused of spending money foolishly, he would probably be pairing her with those stimuli at the moment, e.g., "You think money grows on trees! You have no concept of how hard I have to work for it."

[Verbal pairings occur quickly; thus they are difficult to capture for analysis, at least before some degree of practice has occurred. Hence, readers might wish to pick up some memos or emails from colleagues and note any pairings in them; this can be quite informative.]

Denials

People may deny that those things they are pairing with aversive stimuli are really aversive to them, but such denials must be accepted with great caution. The man who calls his company "cheap" may protest that he really likes his company; this is doubtful. Likewise, the individual who pairs his wife with aversive stimuli may protest that he loves her; that, too, is doubtful.

A leader of a group devoted to women's liberation may protest the idea that she dislikes men. Such protests are doubtful if she makes comments such as, "Men have abused women for generations," and "Men admire aggressive men, but the same men always label aggressive women as bitches," and "Men get very defensive and hostile when women start attacking the glass ceiling." Such protests are reasonable, however, if she makes comments like the following, "Treating women equitably is good for everyone," or "Fairness in pay for both sexes is the mark of an enlightened society" or "Respecting competence is not a gender issue." (Do you feel the aversive pairings have more impact?)

195

Readers might wish to ask some people, "How do you feel about ...?", then note their pairings. You can, of course, ask about anything: people, ideas, places, movies, etc.]

Logic and Objectivity

The opposite of a reinforcing stimulus is not necessarily an aversive stimulus.

The women's liberationist may find men aversive, but may not find women reinforcing. If she did find women reinforcing, she would be as inclined toward pairing women with reinforcers as she is toward pairing men with aversive stimuli. That a black person hates whites ("Whitey is a honkey.") does not mean that he likes blacks; indeed, he may hate both equally ("Most blacks are Uncle Toms.")

The person with an acute authority problem may readily express anger toward senior managers; this does not mean the like non-exempt employees. Thus, hating what is evil does not necessarily mean loving what is good. Many people find unjust people quite aversive and are quick to say so; this does not mean they find fair people reinforcing. They may be reinforced by attacking unjust people but not by complimenting fair people. In sum (on a more philosophical note), if we loved good, in the loving, we would be good. But if we go through life merely hating evil, in the hating, we will be evil.

Readers are asked to determine what they dislike most in their manager. Does this mean you like its opposite? Suppose you dislike your manager's apparent lack of interest in your work. But if she had more interest and involvement, would you label her a "micro-manager?"]

Every Alternative is Aversive

That opposite stimuli are not necessarily reinforcing and aversive is an important phenomenon. Since aversive stimuli are so often used in our society, opposites and alternatives may all have been paired with aversive stimuli and be aversive themselves. This is called an avoidance-avoidance conflict, and its effects are devastating, despite its frequency of occurrence.

The mother may punish independent behavior one day ("If you ever do something like that again without asking my permission, you'll regret it.") and punish dependent behavior a day later ("Why do you always bother me with such questions? You're old enough to take care of yourself.") The married person may dislike living with their spouse, but dread the alternative of living alone. The employee may find staying with his company aversive, leaving his company aversive, and joining a new and unfamiliar company aversive. The highly independent salesman may find his manager's statement, "I will help you," aversive; but he may also find his manager's statement, "All right, I won't help you," aversive.

How do we know when we, or others, are in an avoidance-avoidance conflict? When we vacillate, when we're indecisive. A married person may undergo a great conflict if he/she is having an affair. Part of the conflict may be due to the idea that leaving either person, the spouse or lover, is aversive to them. Thus, the person may miss his/her spouse more when in the presence of their lover and miss their lover more when in the presence of their spouse; the closer he gets to each, the more he loves the other. The pain of "being away" from each is driving the conflict.

Many people stay in abusive relationships because the alternatives are aversive, especially the dreaded "being alone". Many managers find an employee's presence aversive, but the alternative of confronting the employee more aversive, hence avoided.

[Readers are asked to think of some conflicted time in their life. Were all the alternatives aversive? If they were not, conflicts would probably not have arisen and certainly would not have lingered on, because the road most easily and often traveled is the one that is clearly least aversive.]

What Is He Reacting To?

The final method of diagnosing behavior is, first, to note which of an individual's response patterns occur frequently and then to observe what immediately precedes and follows these behaviors. The most important stimuli to observe preceding or following the responses are those involving the behavior of other people, including oneself if possible. This is because the most reinforcing or aversive stimuli to an individual are usually to be found in the behavior of other people.

In the case of avoidance behavior, the stimuli to notice are those involving the behavior of others immediately preceding the response; that particular behavior is usually aversive to the individual. It triggers fear in them. If the individual repetitiously makes excuses, for example, we must determine what type of stimulus immediately precedes his excuse-making behavior.

> Manager: I want you to break that machine down and put in the replacement parts this afternoon.
> Subordinate: I was going to ask you if I could have this afternoon off. I've been getting pains in my chest and I wanted to see a doctor about them.

It is important to note that we are talking about *repetitious* behavior. One "excuse" response by a subordinate does not tell you anything. If the subordinate in the forgoing example engages in this behavior frequently, and we determine that it is usually a reaction to the type of stimulus presented above by his manager, we can conclude that having work demands placed on him by others is aversive (frightening) to him. In the case of reinforced behavior, one must determine what immediately follows the response. Suppose we noted frequent complaining in an individual. We would then look for reinforcing stimuli in the behavior of those to whom he complains:

198

Subordinate: You know, I think we're headed for a lot of trouble.
Manager: How's that?
Subordinate: People are upset with this company.
Manager: In what way?
Subordinate: They feel the salaries are way too low.

Here we might determine that the manager's interest and concern, as reflected in his questions and tone of voice, are reinforcing to the subordinate. Indeed, few managers realize how reinforcing their attention is to subordinates. This manager has unfortunately made his attention and concern contingent upon the subordinate's complaining. He might better have waited for some indications of positive attitudes by the employee and reinforced them with his attention and an exploring focus. Here, again, we are discussing repetitive behavior. Obviously, if a subordinate rarely complains, the manager should objectively explore the reasons when he does.

Diagnosis, even by means of repetitive behavior, is not easy. Does an individual constantly ridicule other people in front of a group because he finds the group's laughter reinforcing or because he finds the ridiculed person's discomfort reinforcing? This is sometimes a difficult question to answer, and trial and error methods may have to be used to change the ineffective behavior.

[Readers are encouraged to think of a frequent, repetitive behavior pattern engaged in by their manager. What is the normal response of people when the manager engages in this behavior? These responses are probably reinforcing to the manager.]

Fear-Driven Behavior Versus Reinforced Behavior

The distinction between behavior controlled by a reinforcer and that controlled by an aversive stimulus is often a difficult one to make. The best criterion is excessiveness. Is the behavior excessive and/or inappropriate? If it is, then it's probably fear driven. Why? Because those things we fear in others could occur at **any** time, hence we must be on guard **all** the time. Thus does fear-driven behavior become excessive and require different approaches if we want to change the behavior.

Does the obsessive-compulsive housewife continually wash her floors because a clean floor is reinforcing to her or because a dirty floor is aversive to her? Probably the latter because the behavior is excessive (the definition of obsessive-compulsive). Since the things we fear usually center on the behavior of others, we can reasonably assume that the compulsive person's behavior, because it is excessive, results from her having been criticized for "being dirty" a number of times. Thus, we can conclude that this person is overly sensitive (fears) to criticism from others and is working diligently to avoid it.

Is the cautious micro-manager bogging down in details because "being right" is reinforcing to him or because "being wrong" is aversive to him? If a response recurs repeatedly and excessively and nothing seems to follow it, the best guess is that it is avoidance behavior and reflects the fact that he's been punished too harshly for mistakes in the past. In general, if behavior is stable and of long duration, it is probably avoidance, fear-driven behavior controlled by aversive stimuli.

Indeed, fear-driven behavior occurs precisely because nothing happens. We avoid the dreaded criticism from others because we're excessively subservient with people. No one would criticize us if we weren't so subservient, but we'll never know that because we're always subservient. We excessively try to impress people because we fear being seen as a failure by others (we were ridiculed in our teenage years). We wouldn't be seen as a failure if we weren't always trying to impress people, but we'll never know that because we're always trying to impress people. We're constantly extolling our physical prowess (macho) so no one will again ridicule us for being a "sissy". No one would see us as a frightened sissy if we weren't so focused on our physique, but we'll never know that because we're always bragging about our physical prowess.

Behavior is complex, but this should not discourage us from analyzing The rewards of such an analysis can be well worth the effort, especiall when it results in more constructive, effective behavior by ourselves and those with whom we interact. At a minimum, an accurate analysis of those in our inner circle (both personal and work-related) can result in more realistic expectations on our part, thus ridding us of unnecessary disappointments and frustrations. Indeed, the analysis of the behavior of ourselves and others probably offers us one of the most potent tools available for developing a sense of realism, and with realism comes more effectiveness, contentment, confidence, and social growth.

[Think of an excessive, inappropriate behavior pattern of someone in your inner circle. What is the fear controlling the behavior? Does recognizing the excessive behavior and the fear driving it lead you to be a little more tolerant of the person? Does it also mean that their fear-driven behavior has less impact on your own feelings and attitudes?]

SECTION 5

CHANGING OTHERS

Is it helpful to have someone work with you on these learning
principles?

Which principles are easier to use, pairings or operant?

Is the ability to use both reinforcers and aversives important?

Do manager-subordinate interactions ever cause both participants
anxiety?

CHAPTER 20

CHANGING THE BEHAVIOR OF OTHERS

We have now covered the basic principles of pairings and operant learning
and can begin to consider how to put them to use. While we all want to
influence others, our major focus always should be: Evaluating other
people and their influence on us and our confidence.

A summary of our principles follows. Remember, however, that the terms
"reinforcer" and "aversive stimulus" refer to what is true of others, not of
us.

Classical Learning Principles

Principle I

To decrease the frequency of behavior controlled by a reinforcer, pair the
reinforcer with aversive stimuli.

Principle II

To decrease the frequency of fear-driven behavior controlled by aversive
stimuli, pair the aversive stimuli with reinforcers.

Principle III

To increase the frequency of a certain behavior, pair the verbal equivalent of the behavior with a reinforcer.

Principle IV

To decrease the frequency of a certain behavior, pair the verbal equivalent of the response with an aversive stimulus.

Operant Learning Principles

Principle V: Reinforcement

Any behavior immediately followed by a reinforcer is strengthened and has a greater likelihood of recurring.

Principle VI: Extinction

Any behavior not immediately followed by a reinforcer is weakened and has a lesser probability of recurring.

Principle VII: Punishment

Any behavior immediately followed by an aversive stimulus is weakened and has a lesser probability of recurring.

Principle VIII: Avoidance Behavior

Following a behavior with the cessation of an aversive stimulus greatly increases its strength and the probability and the frequency of the behavior recurring (fear-driven behavior).

We know that these principles are not as simple as they seem. If readers are overwhelmed by their complexity, however, they would do well to remember that they are not expected to recall all of their many facets, intricacies, and consequences. It is enough if they have grasped some major ideas – the general consequences of extinction, for example, or of using aversive stimuli.

Cautions

Some words of advice: Using the principles successfully takes practice, and mistakes are bound to be made. This is not an alarming prospect, however; we can learn from our mistakes and avoid repeating them.

To believe that using the principles represents manipulation, however, is to deny reality. We use and are subjected to these principles every day, like it or not. The goal is to use our most powerful tool, our mind, to think about what we are doing to others and what they are doing to us. Those who fear manipulation can only fear people "thinking" rationally about what they are doing to others and what others are doing to them.

Can the principles be used destructively? Certainly. Any knowledge can be. Understanding the principles minimizes that likelihood, however, and, we hope, also increases the likelihood that knowledgeable people realize that the confidence of those around them should be a major goal in their lives because that confidence will pay handsome dividends to them.

Remember, too, that the principles should not be applied in all situations. Many interpersonal interactions are too emotional (too reinforcing or aversive) for an individual to apply to them a set of thought-out behavioral principles. If a manager is able to use the principles five or ten percent of the time, that will be more than adequate, as the consequences in the behavior of those around him/her will demonstrate, ideally in terms of increased innovativeness, efficiency and productivity. As the manager sees behavioral changes occurring in others, he/she will be reinforced for using the principles, and this will shape their own behavior so that, consciously or not, they will use them more and more.

Another point to remember is that it is always helpful to have a "partner" who is familiar with management psychology and who is frequently nearby. This person can evaluate the manager's impact on others and provide invaluable feedback, for which he/she should be amply reinforced.

Finally, it is best to begin by practicing just two principles. This more narrow focus avoids confusion, since any real life situation always involves two, three, or four of the principles, as we can see from the following example:

> Subordinate: I would like to delay committing myself to a decision just now.

> Manager: You always want to delay committing yourself to a decision and, frankly, I'm fed up with it!

The manager, by his angry statement, has paired both his subordinate and himself with aversive stimuli (Principle I), has paired the verbal equivalent of a response (delayed decision) with aversive stimuli (Principle IV), and has punished the subordinate's response (Principle VII). One statement thus reflects three principles. (Indeed, Principle VIII is also involved, since the manager now has an aversive stimulus "going" and the subordinate must try to stop it. Whatever behavior does successfully stop it will increase dramatically in strength, even if he stops it by saying nothing.)

The principles that one chooses to use and practice should be contingent upon one's own behavior patterns. Most managers begin with Principles V and VI. These principles can be very difficult to implement, however, if the manager is a highly critical person. She/he is then attempting to change not only others, but also their own behavior, a difficult proposition at best.

Pairings Versus Operant

Although many managers choose the operant principles, there are advantages to beginning with the classical ones. *Operant principles require an immediate reaction to a behavior.* Managers must, consequently, be quick on their feet and able to think and respond rapidly when using them. Classical principles, on the other hand, can be pre-planned and deliberately thought out.

It is true that operant techniques can give the manager quick feedback, since behavioral changes may be seen immediately after the manager's response (which is probably why most managers focus on them). *But classical principles allow much more certainty, because their use is not contingent upon the behavior of someone else.*

Both sets of principles require an intimate knowledge of the individual to whom they are being applied. They require not only an analysis of typical response patterns, but also – and more important – a knowledge of what is really reinforcing and aversive to the individual.

Some managers attempt to list "typical" or "common" reinforcers and aversive stimuli applicable to many people. This leads to mistakes, because typical reinforcers and aversive stimuli do not exist. Some people love attention; others hate it. Some people love being touched or talking about feelings; others hate doing so. Some people love compliments; others hate them. Some people enjoy responsibility; others are frightened by it; a promotion in the latter case can be an intense aversive stimulus.

We might summarize the principles as follows: Classical principles merely require the speaker to pair a stimulus or the verbal equivalent of a response with stimuli reinforcing or aversive to the listener. Operant principles require the speaker to respond to another person's behavior as it occurs. This is because changes in the person's behavior during operant learning occur only as a result of what happens immediately after the behavior, consequences that usually involve the behavior of other people.

[Readers, to use any of the principles effectively, must be able to use both reinforcers and aversive stimuli. This means, to be reinforcing, they must be able to be emotionally expressive.

To check this out, readers are requested here to ask several people in their inner circle, at the risk of embarrassing everyone, what those people feel "their greatest asset is". The reader is asked to agree with their response and emotionally express their admiration for that asset, using several "you-reinforcer" pairings to drive the point home and increase the person's self-confidence.]

Focusing on A Goal

It might be helpful now to apply all eight principles to one simple "target" behavior. Since firing incompetent subordinates seems to be the most emotionally difficult action a manager has to periodically take, let us look at the case of a manager whose goal is to increase the probability that her subordinate, John, will perform this necessary, but uncomfortable, task.

The manager must first determine what reinforcers and aversive stimuli are precluding John from firing incompetent people. Her observations indicate that John has a "strong need to be liked" and, more importantly, a "strong fear of being disliked" by his subordinates. (Most behaviors are controlled by more than one reinforcer and one aversive stimulus, but our example should be a simple one.)

Classical principles

Principle I. Since "being liked by people" is too strong a reinforcer to John, the manager might do well to pair it with an aversive stimulus.

> Manager: John, you seem to go out of your way to be liked by people below you. You know, when subordinates like you, many times they don't respect you. They may even be saying they like you to your face and laughing at you behind your back. So, a need to be liked by subordinates can be a self-destructive thing and give people a lot of damaging control over you.

210

The manager has three times paired "being liked by subordinates" with aversive stimuli. She has increased a bit the likelihood of John firing incompetent subordinates if the occasion arises.

Principle II. Since "being disliked by subordinates" is too strong an aversive stimulus to John, the manager must pair it with stimuli reinforcing to John. (The conversations throughout this example would, of course, take place days apart.)

> Manager: John, you seem to be going to some lengths to prevent subordinates from disliking you. I think you might be making a mistake. When people express a dislike of you, it sometimes means they trust you enough to be open and honest with you. So, if someone seems to dislike you, I hope you'll sometimes see it as a sign that they have confidence in you. And you know, when people indicate they dislike you, they often are indicating that you're important to them, that you've had an impact on them.

The manager has paired "being disliked" with reinforcers. She has decreased, a bit, the intensity of John getting upset if someone indicates a dislike of him. Thus, she has decreased the likelihood that John will avoid firing incompetent people.

Principle III. Here the manager must pair the verbal equivalent of the response pattern (firing incompetent people) with reinforcers.

> Manager: You know, John, I think the manager who fires incompetent people is a rare commodity these days. The manager who does fire incompetent people is usually liked and respected by the good people who are frustrated by a manager putting up with incompetence. Firing incompetent people quickly is the real mark of a truly professional manager; it's a trait often much admired by senior management.

The manager has again increased the probability that John will fire incompetent people.

<u>Principle IV</u>. Here the manager must pair the verbal equivalent of the undesirable behavior (not firing incompetent people) with aversive stimuli.

> <u>Manager</u>: I was talking to Jim the other day, John, about how the inability to fire incompetent people probably leads to more business failures than all other factors combined. As a matter of fact, not firing incompetent people around them can make competent people quite angry toward their manager.

These, then, are some possible classical responses the manager could make to increase desirable behavior in her subordinate. They did not require any response from the subordinate. They could be planned deliberately in a calm, analytical manner. (Is it manipulation when managers "think" about the right thing to say and do? Again, can these principles be used destructively? Yes. Whose problem is that? The manager of the person doing so.)

Operant Principles

Now let us consider operant principles, which require a response on the part of the subordinate. Here we will use a dialogue between manager and subordinate that reflects the four operant principles.

> <u>Manager</u>: John, I feel you aren't firing incompetent subordinates who you should be firing. How do you feel about that? (Aversive stimulus is started)
> <u>Subordinate</u>: Well, there may be some weak people below me, but firing them could upset the others. We'd be in real trouble if everyone walked off the job. (Attempts to stop the aversive stimuli by pairing "firing people" with aversive stimuli)
> <u>Manager</u>: Oh, come on, John. Nobody is going to walk off the job and you know it. That's just an excuse for not doing your job. (Punishment; aversive stimuli still "on")
> <u>Subordinate</u>: But I don't have any replacements for the people I'd fire. (Still attempts to stop the aversive stimuli without committing to engaging in the behavior that frightens him)

Manager: We'd be a helluva lot better off with no one in those positions than some of the people you've got there. My God, we've been living with some of them for years! (Punishment; the manager did not stop the aversive stimuli when John tried the excuse of no replacements.)

Subordinate: Well, I suppose I could call the Personnel Department and ask them to help get me some replacements.

Manager: I think that would be an excellent idea. (Shaping; stops the aversive stimulus by using a reinforcer to strengthen a constructive plan of action. What is a reinforcer? Anything that stops the aversives that cause fear, even temporarily.)

Subordinate: Do you really think I'd be better off without the people though? We're under a tight schedule.

Manager: Not tight enough to carry incompetent people on the payroll. (Mild punishment)

Subordinate: I suppose not. I suppose I should let Jack go. He's certainly been goofing off more than anyone, but …

Manager: John, if you let Jack go, I think everyone around here would have a good deal of respect for you. I know I would. (Interrupts to reinforce)

Subordinate: O.k., I'll do it, but …

Manager: Excellent! (Reinforcement)

Subordinate: But it's going to be difficult.

Manager: Say, how are those two new machines? (Extinction)

The manager has successfully shaped the desired behavior in his subordinate. Clearly, operant learning requires quick thinking and a quick response to ongoing behavior. However, the immediate result – the changed behavior – is there for the manager to see and provides her own necessary reinforcement.

[Readers are asked to think of a behavior they want in a person. What are the reinforcers and especially the aversives (fears) preventing that behavior? Can you think of, and use, some constructive pairings? For example, can you say to someone, "If you don't like and respect yourself, no one else will or should. But if you do like and respect yourself, people will really look up to you, especially the people you care about."]

Gossip as a Distraction

Conversations between a manager and subordinate, like the above example, are usually unpleasant, because they involve stimuli aversive to both people. For this reason, managers often allow themselves to get sidetracked by a subordinate onto irrelevant issues. These side issues often involve a discussion of third parties, because most people enjoy talking about others in their absence. In the forgoing dialogue, for example, the subordinate might easily have swung the conversation off himself as follows:

> Subordinate: Who do you feel I should fire?
> Manager: That's up to you, John.
> Subordinate: Well, Jack's been having trouble lately.
> Manager: In what way?
> Subordinate: I think he's got problems with his wife.
> Manager: What kind of problems?

Soon both people are talking about what to them is a reinforcing topic, Jack's problems with his wife. They not only waste time doing so, but also avoid getting back to the real issue. The reason is that the real issue is aversive to both.

No one can change the behavior of anyone who is not present at the time, since only stimuli that have an impact on an individual's sensory organs can influence his/her behavior. Conversations between managers and subordinates about absent third parties should be held only if the manager is planning or attempting to change the behavior of his listener in relation to the absent third party. Rarely is there any other justification for talking about anyone not present. For too many managers, gossip is a reinforcing and useful device to avoid aversive stimuli.

[Readers are asked to think of some "gossip" about someone not present and mention it when they're in a particularly boring meeting. Did you get everyone's attention? Did anyone reinforce you by asking for more elaboration? Did anyone extinguish you and try to get the group back to substantive issues?]

Is it important to know the reasons for someone's behavior?

Can I change anyone's opinions by punishing them?

Are negative attitudes in the workplace always bad?

How can I increase my self-confidence?

CHAPTER 21

INEFFECTIVE INFLUENCES ON BEHAVIOR, EFFECTIVE GOALS

Let us now explore some of the reasons why much of what we say seems to have little impact on people. Both operant principles and pairings influence a person's subsequent behavior. Problems sometimes occur when trying to change someone's behavior if pairings caused the behavior and operant techniques are used to try to change the behavior, or vice versa.

If aversive pairings, for example, caused some fearful behavior, using reinforcement (operant) principles will only change the way the fear is expressed, but do nothing to diminish the fear itself. A sudden loud noise, for example, will usually frighten a child; lightning is often paired with sudden loud noises (pairing); hence an approaching storm may well lead the child to start crying. The child's reaction can be effectively eliminated by punishing the crying behavior (operant technique). The child, however, will still fear storms.

The "causative factors" can be diminished somewhat by pairing the storm with reinforcers, saying enthusiastically for example, "Look at how beautiful that lightning makes the sky. Gee, I like storms; they're so interesting. And storms make the trees grow and the air so clean."

Conversely, operant experiences are not truly remedied by pairings. If a subordinate finds his manager's approval reinforcing, and the manager makes his approval dependent on the subordinate saying derogatory things about another person (operant technique), the subordinate will increasingly say derogatory things about the person. Even if other people classically pair the third party with reinforcers to the subordinate, it will not stop the subordinate from saying derogatory things about the person in his manager's presence as long as the manager continues to reinforce the response.

Socially pervasive operant procedures can result in widespread response patterns. Failure to stand and "pledge allegiance" to the flag in school may lead to aversive stimuli (punishment). The Protestant ethic leads to the reinforcement of work behavior and, more importantly, the punishment of non-work behavior. Consequently, many people experience uneasiness and/or "guilt feelings" when they are on vacation (or even on weekends) and not engaged in productive activities. This behavior cannot be changed by classical pairings. As a result, many lives are spent striving for goals which, when attained, are soon found to be wanting. The successful attainment of the goal may well eliminate its reinforcing value, but rarely the striving.

Most failures in this area, however, occur when operant procedures are used on responses originally caused by pairings. More specifically, to protect themselves, managers may quickly punish or at least extinguish subordinates who express negative attitudes toward senior management. But if those attitudes are held because senior management has paired itself with aversives, then a direct expression of the employee's negative attitudes may be suppressed, but the negative attitudes still exist. Indeed, they will probably be expressed in more subtle ways, sometimes even in acts of sabotage. This is readily apparent when senior management awards itself large pay increases or bonuses when employees are being asked to make sacrifices.

Many subordinates find the attention of their manager quite reinforcing. Consequently, they may prolong meetings with their manager. Punishing the subordinate for prolonging or disrupting a meeting does little good if the manager's attention remains an overly strong reinforcer to the subordinate. The latter will merely get it in other ways. The effective manager will make the attention contingent upon constructive, results-oriented behavior or classically pair attention with aversive stimuli.

Too often we "let sleeping dogs lie". Bill likes attention too much. It's difficult, however, not to give it to him when he's standing in your office peppering you with questions (no matter how superficial); indeed, that's precisely why he is always in your office. What should we do? Give him attention, thus reinforcing him, when he's working quietly and not seeking it. But if we walk by his office and he doesn't grab us, we're relieved and quietly slink back to our office. We let sleeping dogs lie -- not an effective orientation.

[Readers are asked here to think of someone who frequently annoys them. Is the fact that you're annoyed reinforcing to them? Are you expressing that reinforcer when the person is engaged in behavior you like or when that person engages in the behavior that annoys you? Try making the expression of the reinforcer contingent upon behavior you want in the person, even if that behavior is silence.

If, for example, someone always annoys you by bogging down in details, just smile pleasantly when they do so. But ask them a question when you know they're in a hurry and express annoyance when they only have time to give a quick, superficial response. You will be reinforcing them for cutting you off, a most short desirable behavior on the part of someone who usually prolongs meetings.]

A frustrating inability to influence someone, consequently, often reflects the inappropriate application of our principles, more specifically, the application of pairings to operant-induced behavior or vice versa.

Classical Extinction

A second common reason we have little impact on people involves our inhibitions over using either reinforcers and/or aversive stimuli. Far too often we merely specify desirable or undesirable behavior but fail to pair them with reinforcers or aversive stimuli. Several illustrations follow:

> Ineffective: I think you should buy our product.
> Effective: I think you should buy our product because it will save you a good deal of money.
>
> Ineffective: You should not smoke in this area.
> Effective: If you smoke in this area, you're likely to ignite gas vapors, which could lead to a pretty bad fire.
>
> Ineffective: You should focus more on productivity with your people.
> Effective: If you focus more on productivity with your people, we'll get these jobs done sooner and get the plan superintendent off our back.

[Readers are asked to think of an important behavior they would like their boss to engage in. That's the easy part. Now think of what is reinforcing to the boss and use it in a pairing.

> "I've noticed that when you compliment people, your opinions become very important to them."

Now think of a behavior you want decreased in frequency by your manager. Think of what's aversive to your manager and pair the two, e.g., "I was just reading an article that claims that when people are critical of others, it's because they're afraid of them."

Can you use reinforcers and aversives with equal ease?]

Knowledge of the Principles

Some managers fear that if everyone knows these principles, their implementation may be compromised. This is simply not true. If compliments are reinforcing to an individual, sincerely telling him that he did an outstanding job will have a reinforcing impact on him, whereas insincerely telling him he did an outstanding job will have an aversive impact on him; in both cases the statement will have an impact, whether or not the individual knows these principles.

Indeed, reinforcement theory will be used most effectively in interactions with people we see often, all of whom may be aware of the principles and all of whom give each other frequent feedback about the effect of their behavior on others. This feedback should be constructive; it should not reflect the emotional approach of many so-called sensitivity groups that give love and concern to depressed, self-deprecating souls and short shrift to confident, effective individuals. Quietly telling a manager he has just paired his own subordinates with aversive stimuli can have a beneficial influence on all concerned. Thanking someone for her expressed reinforcement of one's own achievement or pointing out a manager's subtle punishment of new ideas can be effective and quite constructive.

Behavioral impact is contingent upon the effective utilization of reinforcement principles in face-to-face interactions. It is not contingent upon a person's level of authority. Just as managers grossly underestimate their influence on subordinates, so too do subordinates grossly underestimate their influence on their superiors. Many subordinates complain about the lack of feedback from their managers, but few will pair the manager giving feedback to them with reinforcers. Fewer still will reinforce the manager when she/he attempts to give feedback. Indeed, few people realize how many people leave their managerial positions because of the emotional difficulties (fears) involved in managing people, difficulties that emanate from the behavior of subordinates and that become too aversive for the manager to withstand.

A Two Month Trek to the Most Noble Goal

As previously mentioned, if you are on an airplane with a small child and the oxygen masks drop from the overhead bins, whose should you put on first, the child's or your own? Your own. So it is with self-confidence. If you're confident, if you like and respect yourself, you'll almost always say the right thing at the right time to others; in effect, you will increase their self-confidence. If you are driven by fear, however, your ability to increase the confidence of others will be minimal. How do we increase our confidence, recognizing that the people with whom we interact have a strong influence on us?

1.   First, we accept the fact that people do influence our confidence. Thus, we focus outside ourselves, on others and how they are influencing us. We care much less about how others see us because we're more concerned with how we see others.

2.   Because emotional reactions are such a strong reinforcer to most people, we must learn to be emotionally expressive. Why? Because that's how we'll reinforce people. If we can't be emotionally expressive, we can't really reinforce people. If we can't reinforce people, we are extinguishing them or punishing them. There's no alternative. Thus, they won't like us. They'll ignore or even avoid us. Why? Because we don't reinforce them. (And it's difficult to learn to like yourself when the people around you ignore or avoid you.)

So we'll learn to emotionally express our sincere recognition and appreciation for the strengths and assets of those in our inner circle. And we'll do so with neither inhibition, reservation, nor expectation. And we'll do so when we're alone with the person so we don't offend others (despite noble protests to the contrary). And we'll move quickly to another topic after we have reinforced someone so they don't feel manipulated and obligated to reinforce us in return.

3.   Because we're now capable of spontaneously and sincerely reinforcing others, we would do well to consider just what behavior we want to strengthen in them. We know that any response that successfully stops an aversive stimulus will increase in frequency more than any other. And how does a person know an aversive has stopped? Most dramatically, when it's suddenly replaced by a reinforcer?

Now we also know that people influence our thinking and feelings, so let's focus on reinforcing anything that people in our inner circle do that increases our confidence, our coveted liking and respect for ourselves (after we're confident, we'll be in a much better position to truly help others).

What behavior by others most impacts our confidence? Their "you-reinforcer" pairings. So we'll develop an exquisite sensitivity to people using "you" when they're referring to us. And we'll especially note when they pair "you" with a reinforcer or an aversive stimulus. If it's an aversive, we'll remain quiet in order to extinguish this poor judgment on their part.

If it's a reinforcer ("You're really good at that"), however, we'll respond emotionally with appreciation and sincerely felt gratitude for their positive views of us. We won't say, "Aw shucks;" we won't kick the floor in a sign of embarrassed humility; we won't even protest that we could have done much better had we more time. For these reactions are extinguishing and weaken their positive view of us and, worse, weaken their desire to tell us their positive feelings about us. In short, our negative reactions decrease the likelihood we'll ever learn to like and respect ourselves.

We'll also be aware of the fact that if we do extinguish their positive views of us, then there will be no difference in our reactions to their positive or negative views of us. Thus, our ability to extinguish their negative views will be weakened considerably since our bland, monotone extinguishing reactions to their negative views are not contrasted with our animated, expressive, reinforcing responses when they are positive.

> They: That's really a beautiful shirt you're wearing.
> Bad Response: This? Oh, I've had this old thing for years.
> Good Response: Thank you! Thank you for noticing!

***

> They: You did a beautiful job on that report.
> Bad Response: Well, I could have done a better job if I'd had access to those merger figures earlier.
> Good Response: You know, your opinion is very important to me so your saying that really makes me feel good! Thank you!

Following these principles for two months will probably lead us to see a marked difference in who we have become, especially if we contrast it with who we were two months previously.

4.   A reinforcer is most effective if it occurs within one-half-of-one-second of the other person's response. (Courageous readers might try waiting five seconds until they respond to someone saying, "I love you," to them. This should only be tried with those whose love is unimportant to you.) But sometimes people's "you-pairings" are complex and, by the time we've figured out how to respond appropriately, we've already extinguished them. So we need an orientation that is always effective, whether the person is pairing "you" with reinforcers or aversives to us. And we have one. Here are some examples:

> Good They: You really made a beautiful presentation.
> Good Us: Hey, thank you! You've just made my day!

***

Bad They: You really made a crummy presentation.
Bad Us (Upset): Why? What did I do wrong? I get so nervous making presentations. (Reinforcing their hostility)
Good Us (Cheerful): Well, I sure have a lot of fun making them! I love the attention...including yours! (Punishes their hostility)

When in doubt, Be of Good Cheer! Why? Because when you're of good cheer, you'll be reinforcing people who are using "you-reinforcer" pairings. After all, why would anyone pair you with a reinforcer unless they found your happiness reinforcing? More important, being of good cheer is punishing to those who don't like us and who then use "you-aversive" pairings. As we've seen, the reinforcer to those who use "you-aversive" pairings is seeing us hurt and/or upset. This helps explain why hostile people usually stalk the weak, frightened person. Our good cheer is, on the other hand, aversive (hence punishing) to such people. Thus, frequently being of good cheer increases the likelihood that we will surround ourselves with people who like our confidence; more importantly, we will increase the likelihood that those who dislike happy, confident people will avoid us and refuse to be part of our inner circle.

5.   Again, it is important that we hold positive attitudes toward others since they have such a strong influence on our feelings and attitudes and we must interact with people so frequently.
But "people", since they so often constitute the source of our fears, are aversive to many people. Since we pair what we dislike with aversives, "people" are often paired with aversives in our interactions with others.

- People are really selfish.
- People are about as trustworthy as a three-dollar bill.
- Most people don't even know what's going on in the world.

> ▪ Underestimating the intelligence of people never lost anyone an election.

These "people-aversive" pairings are too often reinforced by others because so many of us feel comfortable around those who share our dislike (fear) of people. Indeed, we often feel that those who make these "people-aversive" pairings are likely to remain loyal to us and to not threaten us with their "love" of others. And anything or anyone that alleviates our fear is a reinforcer to us.

While we should extinguish and even punish people-aversive pairings by others, our hope of changing this attitude is probably futile. Why? Because people who are negative about others are so often reinforced by others. Our best bet, if we really want to learn to like and respect ourselves over this two-month period, is to minimize our interactions with such persons, even avoiding them when possible. Above all, we must change the topic when discussions of "people" come up with them. Our ability to be confident interacting with, and reinforcing toward, people will be minimized after being subjected to those who pair people with aversives.

6. Let us now recall some exercises that readers may have already carried out. Because our confidence is so dependent on the behavior of others, we would do well, during our two-month learning period, to identify those with whom we'll interact most frequently and those we'll avoid. In this exercise, we'll be intent on evaluating a person's impact on us; we will not be concerned with influencing, let alone changing them.

What we'll do is engage in the behavior we want to strengthen in ourselves, behavior that will broaden our response repertoire. It may be positive attitudes (especially toward ourselves) or decisiveness or a love of people or our coveted liking and respect for ourselves ("I'm really happy with the job I did on ..."). Whatever it is, we'll force ourselves to engage in that behavior and note whether those with whom we're interacting reinforce, extinguish, or punish us. And for our two-month "personal growth" period, we'll go out of our way to interact with those who reinforce us when we engage in our desired behavior (even buying them lunch), and minimize our interactions with those who extinguish or punish us for engaging in our desired behavior.

If it is difficult for us to make decisions on just who we want to be with, we may have serious problems. Why? Because it could indicate that we like people who are bad for us. That means we'll never grow. We'll always feel comfortable with the same kind of people, the people who made us who we are and who keep us as we are, never to change. Worse, we'll fear and avoid people who could help us change. This is why constantly meeting new people is so important Again, we tend to pick as friends those who share our fears, hence the likelihood of their confronting and alleviating our fears is minimal. But if we seek out those whom we dislike, those whom we fear, then we're more likely to develop a wider response repertoire, to experience personal growth, a most rewarding pastime.

Jim is a very sensitive person. His friends are also quite sensitive. Indeed, they're his friends because they're sensitive and won't criticize him and are sure he won't criticize them.

Mike is a blunt, outspoken person. Jim avoids Mike. Under pressure from his manager, Jim asks everyone around him, including Mike, what his "greatest shortcoming is". His friends tell him he's "just fine". Mike tells him, "You're too sensitive to criticism. I feel like I'm walking on eggshells around you."
Who has the best impact on Jim? Who will encourage personal growth, a wider response repertoire on his part? Who is most likely to alleviate Jim's fears?

Sam is a sarcastic, critical person. His friends are sarcastic, critical people. Mary is an enthusiastic, positive person. She would broaden Sam's response repertoire by extinguishing his sarcasm (unlike his friends) and reinforcing (encouraging) a more positive (balanced) view of life on his part. But because Mary is so enthusiastic and extinguishes his sarcastic criticism, Sam doesn't like her and avoids interacting with her. Can he change, grow, learn to adapt more flexibly to life if he continues to seek out only those who like his critical, sarcastic orientation? Love thine enemy and to thine own self be true.

Do It For Them

Think of those whom you love. What is the best thing you could do for them? Protest your need for them? Protest your undying and faithful devotion to them? No and No. Why? Because you'll still subject them to your fears. Worse, you won't be a force in their life who increases their love and respect for themselves. You'll be too frightened of them finding you less significant, less important if you did.

The best thing you, and any manager of people, can do, is learn to like and respect yourself. Why? Because then you'll admire, seek out, and encourage those around you who like and respect themselves. And when you do, they'll encourage (reinforce) the same in you. And wouldn't that be a glorious world in which to live!?

SECTION 6

INTERVIEWING

What factors should be considered in a selection/promotion decision?

Should promotions be based on performance?

Is reviewing a job description adequate preparation for an interview?

CHAPTER 22

INTERVIEWING

Speech is the index of the mind. (Seneca)

There are three general reasons for including a chapter on interviewing in a book on management.

- *First, good interviewing techniques are good management techniques.* A large part of a manager's job is to ascertain the ideas and attitudes of her subordinates on a day-to-day basis. This not only provides the manager with useful information in the form of helpful suggestions for getting the job done, it also allows her to better understand her subordinates' behavior and its causes.

Through good interviewing techniques, the manager can monitor not only the work activities of subordinates but also their attitudes about various facets of their projects and responsibilities–both of which will have a strong impact on how well those responsibilities are, and will be, carried out. That is, interviewing helps a manager spot trouble areas before they reach unmanageable proportions. It allows perceptive managers to pick up subtle clues that tell them that results are going to be disappointing and action is required. The alternative is waiting for the results themselves to tell the manager there are problems, an approach that often dictates precipitous action after the proverbial horse is out of the barn.

Thus, interviewing often allows a manager to predict job performance before that performance (and possible failure) has occurred (negative attitudes expressed by a salesperson toward a customer probably indicate poor sales calls will be made on that customer, a problem that should be addressed before the potentially damaging sales call is made.

- *Second, effective interviewing is also a strong motivating force;* it tells subordinates someone else in the world is concerned about what they are thinking, feeling, and doing. Having one's attitudes and opinions focused on in a non-judgmental way (see next chapter) is one of the more rewarding experiences of life. The techniques of good interviewing, consequently, should be used by the manager *daily* in his/her interactions with subordinates.

- *Third, selection-promotion decisions are probably the most important decisions a manager will ever make.* At the highest level, the board of directors, selection of the chief executive officer may determine the fate of the organization for years to come. At any level, however, a manager's selection and promotion decisions will impact everyone in the organization, constructively or destructively.

Performance a Poor Criterion for Promotion

Some might say that interviewing is not necessary in a promotional decision, since the employee's performance is already a matter of record. There are three reasons, however, why promotions should not be based on a person's performance in her present position.

First, performance is difficult to interpret objectively; there are no objective objectives in this world; everything is "subject" to subjective interpretation. Second, successful or unsuccessful performance is always the result of numerous variables, many of which the individual cannot control (e.g., the salesperson's best customer moves their operations offshore). Third, promotion means moving a person into a new environment where, as we have seen, he/she will confront new reinforcement contingencies, new personalities, new duties, and responsibilities; in short, an entirely different set of interactions.

Consider, for example, the following case: A large Eastern company took over a small family-owned Midwestern company. The large organization tried to show its faith in the small company (and minimize negative reactions) by promoting the vice president of purchasing for the small company to the corporate vice presidency of purchasing for the entire corporation. Despite the fact that the two functions were essentially similar in that they both dealt with the same product lines, the man became an alcoholic within six months. This was because he had moved from a friendly, "calling-the-president-by-his-first-name", family-type atmosphere into a cold, aggressive, hypercritical atmosphere in which "survival of the fittest" was the dominant theme. He could not adapt.

The criterion for promotion decisions should be our best estimate or prediction as to how a person will respond in the new situation. We will base our inferences, of course, on the only data we have available, those concerning the *present behavior* of the individual, rather than solely on his/her present performance. And one of the most effective situations in which to elicit and analyze behavior objectively is the interview.

[Readers are asked to think of "failures" in those promotion decisions with which they have some familiarity. What factors were the bases of the decision? Why did the person fail? (90% of firings are due to personality factors) Could the failure have been predicted? Did the failure occur because of an underlying, but overlooked, fear in the person or the manager?]

Preparation for the Interview

A good interview requires preparation in two areas. First, we must know the job responsibilities the interviewee will assume in the new position and the personalities of the people with whom she/he will interact, especially that of their immediate superior. Lacking this information, we are merely sending a person into a vacuum.

The fact that one superior is a precise, thorough, detail-oriented person, whereas another is an impulsive, fast-paced, aggressive person is critical when we attempt to estimate the success of any given individual under these managers. Even if the job duties are quite similar under the two managers, the same person could find himself a stunning success under the one and a miserable failure under the other. Like it or not, success in a given position is determined, to a large extent, by what the manager of that position says it is.

The subject of job descriptions needs further explanation. A job description is normally a series of physical facts that are of little help in predicting performance. To be useful, these physical facts must be translated into behavioral terms. The position of plant controller, for example, may list as one of its responsibilities the coordination of materials inventory. This tells us little. If, however, we know that the inventory consists of small parts that are rapidly moving in and out of the plant, we can infer some of the behavioral characteristics necessary for the position. In this instance, for example, responsibility for the inventory may require that the applicant be detail-oriented, capable of handling a number of variables at one time, well organized, and able to make quick decisions.

These are behavioral characteristics we can determine from an interview of the person. They will tell us more than we can learn by simply asking a person if he is capable of handling inventory and/or relying on supposed past experience in that area. If job descriptions are translated into behavioral terms, the behavioral description of a given applicant can then be compared with the required behavior traits of the position.

It might be helpful to list some basic behavioral terms that could be relevant for some positions (see addendum for a much more thorough list). The reader should not approach these as a cookbook, but as a stimulant; the evaluator should always attempt to describe the uniqueness of a position (and every position is unique).

APPROACH TO PROBLEMS

Detail orientation
Thoroughness
Follow through
  (finishes tasks)
Organization
Creative

Quickness
Efficiency
Judgment
Risk orientation
Factual

APPROACH TO RESPONSIBILITIES

Emotional stability and
  expressiveness
Attitudes (toward
  authority)
Decisiveness
Independence

Initiative
Conscientiousness
Aggressiveness
Cooperativeness
Pace
Determination

APPROACH TO PEOPLE

Persuasiveness
Tactfulness
Forcefulness
Openness
Sincerity
Friendliness

Reaction to
criticism & feedback
Humor
Listening skills
Responsiveness

Approach to Managerial Responsibilities

Managerial responsibilities will not be elaborated upon here, since this is the primary thrust of the entire book. Suffice it to say, it is important to evaluate the following: What is the candidate's behavioral impact on subordinates; what does she/he find reinforcing and aversive in the behavior of others? Is the candidate realistically critical evaluating subordinates? Will the candidate select/promote competent people, fire incompetent people, develop people by giving them frequent feedback? Most important, does the candidate like and encourage confidence in subordinates?

[Readers are strongly encouraged to list what they feel are the five most important behaviors needed in their present position. Then ask your manager to do the same for your position without revealing your list. Compare the lists. Interesting?

Agree on seven or eight behaviors as being important. Ask your manager to rate you on those behaviors. (The areas in which you are rated low may well reflect your shortcomings and/or your manager's fears. In either case, you would do well to pay attention since doing so may prevent surprises in your manager's evaluations of you and in your career with that manager and that organization. Your low rated areas might also tell you what your manager may be saying about you [what aversives he is pairing you with] to others in the organization.)

If, for example, your manager feels you're too sensitive to criticism, he may be saying that he fears confrontation, that you're too argumentative when criticized, or both. In either case, you will want to express enthusiastic appreciation for his feedback, even if you disagree with it. Indeed, you might do well to ask for his advice periodically, reinforcing his good judgment when he is gracious enough to give you some words of wisdom.]

Criteria Mistakes

We might note that three of the most overrated criteria on which selection-promotion decisions are based *at the managerial level* are intelligence, experience, and technical knowledge.

We are not asking people in business to analyze the works of Kant or Plato. The basic problems of an organization do not require an Einstein (indeed, Einstein might well have been a poor manager); their solutions are usually found in the reinforcement and aversive contingencies and the behavioral interactions discussed earlier. The problems of many managers are more emotional than intellectual.

Experience in handling a function tells us little about a person's ability to handle it well and nothing about many of the crucial aspects of his job. (Whom does he select? Can he fire incompetent subordinates? Does he communicate with, and reinforce subordinates for, a job well done? Are practical results more reinforcing to him than merely getting along with others? Does he develop subordinates by giving them frequent, constructive feedback?)

Technical knowledge becomes more important as one *descends* the managerial ladder. The steel mill foreman had better know what is happening at a technical level. The steel company president, however, needs little technical knowledge; most of his contributions will be reflected in his selection/promotion decisions and in his impact on the behavior of other people in the organization.

Why Interviewing?

It is unfortunate, but not surprising, that an effective two- or three-hour interview generally tells a manager more about an individual than does managing her for two or three years. This is not only because of the manager's fears and prejudices, but also because the vast majority of even competent managers focus only on the results of behavior, rather than on the behavior itself and what causes it.

If three subordinates submit the same report with the same error, most managers focus on the report and the error. Effective managers go one step further. They analyze their subordinates' frequent, repetitive behavior patterns and may conclude, for example, that the same error is the result of a repetitious negative attitude problem in subordinate A, a repetitious lack of focus on details in subordinate B, and a repetitious indecisiveness in subordinate C. By dealing directly with these behavioral characteristics, the manager gets at causes and eliminates the need to put out the fires constantly caused by these characteristics.

[Readers are asked to think of two people who repetitiously make the same kind of mistake. Are the reasons different for each? Do they each engage in this behavior in order to elicit and/or prevent certain behaviors from others?

Do you know, for example, two people who are excessively critical? Might one person be so in order to avoid intimacy with others, using his pattern of being overly critical to prevent anyone from getting too close? Might the other person be overly critical in order to be one of the "guys", i.e., to prevent rejection from the other critical people in their inner circle?]

When can I believe what a person is telling me in the interview?

What is the difference between content and behavioral interpretations?

Why is a short interview unreliable?

Isn't it easy for people to change their behavior just for an interview?

CHAPTER 23

INTERPRETING BEHAVIOR

Because our goal is accurate interpretations and predictions of a person's behavior, let's look at some principles of evaluating behavior before we look at how we might best elicit behavior.

The purpose of the interview is to elicit a sample of the interviewee's typical behavior for interpretation. The first ten or fifteen minutes of the interview should be used to relax the interviewee. Interpretations in this initial phase should be much more tentative than those made in the later stages of the interview.

The goal of interpretation is to determine the interviewee's most *frequent, repetitive* response patterns in the work setting and the stimuli that are most reinforcing and aversive to him/her. (A person's frequent, repetitive behavior patterns reflect the best and most accurate description of that person. Fear, as we've seen, leads to excessive behaviors. What meets the criterion of frequent, and repetitive more accurately than excessive? Ergo, we don't know a person unless and until we know their fears. And when we know their fears, we'll know a lot about them.)

It is important to note that an individual's present behavior and their interpretation of past events are determined by what and who he/she is now. Thus, two interviewers should be able to probe two completely different time periods in an individual's life and arrive at the same

239

conclusions regarding the most probable response patterns of the person and the reinforcers and aversive stimuli influencing him/her.

If we have difficulty interpreting behavior, we naturally feel we need training and help in interpretation principles. This is rarely the case. Difficulties in interpretation originate more from poor interviewer questioning (see next chapter) than from lack of knowledge of interpretation principles. Consider the following all too typical factual interviewer questions:

> What was the name of the company you joined?
> Where was the company located?
> What was your position title?
> How long did you stay with the company?
> Did you hold any other position with that company?
> What were the titles of these positions?
> What was the date you left the company?

The most highly trained and skilled interviewer in the world would have difficulty making relevant interpretations based on a typical interviewee's responses to these formal, factual, patterned questions. Yet, too many interviewers focus on interpretation principles when it is really their poor interviewing skills that preclude them from gaining insight into the interviewee. What is the goal of most of our interpersonal interactions? Too often, it is to influence the other person's thinking and feelings, about us or any number of things (again, the only reason we say these things we call words is to influence others). Too rarely is our goal to evaluate the other person, to find out who they are and what they think and feel. This is unfortunate because we would do a much more effective and efficient job of influencing people if we spent more time assessing them, their thoughts and feelings. Most of us spend 90 per cent of our time with others trying to influence them and 10 per cent of our time evaluating them. These ratios should be reversed.

Many interpretation problems, consequently, stem from the emotional difficulties involved in interviewing, since trying to influence someone should never be part of an interview. It can, of course, be frustrating to listen to another person's point of view without being able to venture your own insightful, profound opinions, or tell her how wrong she is or how stupid his judgments are. This frustration and the resulting interviewing ineptness are apparent in both selection-promotion decisions and manager-subordinate interviews. Hence, effectively eliciting the behavior of another person is a rare and invaluable skill in any position in an organization (and in any interaction in any area of life).

Committing Oneself

Interpretations should always be put into written form for two reasons. First, written interpretations should be subsequently used to check the efficacy of each interviewer. This is accomplished by correlating the interviewer's interpretations with the interviewee's behavior on the job several months later. Most organizations discuss interpretations via an informal, word of mouth process. This approach is worse than ineffective because everyone straddles the fence. If the interviewee eventually succeeds in their new position, everyone recalls their positive interpretations; if the interviewee fails, everyone remembers their doubts about the person.

Second, permanent stimuli (a written report focusing on the interviewee as a person) should be made available to the interviewee's manager. These written interpretations should be a constant reminder to managers that they must focus on the person and her/his shortcomings rather than solely on the consequences of those shortcomings. Most good managers are focused on results. Excellent managers, however, focus on the cause of those results, especially the causes over which they have some influence; this is the behavior of their subordinates.

Keeping these points in mind, let us now consider three basic principles governing the interpretation of interviewees' behavior.

Be Hypercritical in Your Interpretations

Pleasing the interviewer is probably the most important goal (reinforcer) to most interviewees, especially in selection-promotion decisions. Most of his/her efforts will be aimed toward avoiding any negative opinions on the part of the interviewer. If the interviewer notices a negative trait during a two- or three-hour interview, consequently, imagine how blatant this shortcoming will be when the interviewee is spending 40 or 60 hours a week in the work setting, where he is more spontaneous and not always intent on pleasing anyone.

Good interviewers are highly critical people. They are, consequently, rare people, since it is aversive to most individuals to have to criticize someone whom they hardly know and who has never done them any harm. This is especially true of the typical human resource specialist who is often in this position precisely because she/he is such a "nice" person.

Being realistically critical is even more difficult, however, for managers who are trying to fill positions under them. Having an open position is frustrating to everyone, but especially to the manager who has to screen all those candidates. To alleviate this frustration, shortcomings shown by the interviewee are too often overlooked or minimized by the hiring manager. Thus, responsibility for realistically critical interpretations should fall on people who are not under this kind of pressure—a good human resource evaluation specialist.

[Readers are encouraged to ask the opinion of a good friend about someone in the public eye. Then ask yourself how in-depth, how logical and objective their views are and how articulate they are in presenting those views. Are you being realistically critical?]

Base Your Interpretations, Whenever Possible, on the Obvious

The obvious response patterns are those most likely to recur in the work setting. If the interviewee is obviously loud and boisterous, describe him as loud and boisterous! Do not look for deep, hidden meanings in a person's behavior. Because an individual crosses his arms does not necessarily mean he is rejecting ideas; he may be cold.

Interpretations should, moreover, be based on the most frequent, repetitious response patterns of an individual, not on his possibly true, but infrequent response patterns. In fact, *any valid interpretation should be confirmed by at least three repetitious instances of behavior during a normal interview.*

[Readers are encouraged to think of what they feel is the most obvious, frequent, repetitive behavior of their manager. Describe your manager to someone in those terms. Do they find you insightful?]

The Crux of Valid Interpretations

There are two ways we can respond to a person's behavior. First, we can focus on what we have always focused on: the content of what they are telling us; creatively, we'll call this is a "content" interpretation. Or we can focus on their behavior, on what that content, no matter what that content is, tells us about them as a person; we'll call this a "behavioral" interpretation. By far, most valid interpretations will be based on behavioral interpretation, not on content interpretations.

Suppose, for example, someone says to us: "I went to Greece last year; it was beautiful! The water was unbelievably clear. The people were warm and friendly. It was one of the best vacations I ever had."

Content interpretation: Maybe I should consider going to Greece on my next vacation.

Here we are not thinking of the person doing the talking, just the thing they are talking about: Greece. This is the way we have been taught to think and the way we should think most of the time.

Behavioral interpretation: This person is capable of being positive and enthusiastic.

243

How do we know? They just were. Here we're looking at what the person is saying only insofar as it is telling us something about them. We don't care about the topic, Greece, nor are we focused on it. The person could just as easily have been talking about widgets, dogs, or a house. (Remember, however, we will judge people in terms of their frequent, repetitive behavior; one response tells us little. If they speak this way several times in the interview, we'll describe them as positive and enthusiastic.)

Let's consider another example: "I went to Athens last year. It was awful! The air was filthy, the people were surly, and driving was impossible because they have no inkling how to drive a car."

Content interpretation: I should think twice about going to Athens on vacation.

The speaker has paired Athens with aversives and tried to influence our views about that particular city. And Athens (content) is what we're focused on and reacting to. If they had spoken of widgets as negatively, our views about widgets would have been impacted as negatively.

Behavioral interpretation: This person is negative and critical.

Here we're focusing on the behavior and what it tells us, not about Athens, but about the person. We don't even care about Athens. Again, frequent, repetitive behavior is the criterion; that's why we repeat this admonition frequently and repetitively.

The difference between content and behavioral interpretations is sometimes a subtle, but always a critical, point. It is the essence of correct interpretations. If we ask an interviewee to describe a previous boss, we have no way of knowing whether her description is accurate nor should we care. We do know, however, what the interviewee emphasizes in her description, and this is the material to use for interpretation.

Likewise, if an interviewee elaborates at length on his having worked full-time while completing his bachelor's degree at night, we must base our interpretation on his need to elaborate this point, his need to impress us with this information. That he worked full-time and completed his bachelor's degree at night is a fact we do not know is true; even if it were true, it could have been influenced by many variables the interviewee is not sharing with us, such as the fact that his full-time job was night watchman and he had little to do but study during work hours.

Few interviewees are going to tell us they were fired from their last job, nor should we expect them to. Indeed, that they were fired may be more a reflection of their previous manager than of them. To judge the situation would be impossible and irrelevant. That the interviewee, however, frequently and repetitiously pairs superiors with aversive stimuli during the interview is relevant and important.

People can easily change the content (and always do) of what they say to us. If a fellow dislikes Joe, he will probably pair Joe with different aversives at different times to different people. He may easily change the content but his negative orientation toward Joe may never change. It is very difficult, however, for a person to change their behavioral orientation. It would be difficult, for example, for someone with a strong need for precision not to be precise in the interview. ("I was with that company fourteen months; no, actually it was a little over fourteen months, about fourteen and a third months.") So too would it be difficult for a negative person to suddenly be repetitiously enthusiastic in an interview, for an indecisive person to become frequently decisive in an interview.

Suppose we ask an interviewee to describe the atmosphere of a company he worked for ten years ago. We do not know if his description is accurate, nor is this important. We do know what he focused on when describing the atmosphere of his former company. More important, his behavior may be well organized, and/or direct and succinct or highly tangential, and/or overly self-deprecating or self-aggrandizing. The point is the interviewee's behavior tells us a good deal about who he is and who he will be as an employee.

Some interviewees are quite adept at weaving good stories (especially salespeople). Focusing on the content of their stories, rather than their behavior, is the most common error made in interpretations.

[Readers are encouraged to ask someone significant in their life how they feel about you -- e.g., to a spouse, "How am I as a husband?"; or to a child, "How am I as a parent?"; or to a boss, "How am I as an employee?" Can you, as they respond, focus on their behavior and not on the content of what they're saying about you?

> You (to your spouse): How am I as a spouse?
> They: Well, frankly, sometimes you're pretty self-centered.
> Possible content interpretation and response by you: So are you! Hell, you're far more....
> Possible behavioral interpretation: My spouse is pairing me with an aversive. Am I reinforcing him/her sincerely, spontaneously, and frequently enough?]

Effective Interviewer Interpretations

The variety of human behavior is infinite. To attempt to categorize various response patterns by assigning them to specific personality types would be difficult, if not impossible and misleading. It will be more helpful to consider some examples of effective interviewer interpretations during an interview. The interpretations in the following examples are obviously tentative and would require confirmation in several more instances of similar behavior during the remainder of the interview.

> Interviewer: Well, could you tell me a little about your business background? You might start with the day after you finished school if you like.
> Interviewee: Did you want me to start with the day after high school or the day after I graduated from college? (He answered a question with a question.)

Possible interpretations: Ambiguous situations are aversive to the interviewee and make him uncomfortable; he actively seeks structure and clarification in such situations; thus, precision and accuracy are reinforcers to him. This could be a problem if the interviewee is assigned to work under a manager who expects independence and initiative and does not monitor and direct subordinates closely.

****

Interviewer: What was the atmosphere of the company like?
Interviewee: Well, people pulled together. There wasn't a lot of this backbiting you see in a lot of companies. When someone needed help, we all pitched in to get the job done. (Focuses on interpersonal relations; we still really know nothing about the company, nor does this matter.)

Possible interpretations: The interviewee finds competition with her peers aversive; she will not be motivated by internal company contests. She should not work under a manager who encourages competition among her subordinates. Support and cooperation from people around and over her are reinforcers that can have a strong motivating impact on her. She must feel she is an integral member of a team; being an outsider or isolated is aversive to her.

****

Interviewer: What happened then?
Interviewee: I was promoted to supervisor of accounts receivable.
Interviewer: How did it go?
Interviewee: Pretty well. I had a lot of older people under me and, as you know, they can be difficult to deal with.
Interviewer: In the sense of . . .?
Interviewee: Well, we tried to put in some new methods, but changing the habits of people who have been doing something for 20 years isn't easy, but I was patient and didn't press the issue and they really appreciated me after a while.

Possible interpretations: The interviewee is uncomfortable with authority over other people (aversive stimuli) and lacks a commanding, confronting presence. He is more likely to allow people to go their own way than to lead them. He would have difficulty managing aggressive people (aversive stimuli) and would, consequently, probably select weak people as his subordinates.

****

Interviewer: How many people were you over?
Interviewee: About 25.
Interviewer: How were they?
Interviewee: What do you mean?
Interviewer: Good or bad?
Interviewee: Good, I suppose! Everybody got along well with everybody else. Not a single person left the department in the year and a half that I managed them.

Possible interpretations: Maintaining positive interpersonal relations is a strong reinforcer to the interviewee; on the other hand, disruptive interpersonal relationships probably are overly aversive to her. She has difficulty taking adverse action when necessary and is probably too lenient and superficial evaluating subordinates (it's unlikely that 25 people are all good; but, again, we will reach this conclusion only if her assessments of her subordinates and people generally throughout the interview frequently and repetitiously reflect this overly positive orientation on her part).

****

Interviewer: What happened then?
Interviewee: I left the company.
Interviewer: Because?
Interviewee: Well, there were three things I disliked. First, the whole place was too fear-driven, kind of a "protect your rear" atmosphere. Second, the pay was quite low. Third, there was no place to go in the organization.

Possible interpretations: Decisive (she answered the question in a direct, succinct manner). Organized (she lists the liabilities of the company in a systematic, highly organized, one-two-three manner).

248

Interviewer: What position did you report to at that time?
Interviewee: Vice president of operations.
Interviewer: What kind of guy was he?
Interviewee: Good, one of the best managers I ever had.
Interviewer: How so?
Interviewee: Well, he let you do a job the way you saw fit. Then if he felt you were doing something the wrong way, he wasn't afraid to tell you about it. You knew where you stood with him. I probably learned more about myself from him than from any other boss I ever worked for.

Possible interpretations: The interviewee finds constructive criticism and an open atmosphere reinforcing. He is motivated to develop his own personal skills and needs a confident, decisive manager over him who will delegate responsibility.

****

Interviewer: What kind of manager was your boss?
Interviewee: All right, I guess. He was a bit sneaky, though.
Interviewer: How so?
Interviewee: Well, he'd take credit for things you had done. But, boy, if anything went wrong, your name was the first thing out of his mouth.
Interviewer: He was pretty quick to put the blame on people under him.
Interviewee: He sure was.
Interviewer: He was somewhat like that other boss you talked about in that respect.
Interviewee: That's right. I haven't had too much luck with my bosses. I think the power goes to their head too much.

Possible interpretations: The interviewee has an authority problem; anyone in a position of authority over him is an aversive stimulus he will attack by pairing with aversive stimuli (which he did in the interview).

Many interviewers mistake an authority problem for aggressiveness, a deadly mistake that can and often does lead to much harm to an organization.

****

Interviewer: What school did you attend?
Interviewee: The University of Chicago. How about yourself? Where did you get your degree?

Possible interpretations: Controlling. Dislikes being in a subservient role and actively attempts to dominate others (whoever asks questions in an interaction controls that interaction). (Incidentally, never answer an interviewee's question about yourself (see next chapter). Proper response: "Well, we can talk about me later if you'd like. How did you like the University of Chicago?" (Always return to a question and regain control or you will suddenly be in an adversarial interaction.)

****

Interviewer: How was the company?
Interviewee: Well, it had good and bad points.
Interviewer (later): What kind of guy was your boss?
Interviewee: Not the best I've had, but not the worst either.

Possible interpretation: Indecisive.

****

Interviewer: How was the company?
Interviewee: Lousy! The people were clueless!

Possible interpretations: Too intense emotionally. Overly direct, blunt, and abrasive.

****

Interviewee: I joined the company in May of 1992; no, June, I think it was June; no, May, the last week of May; May 28th, that's it.

Interpretations: A strong need for precision; bogs down in irrelevancies.

****

Interviewee: You know, a better question might have been, why did I leave the company.

Interpretation: Has few inhibitions over criticizing an authority figure (interviewers are usually in an authoritative position; after all, the person's future may rest on the recommendation of the interviewer; to be so openly critical usually reflects an argumentative orientation and/or an authority problem; either one is predictive of trouble ahead if the person frequently and repetitively offers his "helpful suggestions" to the questions of the interviewer – and later, if hired, the requests of his boss).

****

Interviewee: When I started on the job, I dropped so many balls that I started to call myself "Mr. Fumbles".

Interpretation: Good sense of humor; able to laugh at himself; people who can laugh at themselves usually respond well to constructive criticism.

****

Interviewee: Well, a bird in the hand is worth two in the bush.

Interpretation: Superficial and trite.

****

Interviewee: Am I going into too much detail?

Interpretation: Overly sensitive as to how he/she is seen by others.

Content Versus Behavioral Interpretations

In many instances, content interpretations will conflict with behavioral interpretation. Behavioral are more accurate.

"I still get butterflies in the old tummy when I'm making cold sales calls."

Content interpretation: Lacks confidence (after all, he just told us he's nervous).

Behavioral interpretation: Has confidence (to verbalize one's fears openly, especially in our "macho" society, reflects good confidence).

****

"I've often dealt with some of the most important, top-level people in business."

Content interpretation: Comfortable with high-level interactions.

Behavioral interpretation: Overly and inappropriately intent on impressing others (even if what he said is true, and we'll probably never know, why did he have a need to say it?)

****

You: I feel at times you might tend to be a little too sensitive to criticism. How do you feel about that?
They: I can't believe you'd say that. Obviously, you don't really know me at all.

Content interpretation: Not sensitive to criticism (just said so).

Behavioral interpretation: Sensitive to criticism; just rejected a criticism given quite gently.

****

You: I feel at times you might tend to be a little too sensitive to criticism. How do you feel about that?

They: Well, I think that's probably true; I think I am a little too sensitive to criticism at times.

Content interpretation: Too sensitive to criticism (just said so).

Behavioral interpretation: Not sensitive to criticism; just accepted feedback given gently.

Incidentally, the above examples concerning criticism should be part of every manager's repertoire and often used as the first issue confronted in feedback sessions. If a subordinate has 14 shortcomings, but one is an overly strong sensitivity to criticism, that sensitivity must be successfully worked through before any other shortcoming is addressed. Confronting a person with another of their "liabilities" always involves criticism, implied or otherwise. If the person is too sensitive to criticism, addressing another liability will be "shooting" them with two barrels, criticism and the shortcoming being addressed; consequently, it's unlikely they'll accept either.

Summary

The most important rule in interpretation is to base one's judgments, as far as possible, on the present behavior of the interviewee, not on the content of events he says happened two years or even two days ago.

Many companies relegate interviewing to an unimportant level, despite lip service to the contrary. This is because of their lack of focus on the people in their organization. This attitude usually originates with the chief executive officer who often finds it more rewarding and much more comfortable to focus his attention up (board of directors) and out (big customers or presidents of other companies or government agencies), rather than down (on subordinates, where it should be because that's from whom results flow). This abdication of responsibility for the behavior of subordinates then permeates the organization, thus increasing the comfort of all the managers.

253

The other reason interviewing is assigned an unimportant role is that there are so few good interviewers around who carry out the function effectively. After all, it's a lot more fun, and a lot less frustrating, to influence someone than to evaluate them. This orientation often results in superficial interviews that lead to a high error rate, one for which any organization will pay dearly.

Won't we be more consistent interviewers if we are all asking the same questions?

Is the purpose of the interview to "sell" the candidate on the company?

Is it true that the more facts we have about a candidate, the more accurate our assessment?

Is it more professional for the interviewer to control the interview?

CHAPTER 24

ELICITING BEHAVIOR

After engaging in a thorough behavioral analysis of the job and the personal characteristics it requires, we are ready to begin the interview. The type of interview we will describe here is called a conversational interview. It has no tricks or gimmicks. Its purpose is to elicit a sample of behavior in order to determine the interviewee's most likely behavior in the work setting and those stimuli that are most reinforcing and especially most aversive to him/her. In other words, the interview should help the manager predict frequent behavior and should give her information that will allow her to influence this behavior effectively in subsequent interactions.

Interviewing has two basic components: eliciting behavior and interpreting behavior. Eliciting behavior is emotionally difficult; as we've seen, we must suppress our own attitudes and feelings to those of another person, regardless of how wrong and foolish we think they might be. Interpreting behavior is intellectually difficult because we are being asked to interpret the most complex system on earth, a human being.

Principles of Eliciting Behavior

Let us now consider 12 principles which, if implemented, should help the manager to conduct a better interview. While this chapter is written in terms of a selection-promotion interview, it is worth noting again that these principles are essential in day-to-day interactions between managers and subordinates who have been with the company for years and in sales situations in which it is important for the salesperson to truly know the customer.

1. The interviewer must always be nonjudgmental in his responses.

The difference between a good interview and normal conversation is that the effective interviewer does not selectively reinforce or punish the behavior of the other person. This is what is meant by being nonjudgmental. Suppose we ask an individual what traits he likes to see in other people. If we respond to his answer non-judgmentally, his subsequent behavior is likely to reflect his true attitudes. However, if we respond as follows: "I'm surprised you think those traits are important; I think they're kind of superficial," we are trying to influence him and, unfortunately, we might succeed; thus, we are not likely to subsequently elicit his true attitudes.

Most interviewees are quite alert and perceptive during the interview; after all, important decisions are going to be made about them. The basic goal of the interviewee, especially during the selection interview, is to please the interviewer. In other words, they will attempt to pair themselves with stimuli they feel are reinforcing to the interviewer. Any indication the interviewer gives suggesting what she/he finds reinforcing or aversive, consequently, will color the entire interview. If, for example, the interviewer pairs the phrase, "We have a good, aggressive management team here," with an enthusiastic tone of voice, she has increased enormously the probability that the interviewee will try to pair himself with aggressive traits in his own behavior, whether he is truly aggressive or not. For this reason, as mentioned, effective interviewing requires the interviewer to subjugate his/her entire personality to that of the interviewee. The interviewer cannot afford to express attitudes and opinions during the interview.

Selling the Candidate

Many organizations make the mistake of attempting to sell the interviewee on joining their organization before they interview him ("We give our people a lot of freedom."). In selling their organization to the interviewee, they indicate what is reinforcing and what is aversive to them ("We really try to hire people who like this kind of freedom.").

The interviewee quickly pairs himself with these reinforcers in the subsequent interview ("I really enjoyed working at my last job because they gave you a lot of freedom.") and is highly recommended as a result. However, his behavior during the interview may be nothing like his behavior on the job (this interviewee may actually be uncomfortable with ambiguity and frequently seek out direction and reassurance). A high rate of turnover is the result.

An interview should *precede* any other step in the selection-promotion process. Indeed, convincing the interviewee to join the company is much easier after the interview, since the manager should now know what is reinforcing and aversive to the applicant.

[Readers are requested to ask someone a question about an issue the reader finds quite important emotionally. Can you react to their response in a non-judgmental, accepting manner, regardless of how you truly feel? If you cannot, you will have trouble interviewing people.]

2. Ask general, ambiguous questions.

One might best conceive of a human being as a pool of potential responses. Every human being, given the right circumstances, is capable of emitting any human response, from patting a person on the back to shooting someone. Different personalities are the result of the different probabilities or strengths of the behaviors that have been established by an individual's past experience with the contingencies of reinforcers and aversive stimuli, mostly in their interpersonal interactions.

A decisive person is likely to be so because decisive response patterns have been reinforced in his past experience; an indecisive person is less likely to be so because, in his experience, decisive behavior has been followed by aversive stimuli. (Please remember, however, that describing a person as decisive does not mean he is _always_ decisive; again, _frequent, repetitive_ behavior is what we want. Indeed, if a person is _always_ decisive, he is fear-driven, has a narrow response repertoire, and is probably being driven by a fear of being seen as indecisive or weak.)

The goal of the interview, then, is to elicit an individual's most probable response patterns, as evidenced by their frequent, repetitive behavior. This is accomplished by asking general, ambiguous questions, such as "Could you tell me a little about your business background?" or "How was the company?" or "What was the atmosphere of the company like at that time?" or "Was the atmosphere of that company different from the other one you worked for?"

Asking specific, factual, pre-planned, structured questions such as, "Could you tell me how they organized their paper flow in the purchasing department?" may well elicit a response pattern the interviewee is not likely to emit in the general work setting. It also indicates to the interviewee what is reinforcing to the interviewer (in this case, organizing material). Worse, it tells the interviewee she/he must adhere to the interviewer's agenda, rather than being guided by what they truly feel and who they really are.

General, ambiguous questions serve five purposes. First, they make most interviewees feel comfortable because there are obviously no right or wrong answers. Second, general, ambiguous questions elicit different behavior patterns from different people. They allow the individual the freedom to project himself as he really is into his response, rather than confining him to a narrow range of behavior as determined by the interviewer. It is this projection of himself under ambiguous conditions that reflects his strongest (most frequent) behavior patterns.

Third, general, ambiguous questions tell the interviewer what the person wants to focus on, what they feel is most important, and what they will probably focus on in their daily activities if hired. Fourth, the responses to these types of questions tell the interviewer what the interviewee feels comfortable talking about; thus, they are areas that can be safely probed. Fifth, general, ambiguous questions lead the interviewee to feel he/she is not being controlled.

[Readers are asked to consider an issue of some import to them. Can you elicit the attitudes of others about the issue by asking broad, general questions? Are the people you ask responding with their true feelings or are they hesitant because of their concern over your reactions?]

3. Ask value judgment, not factual, questions.

The interview is not a fact-finding mission. Attempting to determine whether a person left a position in May or June of 1994 tells us little about the person. Also, interpretations cannot be based on the factual material the interviewee presents during an interview. We do not know that a person has good initiative merely because they say they worked full-time while attending college at night; the interviewer cannot be sure of such facts without doing reference checks and investigative work; this is far too time-consuming.

As with general, ambiguous questions, we will elicit much more meaningful material (behavior) if we ask the interviewee for value judgments. Asking an individual what their manager was like tells us much more about the person than whether he left a position in May or June. Likewise, the fact that the interviewee was in a management-training program in 1983 tells us little about them; asking them how effective the training program was can tell us far more. The interviewee's assessments rather than their enumeration of past experiences can tell us, for example, whether or not they are decisive, hypercritical, or too detail-oriented. Their assessments can tell us which situations and types of behavior in others they find reinforcing and aversive. (Never ask an individual anything about anyone in the company for which he is presently working, however; the interviewee does not know how you will use that material, and it can be a strong aversive stimulus to them, strengthening a defensive posture on their part.)

[Readers are asked to find someone who has been fired or laid off in the past. Instead of asking them when they were laid off, ask them how they felt about the severance package or what kind of a person their former boss was. Does this tell you more about the person?]

4. Use short, quick phrases for probes.

It is true, however, that broad, general and value judgment questions will often elicit perfunctory responses from most people. That's usually because no one cared about their responses in the past, as evidenced by the fact that, after their response, they immediately focused on something else.

> Father: How was school today, son?
> Son: Good
> Father (yelling to wife): What time are we supposed to be at the Smith's tonight?

We are going to show the interviewee we are interested in them and what they say. How? By probing! More than anything else, probes tell a person we're interested in them and what they have to say rather than, like most people, trying to get them interested in us.

Suppose the interviewer asked, "How was that company?" Now he wants to probe the interviewee's response, "I thought it was a good company to work for." Most interviewers now turn to a different topic, feeling the question has been answered -- it has not been answered.

A much better reaction on the interviewer's part is a quick, soft, interested, "How so?," or "In the sense of?," or "Because?" These are probes. They are crucial to a good interview and to eliciting meaningful behavior.

Consider the two types of interviewing used by a husband and wife below:

> Husband: What kind of guy am I as a husband? (good general question)
> Wife: Well, you're all right.
> Husband (angrily): Just what the hell is that supposed to mean?

The husband becomes judgmental and punishes his wife. This ensures his true goal: not finding out what his wife really does think of him as a husband. A more effective approach for those brave enough to face the truth:

> Husband: What kind of guy am I as a husband?
> Wife: Well, you're all right.
> Husband (soft, but with interested inflection): How so?

Now the husband may indeed find out his wife's true attitudes (a fact which, it must be admitted, may punish his good interviewing techniques).

The importance of these short, probing phrases cannot be overemphasized. Such phrases are used to elicit what is frequently the richest material for interpretation. The question, "What kind of a boss was he?" usually elicits a perfunctory "Good" or "She was really effective." Far too many interviewers go on to a different subject at this point, although little can be learned from so superficial a response.

Following the response with a quick probe, "How so?" will generally elicit a more revealing elaboration. It tells us where the interviewee, when given the freedom, will focus her attention, what she cares about, what she likes and feels comfortable talking about. Moreover, by using short phrases, the interviewer shows that he is truly interested in the interviewee and not merely in eliciting the interviewee's attention and/or admiration

261

with long-winded, repetitious questions about topics of interest to the interviewer. Consider the two following examples:

Interviewee: I thought it was a good company.
Interviewer: Because?

***

Interviewee: I thought it was a good company.
Interviewer: In what sense did you feel it was a good company? You know, there are many facets to a company and I was wondering which ones struck you most about that particular company? Did you feel it was the aggressiveness or the organizational skills of the company? As I'm sure you've heard, our company is quite aggressive and we look for people who can handle that. So, I was wondering how you would describe that one? (At this point, the interviewee may be wondering how he'll be able to stay awake.)

The first interviewer is focused on evaluating the interviewee, the second on impressing and eliciting the interviewee's attention. Because probes tell the person we truly care about what they are saying rather than merely voicing our opinion, they are especially important in sales interviewing (and in social interactions).

A word about stress interviews might be appropriate here. These typically come in the form of obnoxious questions or in terms of using multiple interviewers at the same time. These types of interviews do indeed indicate how an individual will react to stress. They are probably effective when one is recruiting for the CIA or Army counter-intelligence organizations (or for potential employees of chief-executives who have inferiority complexes and manage by means of ridicule and punishment).

In private industry, however, stress interviews suffer from several shortcomings. First, they develop many enemies for the hiring organization. Second, because it is unlikely that an applicant will encounter such stress in the work setting, an accurate prediction of

262

behavior under those conditions is almost irrelevant. Third, rapport is so damaged that eliciting far more important behavior (organized, detail orientation) is virtually impossible. Stress interviewing as opposed to conversational interviewing, it must be said, may be more fun, but only for the interviewer.

Probes are the essence of effective interviewing. Probes are especially important for managers to use frequently and repetitively in their daily interactions with subordinates (and they are often the last thing a manager uses).

> Manager: How's the program going?
> Subordinate: Well, we're having a few problems.
> Manager: Well, make sure they're fixed by Friday!
> (This manager is more interested in expressing her feelings and frustrations than in being effective.)
> Manager: How's the program going?
> Subordinate: Well, we're having a few problems.
> Manager: How so?

This manager is intent on listening and evaluating the problems rather than merely expressing his frustrations and fears. As a result, he will have fewer frustrations and fears later. He'll also be able to efficiently focus on relevant issues and to make much more effective decisions and recommendations.

[Readers might wish to now ask anyone anything about any topic. Instead of responding with arguments, criticism, or attempts to influence and impress them with your brilliant insights, respond with a quiet, but interested, "How so?" Do you think they might be more comfortable and open with you now? Is that so bad?]

5. Do not attempt to anticipate your next question; let the interviewee determine the flow of the interview.

An interviewer's questions should be contingent upon the interviewee's responses. One never knows what these responses will be. (If one did, the interview would not be necessary.) If the interviewer is trying to think of his next question, he cannot possibly be listening to the interviewee. (This is one reason people who are intent on impressing others make poor interviewers; their focus is on how they appear to the interviewee rather than the other way around.)

Attempting to anticipate one's next question will also make the interview stilted and disjointed. Interviewees frequently go off on tangents, after which a question that would have been appropriate two sentences ago should no longer be asked.

> Interviewer: Whom did you report to then?
> Interviewee: To the vice president of manufacturing. (Interviewer is about to ask what kind of person she/he was, but the interviewee continues.) Of course, I was only in that position four weeks when they transferred me overseas.

The patterned, structured interview is likely to elicit responses from the interviewee that have a low probability of occurring in the work setting. They are too dependent upon the interviewer's behavior, not the interviewee's behavior. They tell the interviewee he is to follow the interviewer's agenda, not his own feelings and thoughts. It also leads to "textbook" type responses which too often, unfortunately, impress too many interviewers, but have little resemblance to behavior on the job.

Structured interviews may make the interviewer more comfortable, but the interviewer's focus will be oriented toward his next questions, rather than on the interviewee's behavior. This often leads to an overly formal, stilted, disjointed interview.

The interviewer will learn more about the interviewee by allowing him/her to guide the interview. (If a moment of silence occurs that makes you uncomfortable, the question, "What happened then?" always seems to elicit a natural, spontaneous response.)

Experience in this area is important. As the interviewer becomes relaxed, he will be able to "ride with" the interviewee's direction, just as we all do in social conversations. In the above example, the interviewee's sudden transfer overseas could easily have been responded to with, "How come?" or "Where to?"

In this connection, it is important that the interviewer not ask questions with the goal of determining whether the interviewee engages in specific behavior patterns. The interviewer, for example, should never say to himself, now I will see if he's decisive so I'll ask him, "What was the training program like?" Again, we cannot predict an interviewee's behavior; if we could, we would not be interviewing him. Interviewee's responses to this general question can range all over the place and tell you many things about him or her (e.g., whether they're organized, too detailed, negative, and so forth), sometimes everything except what you are looking for, whether he is decisive or not.

Basing one's questions on the interviewee's last response is also important because it allows the interviewee to feel they are in control and, more important, that someone is really interested in what they are saying. Let's return to a previous example:

> Father: How was school today son?
> Son: Good
> Father: How so?
> Son (somewhat shocked): What? Who are you?

Whoever asks the questions controls the interaction. This is why interviewing is so important in management, sales and all other areas of life. While we want others to feel they are controlling the interaction (so we base our questions on their responses), it is those who ask the questions who truly do. If you are in an all day meeting with six senior executives and you speak less than five per cent of the time, but that five per cent is spent asking questions, you will probably control much of the meeting.

[Readers are again requested to ask anyone anything about any topic. Whatever their answer, base your next question on some part of their last response.

<u>You (at a party)</u>**:** How long have you lived in New York?
<u>They</u>**:** Actually, I just moved here from Chicago six months ago.
<u>Good You:</u> Well, how do you like New York so far? (then a probe), or How was living in Chicago? (then a probe), or How would you compare New York and Chicago? (then a probe).
<u>Bad You:</u> I was in Chicago on a business trip recently. Actually, I travel quite a bit because people seem to need my guidance a lot. Have you ever heard of me...say, where are you going?]

6. Maintain an interested, conversational tone of voice with appropriate inflection.

No variable is more important in eliciting spontaneous behavior from an interviewee than is the interviewer's tone of voice (as we've repeatedly seen in our discussion of reinforcers). Unfortunately, no variable is more difficult to master, especially for men. Since they often determine whether or not the interviewee gets a job, most interviewers are in a strong position of power. This power is often reflected in their opportunistic attempts to impress the interviewee with their dominating confidence, reflected most openly in their tone of voice, which is likely to be flat, forceful, and authoritative (like John Wayne).

The best interviewing tone, however, is soft, gentle, concerned, and interested. Its softness connotes respect for the interviewee, if only for the pragmatic reason that a commanding tone will elicit only the response patterns evoked by an authority figure, whereas the goal of the interview is to elicit the interviewee's most probable, spontaneous behavior in all situations. The interviewer's gentle inflection connotes a respectful, non-judgmental interest in what the interviewee is saying.   This is likely to be quite reinforcing to the interviewee and will increase the probability of his responding openly during the interview.

Any interviewer who cannot elicit two hours of useful behavior is not using the proper tone of voice. A commanding or uninterested tone can be a severe aversive stimulus. Such a tone decreases the probability that the interviewee will respond spontaneously and openly and increases the likelihood the interviewee will respond in a short, factual, concise manner; this may well have little to do with how they truly feel and who they really are. ("Macho" men often have difficulty interviewing because they cannot bring themselves to leave the flat, aggressive "John Wayne" tone and adopt the more inflected, gentle tone necessary for effective interviewing.)

The reinforcing interest of the interviewer is, of course, a response to everything and anything the interviewee says. If it occurs only when an interviewee says certain things, shaping will take place, and the interviewee will soon be focusing his attention on those certain things. The interviewer who communicates interest only when the interviewee talks about the technical areas of his previous responsibilities will quickly find the interviewee discussing only technical matters, even if her on-the-job orientation is directed much more toward other people.

The reinforcing concern of the interviewer, therefore, must be a constant, pervasive stimulus that is contingent upon whatever the interviewee says. Providing reinforcement periodically and contingent upon specific content areas of the interview will lead to a distorted, inaccurate picture of the interviewee.

[Readers are asked to tape-record some of their interactions with others, especially in interviews (informing all parties, of course). Is your tone of voice inflected, gentle, respectful, interested? Get the opinion of others.]

The above principles are the basics of interviewing. They should be absorbed, practiced, and implemented frequently by every manager. What follows are some points for those who wish to sharpen their interviewing skills to a really fine edge.

267

7. Ask questions on subjects external to the interview.

One of the major goals of the interview is to create a spontaneous, conversational atmosphere. Questions such as "I haven't heard of that company—what do they do?" are the sort one would ask another person at a party. If this type of question is asked sincerely, the interviewee will feel the interviewer has "left the interview" and is genuinely interested in what that particular company does. Such questions will often elicit more spontaneity from the interviewee. As a result, her responses will be similar to those likely to occur in the work setting; they will not simply reflect the interview setting.

This is a subtle, but important, point. The word "you" should be dropped from questions whenever possible, because use of the word "you" is likely to put the person on guard: "How did you find the people in Kansas City?" A better question is: "How were the people in Kansas City?" The focus of the latter question is on the people of Kansas City, the former on the interviewee's opinions. The response of the interviewee to the question that does not use "you", however, will tell us much more about the interviewee than about people in Kansas City.

8. Be naïve; ask simple, basic questions in the interviewee's field of expertise.

Good interviewers have sufficient confidence in themselves to adopt a naïve, somewhat subservient manner. They are not afraid to ask basic questions which might reflect a lack of knowledge, for example, "What is a steel ingot?" "How do you drill for oil?" or "What is a preferred stock?" These basic questions in the interviewee's field of expertise put the interviewee in a dominant position; they also encourage her/him to be relaxed and spontaneous. Many interviewers are so intent upon impressing the interviewee that they shy away from topics that would reveal their ignorance. This is a critical mistake. The effective interviewer makes the interviewee feel more expert, more knowledgeable, than anyone else in the room.

9. Probe choice points and unusual situations.

Choice points refer to situations in which an individual has made a choice—by changing positions, for example, or by selecting a school or refusing a promotion or transfer. ' It is in these situations that the reinforcers and aversive stimuli controlling the interviewee's behavior are most apparent.

Unusual situations also involve stimuli that are intensely reinforcing or aversive to the interviewee. Why a man left his father's company when he was obviously going to inherit the presidency and ownership is a critical question that must be answered. The information is best elicited, not with long-winded or emotionally skeptical questions, but rather, with a soft, quick, interested "How come?" or "Why leave?"

Choice points and unusual situations are, oddly enough, the only two areas an interviewer could be justifiably criticized for not probing. Interviewing a 40-year-old person thoroughly would take 40 years. Two interviewers should be able to probe and skip entirely different segments of the interviewee's life and arrive at the same conclusions. This is due to the fact that the repetitious behavior patterns of the interviewee should be evident in both interviews, regardless of what's discussed. If the interviewee is an obviously thorough person, he will be thorough describing an event that took place ten years ago as well as eight years ago as well as yesterday.

10. Interrupt the interviewee.

When we are interacting with people in a relaxed atmosphere, we interrupt them. An interruption may be mildly aversive if the interviewee is intent upon getting a point across or if interruptions occur too frequently. An interruption can also be reinforcing, however, in that it tells the interviewee we are actually listening to her. Silence is not necessarily listening. In fact, silence, as we have so often seen, extinguishes the behavior of the interviewee and can prove quite frustrating to them. Listening is an active response involving overt behavior that has an impact on the speaker. When we interrupt the interviewee and ask for clarification on a point we do not understand, we are often pairing ourselves with stimuli reinforcing to him.

Silence, of course, can be useful in some situations. Since silence extinguishes behavior, it can be used by the manager to reduce a subordinate's overly strong emotional involvement in a given matter, such as a decision made by management. Suppose, for example, a subordinate frequently and bitterly complains about a new company policy. The manager would do well to elicit his subordinate's feelings with good interviewing techniques (nonjudgmental, but probing questions). The subordinate's angry responses should then be met with silent pauses by the manager. This "ventilation" will usually decrease the intensity of the subordinate's feelings on that issue. Too many managers, however, elicit the feelings and then respond with sympathy or emotional counter-arguments of their own; these positive and negative emotional managerial reactions are often reinforcing to the complaining subordinate and can increase the frequency and intensity of his complaints.

11. Reflect the interviewee's statements.

Reflecting the interviewee's comments is another way of telling her we are listening to what she is saying. This is true, however, only if the reflection sounds interested and concerned, as in the example below. If we reflect in a flat monotone, we may well be pairing ourselves with a stimulus aversive to the interviewee, which will decrease the likelihood of her responding openly in the interview.

Interviewee: So I was pretty excited over the promotion.
Interviewer (with inflected concern): It was an exciting moment. (Reflection)

Reflections of negative events should always underplay the aversiveness of the situation. That a reflection is effective is determined by whether or not the interviewee accepts it. If the interviewer makes the reflection too aversive, the interviewee will reject it.

Interviewee: So I was a bit disappointed that I didn't get the job.
Interviewer: It was a really disappointing moment for you. (Overstated reflection)
Interviewee: Well, not really. Actually, I had two other job offers at the time. (Reflection rejected)

****

Interviewee: So I was a bit disappointed that I didn't get the job.
Interviewer: You were a little disappointed at the moment.
Interviewee: Yeah, it would have given me a chance to see Europe. (Reflection accepted)

12. Respond with emotional interest.

If the interviewee's eyes light up and she takes obvious pleasure in talking about one of her accomplishments and its consequences, the interviewer must respond with the appropriate emotion in order to maintain rapport. Suppose, for example, the interviewee has told us about an extensive study she made on a given project. She then states, "As a result of my input, they gave me total responsibility for implementation of the entire project throughout the company!" Here the interviewer must respond with an appropriate reinforcer. He might, for example, smile and say with an enthusiastic inflection, "Really!" This is just the reaction (reinforcer) the interviewee was attempting to elicit. If the interviewer does not react at all or reacts in an uninterested monotone, he will extinguish the interviewee's response, frustrate her, and decrease the probability that the interviewee will again respond in a spontaneous, open manner.

[Readers are asked to video record some interviews, even with colleagues or those whom you know well. Watch the tapes with others. Get feedback on both your eliciting and interpreting skills. Do this periodically throughout your life; it's truly that important.]

Summary

Few skills are as important in getting through life as that of interviewing. Interviewing people effectively makes the tactless, abrasive person more gentle; it makes self-centered folks more focused and concerned with others. Good interviewing increases the likelihood managers will be motivating to others, focused on relevant matters, efficient in finding and dealing with real issues, appropriate in handling the various nuances of subordinates' behavior, and more inclined toward making the right decision at the right time.

Interviewing effectively allows salespeople to build rapport with customers, to know the fears of customers, and how to alleviate those fears, thus helping everyone. Knowing how to interview encourages the most shy, frightened person to become more confident in social interactions, partially because the focus is on others (while the control is not).

Good interviewing is an emotionally difficult process, made even more so by the frustrations involved. Yet, if the purpose of interviewing is to elicit relevant behavior and interpret that behavior, in what area of life is it not essential? Good interviewing is a way of life, a way of relating effectively to people. It would eliminate many of the problems in interpersonal relations. It is essential in selection-promotion decisions, daily management interactions, counseling, sales calls, social settings, and especially in marital and parental relations. People who use interviewing techniques out of habit will find their decisions in life much wiser, their expectations of others much more realistic, and their actions and decisions much more appropriate.

SECTION 7

THE ART OF CONSTRUCTIVE FEEDBACK

When is the best time to give someone feedback?

In a feedback session, should the manager focus on results or
behavior?

Is it appropriate to combine a salary review and a performance review?

CHAPTER 25

FEEDBACK PERSPECTIVE

The primary responsibility of managers is the behavior of people below
them, because that behavior will play a strong role in determining whether
or not the manager's department meets its objectives. The behavior of any
person will undergo only minimal changes, however, if the person
functions in a vacuum or in an unusually stable, rarely changing
environment. Continuous feedback from others is necessary before almost
any constructive behavioral changes can take place.

Thus, dealing effectively with behavior requires managers to give
feedback to subordinates. Most managerial feedback comes, as we have
seen, in the daily interactions with subordinates involving work-related
topics. There will be some occasions, however, when the manager must
focus his discussion solely on the subordinate's behavior. Ineffective
repetitious behavior requires the attention of the manager in and of itself,
not simply in relation to a specific project or problem. Moreover, such
behavior should be discussed frequently, not once or twice a year as in a
performance review.

Causes, Not Consequences

If, on the other hand, the manager deals only with the consequences of
behavior in specific situations, as many managers are inclined to do, the
behavior will continue. The manager will then find himself on a treadmill,
devoting too much of his time to straightening out situations that would

275

never have occurred had he dealt directly with the behavior itself and its causes.

A late report by a subordinate should be addressed directly by the manager. When reports from the subordinate are frequently, repetitiously late, however, the subordinate's behavior must be addressed in and of itself. Repetitious mistakes by an employee should lead the manager to shift his focus from the mistakes per se to the behavior of the employee.

Managers often focus on consequences (mistakes, late reports) because they are clear cut, readily apparent, and the individual responsible is usually apologetically subservient. But cursing late reports and repetitious mistakes may have minimal impact on the individuals involved. Thus, they will continue, as will the manager's frustration over having to endlessly put out the fires caused by the subordinate's behavior.

Timing of Feedback

Most managers give feedback at the worst possible time—when they are most motivated to do so. Suppose a plant manager finds that his plant superintendent has misread the blueprints of a given job and is assembling the job in the wrong way. It is at this point that the plant manager is most motivated to give his superintendent critical feedback. This is especially true if the superintendent's mismanagement of the project will cost the company money and might reflect poorly on the competence of the plant manager.

This is the worst possible time to give critical feedback. The plant superintendent is not motivated toward learning; he is feeling defensive, and anything the manager says will be an aversive stimulus to him. In fact, he is probably going to engage in avoidance behavior if confronted by the manager. More important, the superintendent has paired himself with a stimulus intensely aversive to the plant manager (mismanagement of the project). Hence, the manager is probably angry. The most reinforcing stimulus to angry people is seeing someone suffer, especially if that person is the cause of their anger. As a result, the goal of the plant manager at this moment is unlikely to be helping the superintendent grow and improve, but rather, seeing the superintendent hurt or at least as upset as the manager is.

The manager's comments and remarks, consequently, will be spoken in a negative tone of voice with the goal of hurting, rather than helping, the superintendent. He will, in effect, punish the superintendent. In sum, the plant manager is highly motivated toward giving feedback, but it's a form of feedback that will most likely have destructive consequences. (Indeed, if the superintendent brought the mistake to his manager's attention, that response will also have been punished by the manager's anger. Few subordinates will bring mistakes to the manager's attention subsequently, thus increasing the likelihood of a breakdown in communications.)

The Right Focus

Obviously, the plant manager must immediately point out and rectify the superintendent's mistake. For the moment, he must focus on the effects of behavior and not on its cause, but his interactions should be factual, non-emotional, and kept to a minimum. If he is irritated, any attempts to "develop" his subordinate are doomed to failure because seeing his superintendent "grow personally" is probably the last thing on his mind at that moment (seeing him wallow in pain is probably the first).

The best possible time to develop subordinates through feedback is when everything is running smoothly, that is, when the manager is least motivated to do so. When a subordinate is not an aversive stimulus to us and we are intent upon helping him grow personally, we will be much more likely to give our criticism in a helpful, constructive manner. Unfortunately, these are the times we are least motivated to give anyone feedback. After all, giving feedback is a scary task; why would we want to confront that dragon when everything's going well? To overcome this hesitancy toward giving critical feedback, most organizations have adopted a policy of forcing their mangers to give annual or semi-annual performance reviews.

[Readers are encouraged to think of an episode in which someone "upset" them. Can you guess the reason they did (which fear of theirs drove them to the dastardly act)? Could you address that issue (fear), the cause of their evil behavior, with them rather than the specific thing they did to upset you? If you address only the specific act, and not the causes, they may commit similar acts in the future. If you address causes, on the other hand, they may be less inclined to engage in any acts of that type.]

Performance Reviews and Their Shortcomings

There are two basic shortcomings to the maintenance of a performance review policy by an organization. First, while most managers will have discussions with their subordinates at company designated intervals, thereby avoiding their superiors' wrath, what actually takes place in these so-called performance reviews is quite another question. If the manager finds confronting and criticizing a subordinate aversive, she will continue to avoid it (e.g., by doing an overly favorable evaluation) even though ostensibly she has sat down with a subordinate and given him a review.

Second, it is naïve to assume that behavioral changes can be effected and maintained through the use of annual, semi-annual, or formally scheduled reviews. Meaningful changes in behavior come about only as a result of the daily subtle, and not so subtle, interactions between a manager and her subordinates. Compared with these, one or two meetings a year have little impact.

The function of a performance review, giving constructive feedback to a subordinate, is important. It should be done far more frequently than once or twice a year, however. Moreover, it should be made reinforcing to managers through adequate training in the nature of human behavior. Punishing a manager for neglecting a performance review will only make the process more aversive to her; it will not lead her to do it well.

Combining a Salary Review with a Performance Review

Another self-defeating policy is that of combining the performance review with a salary review. Making financial compensation contingent upon a manager's evaluation of a subordinate at a given moment is not the best way to motivate the subordinate to view his own shortcomings objectively. The primary goal for most subordinates under these circumstances will be changing the manager's mind about negative points in the evaluation in order to maximize their salary increase or bonus; they will rarely focus upon the points themselves, least of all on any perceived shortcomings on their part. For this reason, the salary review should properly be held one or two months prior to the performance review. (Reversing the two sets up the same destructive contingencies as does holding them together.)

The Real Goal

Most organizations would do well to examine their performance review policy. The ostensible goal of a performance review is behavioral change and growth on the subordinate's part. But the real reinforcer to top management often consists of having on file a recent evaluation of the subordinate. These two goals may be quite incompatible.

Most managers have difficulty being realistically critical of someone with whom they interact frequently. When their evaluation must be submitted in written form to top management, realistic criticism of subordinates is made even more aversive. That is, since managers are already too lenient evaluating subordinates (as numerous studies show), the requirement of submitting the evaluation to senior management, or making it part of a permanent record, or requiring a signature by the subordinate, makes it even less likely that the subordinates will get realistic, effective feedback. Companies might do a better job in this area by insisting that managers periodically (every month or two) discuss what they feel are one or two major shortcomings with their subordinates, rather than an entire evaluation. This should help desensitize everyone to feedback sessions.

[Readers are encouraged to frequently solicit "progress" reports from their managers in areas they have agreed need shoring up. This can help prevent surprises at scheduled performance review sessions. Please don't forget that most important question, "By the way, right off the top of your head, what do you think my greatest shortcoming is in the work setting?"]

Why is it important to reinforce someone in a feedback session?

Is the goal of feedback to address "truth" and let the subordinate know what the manager thinks of him/her?

What should the manager do immediately after pointing out a subordinate's shortcoming?

CHAPTER 26
GIVING FEEDBACK: Part 1

Having looked at the problems connected with performance reviews, we will now consider the principles governing a constructive approach to giving feedback. These principles, in fact, should be considered in all situations where critical feedback is necessary; their usefulness is not limited to formal performance reviews.

1. Establish rapport.

Any time two individuals interact in a feedback situation, there will be some minor apprehension or nervousness, even if the individuals have been interacting for years. These minor anxieties should be extinguished before the actual feedback starts. This is best accomplished by "chit-chat". The subordinate might be asked about his family, the home baseball team, or any other non-working interests or innocuous work activities with which he is involved. Stimuli that are aversive to the subordinate must be avoided at this stage. Discussing some recent mistake he has made, for example, will only increase the tension.

Following these preliminaries, the manager should move easily into the feedback session with an introductory comment such as, "As you know, Jim, I wanted to sit down and share some of my thoughts with you about your performance here at work." This introduction is crucial. Since minor, subtle stimuli from the manager can have a dramatic impact on the atmosphere of the interaction, a mere change in phrasing on his part can set the stage for an aversive encounter. If, for example, instead of saying, "I wanted to …" the manager had said, "As you know, Jim, the company requires us to …," or "I have to…" he would have paired the entire situation with aversive stimuli (and indicated his true feelings about the company and its policies as well).

It is important that the manager be relaxed and comfortable during the review. If he is not, this too will pair the entire session with aversive stimuli; his discomfort will be apparent in his tone of voice, his facial and body gestures, and the words he uses. The subordinate will quickly perceive that the situation is aversive to the manager and will become uncomfortable himself. This is another reason feedback should be given in small, frequent, "spontaneous" doses; everyone's fear of anticipating of a long, formal process then is not allowed to build.

An understanding of human behavior should increase the confidence of the manager during a feedback session. Indeed, an objective discussion of several of a subordinate's shortcomings, given with the goal of helping the subordinate, rather than hurting him, can be one of the most reinforcing, intimate exchanges two people experience. It can establish a strong sense of trust, openness, and confidence. It tells an individual that if something is wrong, this manager will address it openly and quickly; this prevents the all too common phenomenon of leaving the subordinate wondering what her manager "really" thinks of her. It can also be a powerful motivating force for both participants, since a sound exchange reflects mutual concern, but especially that of the manager for her/his subordinate.

2. Always start with stimuli reinforcing to the subordinate.

Two influences have a good deal to do with determining our reactions to an individual. The first is the past history of our interactions with them and whether or not they have paired themselves with stimuli reinforcing or aversive to us. The second influence consists of the most recent pairing we have experienced with the individual. For example, a man may have experienced numerous and frequent pairings of reinforcers with his wife. If, however, she is 15 minutes late for a luncheon date, she will be an aversive stimulus to him *at that moment*. Within a short time, however, the overall history of the previous reinforcing experiences will take precedence over the most recent pairing, and the man will again "fall in love" with his wife.

This is another reason managers should reinforce subordinates frequently in their daily interactions. It builds a positive history of experiences that can take the relationship over the minor "bumps" any relationship encounters. In any event, the manager would do well to take the initial moments of the feedback session to pair himself with stimuli reinforcing to his subordinate. He does this most easily by pointing out some of the subordinate's strengths (and every individual has some strengths).

He might say, for example, "You know Jim, I feel you're quite thorough when you work through problems; I feel you watch details closely, and the precision in your work is excellent. I have little doubt but that when you're given a job to do, it's going to be done properly and I really appreciate that orientation."

These statements pair both the feedback session and the manager himself with stimuli reinforcing to the subordinate. Also, the probability of constructive behavior in the future and the positive atmosphere of the review are enhanced by pairing the effective behavior patterns of the subordinate (precision) with other reinforcers (excellent and appreciated). The goal of feedback is not only to weaken shortcomings, but also to strengthen the person's assets.

We are assuming here that "normal" stimuli are reinforcing or aversive to the subordinate. If this manager is disliked by his subordinate, then the manager's "appreciation" would be aversive, thus weakening his subordinate's concern for precision. (There are occasions when normally positive traits are seen as aversive and negative traits as reinforcing to some people. Reviewing a psychological evaluation with one individual, for example, elicited ready agreement to negative traits and strong arguments against positive traits.

This person lacked confidence and was quite tense when given new responsibilities. He subconsciously attempted to avoid these aversive situations by constantly downgrading himself to top management. In this way he also elicited the friendship of people around him (reinforcer), since most people like individuals with "humility". Lacking confidence also meant he didn't like and respect himself, hence compliments were being directed toward someone he didn't like and respect—so he disagreed with them. Criticisms, on the other hand, were also being directed at someone he didn't like and respect—so he felt comfortable with them and agreed.)

The manager must, of course, sincerely believe his own reinforcing statements about the subordinate. If he does not, that fact will be apparent in his tone and gestures. This will quickly be perceived by the subordinate, for whom the manager and his comments will then become aversive stimuli rather than reinforcers.

[Readers are encouraged to learn to start a feedback interaction by: one, establishing rapport with someone informally (at the water cooler) with "pleasant chit-chat" and, two, emotionally expressing your appreciation for one or two of the other person's strengths. An interaction with your significant other along these lines might prove to be beneficial. This ability to address and reinforce someone for some of their strengths and assets could actually be a helpful part of your repertoire when entering almost any potentially negative interaction.]

3. Use tentative, soft language when criticizing someone.

After his initial reinforcing statements, the manager is ready to address a shortcoming of the subordinate. The purpose in presenting the criticism is not to reduce the subordinate to tears nor to make him jump out of his chair; moreover, it is not to encourage him to apologetically confess to his sins nor even to agree enthusiastically with your profound insights. It is to effect permanent, constructive behavioral change.

Aversive stimuli cannot be avoided in criticizing a subordinate, but they can be made so mild that the subordinate will seriously consider the criticism rather than withdrawing or attacking the manager. Managers, after all, have enormous power over subordinates, often far more than they realize; when a manager whispers, most subordinates hear it as a shout.

Let us assume that a manager feels that his subordinate is indecisive. Using tentative, soft language, he might say, "Jim, I feel at times that you tend to be a bit indecisive." The tentative phrases are "at times", "tend to be", and "a bit". Since the manger has softened the aversiveness of the criticism, the subordinate, unless he is unusually sensitive, should be able to consider it seriously.

Contrast this with the manager who is intent upon "calling it like it is" (thereby proving his toughness and love of Truth), "Jim, you're just too damn indecisive, too weak, too wishy-washy!" This comment may be so intensely aversive to the more passive subordinate that he agrees with it in order to escape. If, on the other hand, the subordinate has successfully stopped aversive stimuli in the past by attacking, he will attack the manager who has paired him with so severe an aversive stimulus. One thing is certain: the subordinate's focus will not be on his own indecisiveness; it will be on his manager and either fleeing from him or fighting him.

4. Use a concerned tone of voice when presenting criticism.

A harsh, authoritative tone of voice has a deadly effect on critical comments. The tone of voice must be concerned; it must "persuade" the subordinate that the manager is intent upon helping him, not merely criticizing him. Indeed, the manager's major goal or reinforcer in a feedback exchange must be helping the subordinate to "grow". If the manager is frustrated and his major reinforcer is seeing his subordinate hurt, on the other hand, this will show in his choice of words and especially in his tone of voice.

Remembering the dangers of "but, however" pairings, the manager must avoid "coupling" the reinforcers (compliments) with aversive stimuli (criticisms). He must not, for example, say, "Jim, I feel you do precise work that is excellent, *but* I feel you're not quite as decisive as you should be." Such a pairing of reinforcers and aversive stimuli would soon turn any reinforcers into aversive stimuli. The manager's sincere reinforcing observations would subsequently have little impact on the atmosphere of the review session. The subordinate would always be waiting "for the other shoe to drop".

Positive assets of the subordinate must stand on their own; they must be said in a way that indicates they are as important to the manager as negative statements. This is best accomplished by pairing the asset with a reinforcer, e.g., "Jim, I feel you do precise work and I think everyone really respects you for that." A short silence should follow each positive statement, both to allow the subordinate to respond if he wishes, and to break any possible pairings with subsequent criticisms (even six seconds will do).

5. Always elicit feedback from the subordinate immediately after your criticism.

Following the presentation of the criticism, the manager must elicit a response from his subordinate in order to ascertain her/his emotional and intellectual reaction to the criticism. The simplest eliciting stimulus is a direct question: "How do you feel about that?" Again, tone of voice is a prime variable. It can indicate that the manager wants his subordinate to agree with him so both can be done with this whole disagreeable business. Or, without changing the words themselves, it can indicate that the manager is concerned enough about his subordinate's behavior to want to discuss it with him.

So far, the manager has said only the following: "Jim, I feel at times you tend to be a bit too indecisive. How do you feel about that?" And yet he has already had an impact on his subordinate's behavior. By telling the subordinate he is indecisive, the manager has paired indecision with the aversive stimuli of his tone of voice which, while soft, is slightly derogatory when discussing the shortcoming. Also, the mere fact that the manager brought up the shortcoming at all indicates that he finds the trait aversive. Thus, the manager has already decreased slightly the probability that his subordinate will continue to engage in indecisive behavior.

6. Do not interrupt silence.

Most subordinates will react to the question, "How do you feel about that?" with a short period of silence. This is partly because the manager is discussing what is one of the most important things in the world to the subordinate—himself. It is also because, unfortunately, while they have frequently discussed the effects of the subordinate's behavior (the poor reports he wrote, the sales calls he did not make), previous superiors have rarely discussed the subordinate himself and, if they have, they did not want to hear any arguments, back-talk, or disagreements. Hence, opportunities for the subordinate to voice his views were kept to a minimum.

Many managers find this short period of silence aversive. They attempt to avoid it by jumping into the conversation with another remark. This is a mistake. By allowing the silence to continue uninterrupted, the manager shows the subordinate that this issue is important to him and he will take all the time necessary to discuss it properly. (Managers should never ask subordinates how they feel about a positive statement, however; the statement itself may be reinforcing, but asking her how she feels about it is almost always embarrassing, hence aversive.)

[The reader is encouraged to informally address a shortcoming with someone in a gentle, respectful manner. Then, even if the person obviously starts to become weepy, ask them, "How do you feel about that?"

When they became weepy or responded in a hurt manner, was your tendency to quickly reassure (reinforce) them because of your exquisite sensitivities and your desire to avoid being disliked? Resist. Let the silence hang (then agree with any rebuttals on their part because this is as far as we've gone and we won't know how to respond until we've finished the next chapter.]

What is the goal of giving feedback?

Should I have specific examples of subordinates' shortcomings ready
for discussion?

If the person agrees with my perception of their shortcomings, should I
reinforce them?

How often should I give feedback to someone?

CHAPTER 27

GIVING FEEDBACK: Part 2
THE INTERACTION

1. Reacting appropriately when the subordinate disagrees.

Whatever the reason for disagreement, and there are many, the manager
must be aware of the fact that his presentation of the criticism, or the
criticism itself, was too aversive to the subordinate.

Suppose the subordinate disagrees by saying, "Well, I really feel that's not
quite correct. I feel I do make decisions when they're called for."

Ironically enough, this is the point at which the manager should throw out
a *mild* reinforcer. Why? First, because his goal is to increase the
likelihood of the subordinate being decisive; it is not to get the subordinate
to agree with the criticism. If the subordinate is protesting that he is
decisive, we should reinforce him because we want him to be so. After
this comment, many people will "prove" to their superiors they are indeed
decisive by subsequently going out of their way to be so. Great! That's
our goal, and we'll reinforce them even more intensely when they actually
are decisive, regardless of our suppositions about why they are being so.

Second, the manager should emit a mild reinforcer because, by disagreeing with the criticism, the subordinate has indicated that the criticism and the manager himself are aversive stimuli to him, hence a manager-reinforcer pairing would be helpful.

The perfect mild reinforcer at this point would be a reflection. The manager might softly say, "You feel, then, you will make a decision when one is called for." By pairing the subordinate with decisiveness, this comment on the manager's part will also increase the probability of the subordinate engaging in decisive behavior in the future. The reflection must be spoken in an accepting rather than a questioning tone of voice, however. If the manager's voice rises at the end of the reflection, it will be a challenging question, hence an aversive stimulus.

It is true that by throwing out a mild reinforcer to the subordinate when he disagrees with criticism, the manager also reinforces disagreement responses to criticisms and thereby increases the probability of argumentative behavior in the future. This is a small price to pay, however, if the subordinate leaves the office a more effective person and if the manager has paired himself with stimuli reinforcing to the subordinate. Notice that the manager has not changed his opinion; he has merely reflected the subordinate's reaction.

The manager might even use a stronger reinforcer to increase the probability of his subordinate's decisiveness. In response to the subordinate's disagreement, the manager might say, "Well, Jim, if indeed you are decisive, I take my hat off to you. I hope you keep up a decisive approach and I'm sure I will notice it and applaud you for it." These pairings will almost ensure decisiveness on the subordinate's part, at least when he is in the presence of the manager, thus giving the manager more opportunities to reinforce his decisiveness.

Consider the alternative to reinforcing this disagreement. The subordinate disagrees with a criticism, and the manager responds with a strong aversive stimulus: "Oh, for God's sake, Jim, everyone knows you're indecisive. I could easily get ten people in here who would agree with me!" This increases the probability that Jim will respond to the manager as he would to any intense aversive stimulus. Indeed, Jim will probably sit at home that night thinking, not about himself and decisiveness as we would hope, but about how he might transfer to another department - or about his manager and how he can "get back at him".

The key point is that the subordinate has both disagreed and said he is decisive in one response. The manager who punishes the response is probably doing so because disagreement is aversive to him. By punishing the subordinate at this moment, however, he is also decreasing the likelihood of the decisiveness he professes to desire.

(If, on the other hand, the manager is only interested in eliciting agreement from his subordinate, he might try a different approach. The subordinate is disagreeing with him partially because the manager is an aversive stimulus to the subordinate.

To overcome this problem, the manager might simply pair himself with a string of stimuli reinforcing to the subordinate. He might say, for example, "Jim, as I mentioned before, I feel you're a thorough, conscientious person. I feel you do a job properly when you assume responsibility for it, and I think you have excellent initiative in moving out to get the job done. I feel your relationships with other people in the company are beyond reproach. Everyone likes you and respects you. (pause) I do wonder at times if you may not be quite as decisive as you could be." Most people will be surprised at the frequency with which this chain of reinforcers elicits an agreeable response from the subordinate, "Well, maybe you're right. Maybe I could be a little more decisive at times.")

Agreement with feedback should not necessarily be the manager's primary goal, however. Certainly, when a subordinate disagrees with a criticism, it is a good indication that the manager has become an aversive stimulus to him, but this fact is a secondary consideration to the effective manager. The manager's primary goal should be to make the subordinate more decisive, not to elicit agreement or cooperative responses. Indeed, the subordinate's behavior in the review session should be of minimal importance to the manager. It is the subordinate's frequent, repetitive behavior in his/her subsequent daily activities that the manager should be concerned with influencing.

2. Do not discuss specific examples of shortcomings.

Of all the points discussed in this chapter, this one will probably be the most aversive to the greatest number of people. A fairly common response to the manager's question, "How do you feel about that?" will be, "Can you give me an example of what you mean?" (This reaction is not nearly as likely, however, if the manager is indeed focused on frequent, repetitive behavior and the criticism is presented in a gently, helpful manner at the proper time.)

Let us first recognize the subordinate's question for what it is, a disagreement with the manager's criticism. In the foregoing example, the manager reinforced disagreement. What he was really attempting to reinforce, however, was the individual's constructive statement, "I am decisive."

Asking for a specific example is not a constructive response, however. Hence, the manager should follow it with a mild aversive stimulus in order to decrease its probability of recurring. He should then bring the subordinate back to the issue by repeating his initial statement. Thus he might say, "No, I'm not thinking of <u>any one</u> instance in particular. I just feel that at times you're not quite as decisive as you could be. How do you feel about that?" (Notice the manager is regaining control by asking a question.)

Why No Examples

There are three reasons why the manager should not go into specifics. First, the subordinate who asks for examples is attempting to avoid aversive stimuli (criticism and his manager) by discussing a stimulus other than himself (avoidance behavior). Suppose, for example, the manager falls into this trap and says, "Well, yesterday at the meeting you refused to give any recommendations on buying those computers." The subordinate then responds with, "The reason I didn't give any recommendations was that I didn't get the figures I needed on our present configuration from Bob," to which the manager must reply, "Why couldn't you get the figures from Bob?" In short order, the subordinate and his manager will be discussing Bob, his procrastination, and his inability to communicate the figures when needed, thus successfully avoiding the real issue of indecisiveness.

An individual will always have 101 sound reasons for engaging in a specific behavior in a given situation. The subordinate may indeed be indecisive on many occasions, but discussing any one in particular will always lead him to justify his indecisive behavior in that situation. In short, the manager will always lose these arguments. Worse, to react to these reasons is to put the manager and the subordinate into an adversarial, mutually aversive relationship; this virtually precludes constructive progress in the rest of the interaction.

More important, the interaction will no longer center on its proper goal, changing the behavior of the subordinate. By focusing his manager's attention on a specific situation rather than on its causes, the subordinate successfully avoids aversive stimuli. Many managers are only too happy to be sidetracked in this manner.

The second reason to avoid specifics is that a specific focus may well lead the subordinate to change the behavior involved, but only in that particular type of situation; it will not lead him to alter his general behavior pattern.

In the forgoing example, by focusing his attention on the subordinate's inability to commit himself at the meeting with Bob, the manager may well increase the probability that the subordinate will make recommendations in meetings, especially with Bob, since it is this situation with which the manager's aversive comments are now being paired. However, the subordinate may continue to be indecisive in virtually all other situations because the aversive pairings did not center on his indecisive behavior.

Again, telling an assistant editor that she is not detailed enough in her work, then responding to her request for specific examples by discussing this fault in reference to an edit she did that omitted punctuation marks, may well lead her to focus on punctuation marks in subsequent reports. Her lack of orientation to detail, however, will continue to be apparent in her other activities.

The stimulus to pair with aversive stimuli (criticism) is the behavior reflecting a lack of orientation to detail, not the specific habit of omitting punctuation marks. In other words, stimulus generalization will affect a broad area of behavior if the manager pairs a general behavioral trait with aversive stimuli, but it will affect only a narrow area of behavior if the manager pairs specific situations and the subordinate's behavior in those situations with aversive stimuli.

The subordinate who is overly sensitive to being treated unfairly can be treated unfairly in a thousand different ways. To discuss his reaction in a specific situation may tone down his sensitivities in that situation, but it will have little effect on his overly sensitive reaction to the hundreds of other situations he encounters in which he feels he is being treated unfairly. The manager should focus on behavior, not on specific episodes.

The third reason not to discuss specifics is that the manager should not even be thinking of a specific situation. A feedback interchange should only deal with *frequent, repetitive* behavior, responses the manager has observed many times by the subordinate in many situations. Behavior that is rare or atypical for the subordinate has no place in a feedback session, no matter how egregious it might have been.

If an individual is consistently attentive to details, but makes a careless mistake on one occasion, there is no possible justification for accusing him of not being detail-oriented. The manager who does so is usually getting revenge for the pain he has suffered because of his subordinate's atypical mistake. An insulting remark made by a subordinate toward his boss in front of others may motivate the boss to make it the focal point of a feedback session. If this is unusual behavior for a normally tactful, considerate person, however, it is best ignored.

When Specifics are Appropriate

There are only two occasions appropriate for discussing specifics. The first is during the actual event, when the continuance of an ineffective behavior pattern will lead to considerably more lost time, money, or energy. If a man is cutting the wrong corner off a widget, he must be told to stop immediately and the process corrected. This does not, however, relieve the manager of the need for thinking about the causes of this behavior (which will be different for different people), if it is repetitious, and later dealing with the person in a constructive manner.

The second appropriate time to discuss specifics, if it seems necessary, is during the salary review. It will do little good or harm, however, since the subordinate's focus will then be on what to her is, and should be, the real issue at the moment, money.

3. *When the subordinate agrees with the criticism, the manager's job doesn't end, it begins.*

If the manager is a reinforcer to the subordinate, if he has made his criticism gently, in a concerned, helpful tone, and if the observation squares with reality, the overwhelmingly probable response will be agreement by the subordinate. The conversation might run something like this:

> Manager: Jim, I feel at times you tend to be a bit indecisive. How do you feel about it?
> Subordinate: Well, I think you might be right. I feel I am a bit too indecisive at times.

Less competent managers tend to reinforce their subordinate at this point because they've successfully elicited the only thing they really wanted – agreement. But even some good managers blunder here. They feel they might be hurting the subordinate (aversive stimulus) and forcing the subordinate to hurt himself. They therefore cut this aversive situation short (avoidance behavior) by reinforcing the subordinate with a remark like, "Well, on the other hand, you are quite thorough and precise when you work through a problem." This, of course, reinforces the subordinate's perception of himself as indecisive (and further erodes his confidence)!

When the subordinate agrees with his criticism, the manager's response should instead be a simple question: "Why? Why do you feel you might be a bit too indecisive at times, Jim?"

The subordinate generally has no answer for this question. He does not know why, and it is unlikely that he will say, "It is because my mother did not hug me to her bosom when I was three years old." By asking the question, however, the manager indicates to the subordinate that he is not merely attempting to elicit agreement; he is also trying to help the subordinate explore this shortcoming. Moreover, the effective manager takes this opportunity to pair the shortcoming with more aversive stimuli (tone of voice when asking why), thus making indecisiveness an even more aversive stimulus to the subordinate. Finally, he mildly, but correctly, punishes the subordinate when the latter states, "I am too indecisive," by prolonging the conversation on a topic aversive to the subordinate, thus preventing the subordinate's attempt of avoidance behavior from being successful, thus reinforced.

Even though the subordinate does not know why he is indecisive, the manager should have some hypothesis to propose and pairings to make. As we have seen, the causes of any behavior pattern usually stem from the behavior of other people. Now is the time for the manager to bring the principles of influencing behavior into effect.

This particular subordinate's indecisiveness, for example, may well be a reaction to other people's criticism directed toward him when he did commit himself to a decision or even voice his views on an issue. The manager should have his best possible guess ready before the review session begins. He should then suggest it to the subordinate at the appropriate moment: "I wonder if it's because you might feel at times that someone might criticize your decision?"

This suggestion may well be a presentation of aversive stimuli the individual has been fearing, but successfully avoiding, all his life. By not pairing it with other aversive stimuli and by speaking about it openly and nonchalantly, however, the manager is starting to extinguish "criticism from others" as an aversive stimulus.

The manager's next move should be to pair criticism from other people, since it is aversive to her subordinate, with stimuli that are reinforcing to him. Hence, she might say, "You know, Jim, when someone criticizes you, he is frequently telling you that he likes you. When someone takes a shot at you, he is often saying he cares enough about you and your views to argue with you. Someone criticizing you or arguing with you can really mean he respects you."

This pairing of the aversive stimulus (criticism from others) with a reinforcer (respect from others) will, as we have seen, decrease the probability of the behavior controlled by the aversive stimulus—in this case, indecisiveness. (Moreover, by using reinforcers, the manager pairs herself with those reinforcers, leading the subordinate to "feel good" about the review discussion and his manager.)

4. Pair defense mechanisms with aversive stimuli.

Some subordinates, although relatively few, will use an infinite variety of defense mechanisms to avoid the criticism of their immediate superior in a feedback interchange. These may range all the way from bland acceptance of anything the superior mentions to outright opposition to everything the manager brings up, be it good or bad. In either case, the manager must stop the review, point out the defense mechanism he observes being used, and pair it with aversive stimuli.

When, for example, a subordinate is responding with a superficial acceptance of everything the manager says, the manager might remark, "You know, Bill, I feel you're just accepting everything I say in order to get this discussion over with. I feel I'm wasting my time here." This will usually bring forth a quick denial by the subordinate and a more serious involvement on his part. A similar pairing of oppositional behavior with an aversive stimulus is also usually effective: "You know, Bill, I get the feeling that no matter what I say, you're going to disagree with it. I almost get the feeling that if I were to say black is black, you would say black is white. I wonder if you're taking this approach because you're a bit too sensitive to criticism."

Most subordinates desperately seek feedback. Most live out their vocational lives with gross misconceptions of what their managers think of them. And yet most managers are uncomfortable in a feedback review interaction. It is aversive to them to play God and to make judgments about those things that are so important to their subordinates. Nevertheless, there is no alternative. Managers cannot abdicate their responsibility and the judgments necessary when they assume authority over other people. Failure to give a subordinate any feedback at all is usually a far greater abuse of managerial power than is giving him feedback that is erroneous.

Many people have adopted and maintained ineffective behavior patterns which could have been alleviated or eliminated had their managers taken the trouble to discuss their problems frankly and openly with them. Allowing an individual to continue on an ineffective course of behavior is also playing God; the manager's judgment in this case is a particularly damning, "I will do nothing about it."

The manager who sits in his office and refuses to interact with his subordinates is not, in any case, avoiding the responsibility of influencing their behavior. He is engaging in a massive extinction process, the results of which will be frustration, irritation, and, finally, lethargy on the part of his subordinates. Likewise, the manager who confines his discussion to work-related topics still uses classical and operant principles that have an impact on the judgments, attitudes, and general behavior of subordinates. Disliking the principles, especially their specificity, does not mean they can be avoided. Influencing people is intrinsic to a managerial position; it cannot be avoided.

Summary

Managers must, as we have said, focus constantly on developing their subordinates and on the daily impact their behavior is having on them. When Jim's manager, for example, notices a tentative thrust at decisiveness on Jim's part, he should be ready to quickly respond with a stimulus that is reinforcing to Jim. In effect, he must be ready to shape, through the appropriate use of reinforcers, his subordinate's constructive behavior.

Without doubt, this is a complex task. No one expects that manager to be perfect in her/his dealings with subordinates; even a slight improvement can be dramatically reflected on the profit statement of the organization.

The techniques in this chapter should be part of the manager's repertoire, to be used every day, not once or twice a year. They might be used during a five-minute chat over coffee or in a complex, three-hour meeting. We will look at examples of their daily use in the next chapter.

Feedback sessions can be one of the most rewarding, motivating interactions between a manager and his/her subordinate. They can lead to sincere, and sometimes dramatic, attempts by a subordinate to adopt more effective behavior patterns in the work setting. These attempts will be wasted, however, if the manager does not follow them with appropriate reinforcers. Without follow-up, an annual performance review is useless. With daily follow-up, frequent feedback interchanges can initiate a developmental process that eventually leads to striking personal and organizational growth.

[Readers are asked here to address an important issue with anyone with whom they interact. No shortcoming or ineffective behavior can be addressed without involving some form of criticism. It is essential, consequently, that the person's reaction to criticism be confronted and resolved before any other issue is approached.

The reader, consequently, is encouraged to say to everyone in their inner circle, "I feel you might tend to be a bit sensitive to criticism at times." Now to the next steps:

> Did you then ask them how they felt about that?
> Was your tone of voice gentle and concerned?
> Did you reflect any disagreements they voiced?
> Did you deflect any requests for specifics on their part?
> If they agreed, did you prolong the interaction and ask them why they feel they might be....?
> Did you do effective pairings?
> Are you ready to reinforce instances in which the person asks for constructive criticism?]

SECTION 8

THE MANAGERIAL PROCESS

CASE STUDIES

CHAPTER 28

ANALYSIS OF MANAGERIAL INTERACTIONS: Example 1

We are now ready to consider some examples of manager-subordinate interactions that will illustrate and utilize the principles we have learned. The manager is not expected to emulate the styles of the managers depicted here, but might wish to consider the principles reflected in their behavior. One manager can say, "What the hell did you do that for?" and make it an intense aversive stimulus to a subordinate, while another can say the same words to the same subordinate in such a manner that it constitutes a strong reinforcer.

The first illustration we will examine is an interaction between a general sales manager and his subordinate, a regional sales manager. The regional sales manager is responsible for a specific geographic territory and has eight salespeople under him covering the territory.

One morning the general manager, who has not seen the regional manager for about a week, passes his subordinate's office and notices that he is alone. Recognizing that his primary responsibility involves face-to-face interactions with his subordinates, the general manager walks into his regional manager's office, and the following interaction takes place:

> <u>Manager (smiling and enthusiastic):</u> Hello, Jim, have you got a minute? *The manager has paired himself with several reinforcers—the smile, the enthusiasm, and the respect implicit in asking if the subordinate is busy. Most of us are very much aware of the subtle cues an individual emits when greeting us that tell us whether we are a reinforcing, neutral, or aversive stimulus to him. There are few things more pleasing to many of us than someone "lighting up" when they first see us. It's a reinforcer we might wish to consider openly expressing when we meet people in our inner circle, especially since it is almost impossible for anyone to dislike a person who so obviously likes them.*

Subordinate: Sure, Paul, have a seat.

Manager (slouching low in chair to create a relaxed atmosphere): How's everything going? *A good interviewing question, broad, general, and designed to elicit form the subordinate his most probable responses and greatest concerns of the moment. Had the manager instead announced, "I want to talk to you about your expense report," his statement would have confined his subordinate's behavior to a narrow spectrum; he would also have failed to provide his subordinate the opportunity to discuss any problems or stress the subordinate might be experiencing at the time. Managers might do well to consider starting almost any interaction with a broad, general question.*

Subordinate: Oh, pretty well. Actually, I just found out our sales are running 14% ahead of last year for this time period.

Manager (sitting up in chair quickly, and with strong inflection): Are they really! Excellent! Beautiful!

Subordinate: Yeah, we're all pretty happy. *It is obvious that this manager has, during previous interactions, paired practical results (sales) with reinforcers; if, on the other hand, he had paired lowering the expense account with reinforcers, the subordinate might have focused on that area and said something like, "Our expenses are down ten percent for the month." In this instance, the manager is not only pairing practical results with reinforcers, he is also following his subordinate's accomplishment of increased practical results with reinforcers, thereby increasing the probability that his subordinate will focus on practical results in the future. How many managers would sit blandly by, or ask a neutral, extinguishing question ("Which areas were up most?") after a comment like the one this subordinate made?*

Subordinate: Yeah, we're all pretty happy about it.

Manager (again with enthusiasm): I would be too! You and your people are doing a hell of a good job, Jim. Why don't you bring them all in and take them out to dinner with their wives to the Athletic Club at company expense? *Here the manager is pairing his compliments with a concrete reinforcer. If he were to use verbal compliments continually as reinforcers without pairing them periodically with other reinforcers, their effectiveness would soon extinguish. His suggestion should not, of course, have been made if the subordinate were a withdrawn individual for whom taking his salesmen out socially was an aversive stimulus.*

Subordinate: Do we have enough money in our budget for something like that?

Manager: For that kind of a performance we do. *Follows his subordinate's "concern for the budget" response with a reinforcer and pairs performance with a reinforcer.*

Subordinate: Good, I'll do it.

Manager: How's everything else going? *This type of question, if sincere, can be quite reinforcing and motivating. Again, it indicates a concern for the listener by focusing on his concerns rather than on some preordained agenda or concern of the speaker. It is, moreover, a good broad, general question.*

Subordinate: Well, I'm having a little trouble with the superintendent of our plant down in Atlanta.

Manager: How so? *A good, concise, probe. The manager did not launch into his own negative experience with the plant superintendent several months ago or plant managers in general, a reaction that would have prevented him from finding out about his subordinate's problem. Managing people is somewhat altruistic; the effective manager's focus is almost always on the other person's successes and problems, not his own. This is not as altruistic as it may sound, however; after all, virtually all the joys and pains of life emanate from other people; why not focus on such an important source of our fears and happiness? And certainly the success of a manager should be dependent upon the success of his/her subordinates.*

Subordinate: Well, one of Mary's customers has been calling the plant superintendent and complaining about our late deliveries. The superintendent got hold of Mary and read her the riot act, raked her over the coals. The jerk told Mary to handle her own customers and keep them off his back. Mary was pretty shaken up about it.

Manager: What happened then? *Still doing good interviewing.*

305

Subordinate: I went over to the plant and told the superintendent what I thought of him talking to my salespeople that way.

Manager: Good! *Reinforcement, thereby increasing the likelihood of more aggressive, and probably internally destructive, behavior by the sales manager toward the plant superintendent.* What did he say?

Subordinate: He said our salespeople shouldn't be having their customers call him. I told him if he had any complaints about the salespeople he'd better talk to me about it or keep his damn mouth shut.

Manager: Excellent! (Continued reinforcement of hostility toward operating people.) That guy always has been a big mouth. (Pairs the plant superintendent with an aversive stimulus.)

Subordinate: I don't think he'll be such a big mouth any more. I really pinned the runt to the wall, and some of the plant guys saw it. *His subordinate's hostile remarks, and hostile feelings, are being shaped to greater intensity through reinforcement from the general sales manager; the subordinate has gone from "told him what I thought of him" to "really pinned the runt to the wall".*

Manager: Well, if you have any more trouble with him, tell me, and we'll both go out there. (Reinforcement.)

In this last sequence, the manager has shaped and increased the probability of a hostile response from his subordinate toward the plant superintendent and operations people generally. In particular, he has increased his subordinate's dislike of the plant superintendent by pairing the latter with aversive stimuli in his comments. Likewise, he has decreased the probability that his subordinate will attempt to build rapport with the plant superintendent or even be amenable to others' suggestions to this end. The sequence has therefore widened the chasm between operations and sales, a chasm that always starts at the top through interactions such as this one. The regional manager is now likely to reinforce negative interactions between his salespeople and operations people. Why did his manager reinforce this behavior? Because any behavior by others that hurts operations people is

306

reinforcing to him; after all, his boss, the VP of sales, keeps pairing operations people with aversives to him.

To the credit of the general sales manager, however, he at least focused on the behavior of the person to whom he was talking, albeit not constructively. Many managers would have talked about Mary or the plant manager, thus engaging in nonproductive gossip.

Manager: Anything else happening?   (Good interviewing question.)

Subordinate: No, that's about it. (He feels satisfied; he has been amply reinforced.)

Manager: How's Ed (one of the salespeople under the regional manager) coming along? *Any question that changes the focus of the conversation indicates an issue of importance to the person asking the question. In this case the manager is indicating that his subordinate's salespeople are important to him and he wants the regional manager to focus on them. Since questions frequently function as aversive stimuli or reinforcers, this question will be one or the other, depending on whether previous discussions between the two about Ed were aversive or reinforcing to the subordinate.*

Subordinate (monotone): Oh, he's coming along all right. (An avoidance response; previous discussions about Ed must have been aversive to the subordinate.)

Manager: Is he still whining about everything? *Good response. The manager does not stop the aversive stimulus after his subordinate's superficial answer. Too many managers would have said, "That's good," and gone on to another topic, thus increasing their subordinate's superficial behavior concerning Ed, but doing so because it decreases everybody's discomfort at the moment.*

Subordinate: Apparently. My secretary told me the other day he told her God himself couldn't survive on the money this company pays. (Attempts to stop the aversive stimuli by shifting his manager's focus to a specific situation concerning Ed, and away from his own handling of Ed.)

Manager: Have you talked to him about those attitudes? *The manager doesn't "take the bait". Many would have done so. Since Ed is not present, however, a long discussion about him will have absolutely no impact on his behavior and is merely gossip. Discussions of Ed, therefore, should only be held relative to the regional manager's behavior. The general manager has kept the aversive stimuli going because the regional manager has not yet made a constructive response.*

Subordinate: No, I haven't been able to get to him yet.

Manager (wincing): Aw, Jim. I asked you to talk to him about his negative attitudes three weeks ago. *Appropriate punishment. The manager has followed the response of "not talking with a subordinate" with an aversive stimulus. He has also followed an honest response by his subordinate with an aversive stimulus. How aversive this stimulus was will usually be determined by the subordinate's next response.*

Subordinate: Well, damn it, I really haven't had time.

Manager: Oh, come on, Jim. You know, procrastinators are like chickens; they both sit on things and hope they will hatch on their own momentum. *Effectively punishes a rationalization. The aversive stimuli are still "on". Also pairs people who delay taking action with aversive stimuli.*

Subordinate: You know, it takes a little time and effort to boost sales the way we're doing. *The manager's response was too aversive; had it been a bit milder, a bit more gentle, the subordinate might have responded with, "I know, I'll get to it Friday." The subordinate is now defensive. His last response was fairly constructive, however; it is, therefore, time for the manager to "turn off" the aversive stimuli and pair himself with reinforcers to reestablish rapport.*

Manager: I know you've been working your heart out, Jim. I know you're putting in as many hours as anyone in the company, and, frankly, you've done a hell of a good job in straightening this territory out. Actually, I was telling Mike (the VP of sales) that very thing about you the other day. *The manager, sensing that he has become an aversive stimulus to his subordinate by pairing himself with too many aversive stimuli, overcomes this problem by pairing himself with what to the subordinate are strong reinforcers. He also follows the responses of effort and putting in long hours with the cessation of aversive stimuli; that is, with reinforcers. How effectively he has paired himself with reinforcers will again be determined by his subordinate's subsequent response.*

Subordinate: Well, I suppose I should make time to sit down with a guy who has bad attitudes and straighten him out, but … (The manager was partially successful.)

Manager: I appreciate your saying that. *The manager throws out a quick reinforcer and blocks a potential negative statement. His subordinate has admitted a mistake; to prolong this topic would probably make both the topic and the manager too aversive, so the manager promptly reinforces a constructive response, even though it means interrupting his subordinate, and then moves quickly on to another topic, thus stopping the "but" aversive pairing.* Say, how are we coming with Preston Corporation? Have we made any sales calls over there yet?

Subordinate: Oops, sorry, I haven't been able to get over there either since you asked me to three weeks ago.

Manager (laughing): You louse, I don't think I have any impact on you at all. *The manager had to use an aversive stimulus, but he made it mild by combining it with reinforcers of humor and self-deprecation.*

Subordinate (laughing along with the manager): Why, you know you're all I live for. I'll get over there before the week is out. (The manager's aversive stimulus was not too strong, hence the subordinate responded in a constructive manner.)

Manager: If you go over there, I know we'll get the sale. (Pairs the verbal equivalent of the desired response and himself with the reinforcer.) You know, the people at Preston think very highly of you. *Pairs the customer with a reinforcer, a pairing many managers have difficulty using, but one of the most important a manager can make. The subordinate may not have gone to Preston because it is an aversive stimulus to him.* Anything else

309

we should be discussing? (A reinforcing question. These interviewing questions allow the subordinate to feel he is controlling the interchange as much as the manager—which, indeed, he should be.)

Subordinate: No, that about covers it, I think.

Manager (getting up): Well, back to the grind for me, then. (Pairs himself with a good reinforcer, implying that activities other than talking to his subordinate are aversive to him.)

This was a generally effective manager-subordinate interaction. The manager, whether he is aware of it or not, has been subtly guiding his subordinate's behavior. Many managers feel guilty about such interactions; they feel that they are wasting time with such "chit chat". As a matter of fact, such conversations should occur at least once or twice a week; indeed, they are a manager's primary responsibility.

Consider what the manager has accomplished in this interchange. First, by suggesting dinner at the Athletic Club, he has increased the probability that the subordinate will reinforce his salespeople's efforts. Second, he has increased the probability that his subordinate will confront negative attitudes in one of his salespeople. (These two accomplishments alone will result in increased sales, since the salesman's negative attitudes are undoubtedly hurting his colleagues' motivation and his own sales calls.) Third, the manager has increased the probability that his subordinate will call on Preston Corporation; without this interaction, that sales call might never have been made. In fact, the conversation had only one unfortunate result. The general sales manager has also increased the probability of poor communication, animosity, and lack of cooperation between sales and operations, a situation which his own manager (the VP) had better "chit chat" about with him (and if he doesn't, the president should have a "chat" with him; and if the president doesn't, the problem will become an entrenched chasm that hurts performance and profits).

Because he is an emotionally expressive person, this manager is able to give his subordinates a good deal of feedback. Through the frequent use of reinforcers and mild aversive stimuli, he lets his subordinates know what is expected of them. Many managers, however, are great sources of extinction. They rarely go out of their way to elicit behavior from their subordinates, and, when they do, they rarely respond in any meaningful fashion to that behavior. Hence, there is truth to the frequent complaint of most subordinates that they "don't know where they stand"—even after a two-hour meeting with the manager! Indeed, each of us would do well to consider how often we extinguish those in our inner circle, both professional and personal.

CHAPTER 29
ANALYSIS OF MANAGERIAL INTERACTIONS: Example 2

Our second example is more complex. We will assume that an outsider has been brought into an organization as vice president of operations (manager). He has responsibility for five plants around the country. He has been on board about three months and knows that he is an aversive stimulus to one of his plant managers (subordinate) because this particular plant manager wanted the vice presidency. This is his third visit to this plant manager's location.

Manager: Hello, Dick, how's it going?
Subordinate: Well, you should know that we've had an upsurge in grievances recently, and there's been some talk of a wildcat strike.
Manager: Oh my God, that's all I need. *Since the vice president is an aversive stimulus to his subordinate, his discomfort constitutes a reinforcer to the subordinate; therefore, this response will increase the probability that the plant manager will continue to focus on problems in the plant. As irrational as it sounds, the plant manager's subsequent behavior in the plant may subconsciously increase the problems, since problems in the plant seem to have such a negative emotional impact on his disliked superior. The plant manager, for example, may well be a little more abrupt, a little more abrasive with his subordinates, after this exchange with his superior.*
Subordinate: Well, it looks pretty serious, Frank. The word has come from several sources in the plant. We haven't been able to pin the instigators down yet, but we will. *The plant manager is indicating that employees out on the floor are aversive stimuli to him; vague references to "sources" and "instigators" are aversive pairings used to refer to people who are aversive to the speaker.*
Manager: What the hell do you think is causing all of this? (Still reinforcing his subordinate with his fear-driven concerns.)
Subordinate: I have no idea. I wish I did.

<u>Manager:</u> Do you think it might be Jerry (plant superintendent)? You know he's always treating the foreman and the hourly people like they were something to be tolerated, something to look down on. *The manager pairs Jerry with stimuli aversive to himself, but not necessarily aversive to the plant manager.*

<u>Subordinate:</u> No. I think you're wrong there. *The plant manager punishes his manager's response. Under these circumstances, this probably means the vice president is correct in suspecting Jerry.* Overall, Jerry's doing a fine job. *The superintendent probably shares the plant manager's views about the people on the floor. Indeed, the superintendent probably got these views from his boss in the first place; hence he is a reinforcer to the plant manager because he has likely paired himself with the negative attitudes toward the workers the plant manager likes.*

<u>Manager:</u> Have you talked to him about the way he treats his people? *Good focus on the behavior of the only person he can influence at that moment; avoids discussing the superintendent except insofar as it relates to his immediate subordinate's behavior; has started an aversive which his subordinate will try to stop, constructively or not.*

<u>Subordinate:</u> Yeah, we've discussed it a bit. He feels he's getting the most he can out of the people with the rotten equipment we have here. *The vice president's question is an aversive stimulus to the plant manager, who is attempting to avoid further interaction along these lines by shifting the conversation to another topic, the equipment. The plant manager's feelings toward the company are implicit in his use of the aversive stimulus, "rotten equipment", which he no doubt blames on the company.*

<u>Manager:</u> Well, there's not much we can do about the equipment. We don't have much cash for capital investments now. *The vice president "takes the bait", focuses on the equipment issue, thus stopping his aversive questioning of the plant manager's behavior; then pairs himself with weak, uncomfortable responses, all of which are reinforcing to his subordinate.*

<u>Subordinate:</u> Well, I don't know how the company and those idiots in corporate can expect anything with equipment that should

have been junked thirty years ago. *Blatant pairing of the company and its management with aversive stimuli. There should be little doubt now as to the origin of any negative attitudes in the plant. The subordinate's negative attitudes have also increased in intensity because his manager's uncomfortable feelings are reinforcing them.*

Manager: I know. I'll do everything I can to get some money for this plant. *The plant manager is now controlling the interaction, a not infrequent situation when one remembers that interpersonal factors take precedence over other stimuli, including position titles, in influencing behavior. He is able to assume control because someone complaining and confronting him is an overly strong aversive stimulus to his fearful superior, who has apparently stopped similar aversive stimuli by "passive agreement" responses. This is a major problem with fear; it always gives others control over us.*

Subordinate: I'd sure appreciate that. *The subordinate adeptly reinforces his manager's passive subservience by stopping the aversive stimuli inherent in his previous complaining responses.*

(Let us assume that this conversation is interrupted by a call from the president to the vice president. The president asks the vice president what is going on in this plant, since he has heard rumors that a wildcat strike is imminent. The vice president says he is exploring the situation. The president says, "I know what the problem is, it's that plant manager out there. If you don't do something about him or get him the hell out of there, you're going to have real trouble yourself." The president has just paired the plant manager with an aversive stimulus and "lack of action" on the vice president's part with intense aversive stimuli. The vice president walks back into the plant manager's office a "tougher" manager; he now knows that the plant manager is an aversive stimulus to the president and that he must take action to save his own skin.)

Manager: Anything else happening I should know about? *Normally a good "concerned" question, a concern that is aversive to this subordinate because it involves a potential "interference" in his domain.*

<u>Subordinate</u>: No, that's about it. *Attempts to extinguish his manager's behavior—and presence.*

<u>Manager:</u> Exactly what did Jerry say when you talked to him about his negative attitudes toward the people on the floor? *His subordinate's displeasure, an aversive stimulus to this manager prior to the president's call, is now a reinforcer.*

<u>Subordinate:</u> Just what I mentioned.

<u>Manager:</u> You didn't mention anything. *Punishment; an aversive stimulus which knocks out the subordinate's previous response and sets the stage for further attempts at avoidance behavior by the superintendent. The aversive stimulus here is not only the manager's "attack" response, but also his new confident manner, born of the fear instilled by the president; hence the confidence is temporary.*

<u>Subordinate:</u> Well, we discussed the people and how they weren't producing. *Avoidance behavior. The subordinate attempts a subtle switch to another topic, the "people". Again, a blatant pairing of people in the plant with aversive stimuli by the person responsible for them, a certain precursor to a drop in productivity.*

<u>Manager:</u> I didn't ask you about your discussions about the people. I asked you about your discussions with Jerry and <u>his</u> negative attitudes. *Punishment; continues the aversive stimulus, which again knocks out the subordinate's previous response.*

<u>Subordinate:</u> Well, I really don't think his attitudes are all that bad. *What was punishment prior to the president's call is now a reinforcer to the manager. That is, the subordinate's uncomfortable feelings, aversive to the manager a short while ago, are now reinforcing his "attack" responses.*

<u>Manager (angry):</u> Do you know why you don't?

<u>Subordinate (angry):</u> No, why?

<u>Manager (angry, an anger born of the fear instilled in him because of the president's call):</u> Because you have the same attitudes. Because he gets his lousy attitudes from you. Because you're the guy who's causing us all our problems out here. *A correct*

316

diagnosis of the subordinate's behavior would have shown negative emotional reactions by others (e.g., fear and anger) to be reinforcing to him, a fact explaining most of the problems in the plant. The manager's discomfort and irritation are born of his fears and are reinforcers to his subordinate; hence the subordinate's rebuttals are now being reinforced again. To have punished the subordinate and decreased the probability of further "attack" responses, the manager could have smiled and quietly stated, in a calm, confident manner, "My friend, our discussion is over ... for now."

Subordinate (angry): Well, if you don't like me here, why don't you fire me? *Still attacking, because he is being reinforced by the manager's discomfort.*

Manager: I know what my prerogatives are. I don't need you to tell me. I want this plant straightened out and your negative attitudes stopped or some action will be taken. *The manager is still reinforcing his subordinate with fear-driven, negative emotional, withdrawal reactions.*

Subordinate: That's fine with me. *For long-term development, the manager would need to pair "negative emotional reactions" by others with stimuli aversive to this subordinate. He does not really have time to do this, however, since the plant is in serious trouble. He should, therefore, have accomplished one pairing, at least, by saying to the subordinate, "You seem to find people getting upset quite rewarding—for that reason, you are no longer working here, you're fired." He should then have gone to the plant superintendent and said, "People are expressing too many negative feelings around here, so I've fired the plant manager— and if these negative reactions continue, you won't be around long either." Interestingly, to be truly aversive to this type of person, these statements would have to be made calmly and quietly.*

This vice president obviously should not have been hired. Had his interviewers focused on what kind of manager was needed in the plants at this time, and had they focused on this candidate's frequent, repetitive behavior, rather than relying on his previous technical experience, it is likely they would have picked up on his fear of confrontation. Indeed, recognizing the fears of any manager will usually be quite predictive of problems in his/her area since fear so readily leads to excessive, inappropriate behavior. This is especially crucial when looking at CEOs because it is not merely their attitudes that will permeate an organization, but most especially and dramatically, their fears.

CHAPTER 30

ANALYSIS OF MANAGERIAL INTERACTIONS: Example 3

In our final example, let us look at an interaction between the vice president of administration and her subordinate, the director of communications. The subordinate, in this case, is a meek, passive, indecisive fellow whom the vice president has given herself three months to develop or she will have to let him go. The director of communications does not know this, however.

Manager: Well, Bill, how's it going?
Subordinate: Oh, pretty well.
Manager: How's the new computer running? *Extinction; should have at least said, "Good," then gone on to her question. Is this petty? No! It's important [God is in the details in interpersonal interactions, too].*
Subordinate: Well, it seems to be doing all right.
Manager: Seems to be? *The manager has emitted a stimulus aversive to the subordinate, thereby punishing the subordinate's weak response to questions.*
Subordinate: Well, I mean the work's getting out.
Manager: Then the programs are running fine.
Subordinate: Yes, they're doing a good job.
Manager: Excellent! *The manager's delight seems to refer to the functioning of the new computer programs, but actually, since it follows a firm statement by the subordinate, it reinforces firmness on the subordinate's part.*
Subordinate: Will we be getting some extra help when the system is fully up and running?
Manager: Will you need some extra help?
Subordinate: Well, I'm not sure. If the system runs smoothly, we probably could get away without hiring anyone. But if the system breaks down or has a lot of bugs, we could be in an awful lot of trouble. *The manager remains silent, thereby extinguishing her*

subordinate's indecisiveness. I suppose we might ask the people to work overtime if the system breaks down.

Manager: Excellent idea! *Reinforces initiative and decisiveness in her subordinate, who has committed himself to a plan of action without guidance from others.*

Subordinate: I don't know if they will do it, though. It depends on how long we have to ask them to work, I suppose. *The manager remains silent and again extinguishes this type of indecisive response.* But I guess we wouldn't have too much trouble. They would sure enjoy the extra pay.

Manager: I think you're absolutely right. *Reinforces a more optimistic, decisive response by her subordinate; is she running a risk of encountering real problems? Yes. But this subordinate's fearful indecisiveness is excessive, hence she is focusing on changing his behavior at the moment; if she doesn't, she'll be constantly putting out the fires his indecisiveness causes. If she is unable to change him after concerted efforts on her part such as this, she'll have to fire him.*

Subordinate: I'll have some overtime schedules drawn up that we can implement if the system doesn't function as well as we'd like.

Manager: Sounds great! I'll give you all the help you need with people from other areas, too. *The manager has selectively and successfully reinforced and shaped a more aggressive action program on the part of her indecisive subordinate.* How's Ed (the director's subordinate) coming along? *Ed has been drinking heavily for two years, and the vice president wants her director of communications to fire him. Firing the man, and the confrontation that might occur, is intensely aversive to the subordinate, however.*

Subordinate: Well, not too well. He missed two days last week.

Manager: Oh, God! Missing days at a time like this is inexcusable. *The manager has punished her subordinate for bringing her bad news, decreasing the probability that the subordinate will tell her "bad" things in the future. However, the manager has also paired Ed's behavior pattern with an aversive stimulus. Moreover, she has presented an aversive stimulus to the subordinate which the latter must now stop.*

Subordinate: I know. I'm going to talk to him about it this afternoon. *An attempt to stop the presentation of aversive stimuli by the manager.*

Manager: Talk to him? What good is that going to do? We've already talked to him twenty times about it! *The manager has followed "talking to Ed" with strong aversive stimuli and effectively punished a response pattern that should normally be reinforced; it may be appropriate here, however. But she has also paired herself with the same intense aversive stimuli, a pairing that is almost certain to elicit a hostile remark, even from this passive subordinate.*

Subordinate (with some anger): I know you want me to fire him, but that's the easy way out. *The subordinate is pairing both the behavior he does not want to engage in, firing the subordinate, and his manager with an aversive stimulus, "the easy way out".*

Manager: Well, I don't really feel it's quite that easy. (In a gentle tone of voice): I think firing someone can be quite difficult emotionally. *Bad response, although it may help reestablish rapport and help her "win" the argument; by pairing "firing someone" with an aversive stimulus ("quite difficult"), the manager has made this behavior more aversive to her subordinate. She probably focused on winning the argument when her subordinate became aversive to her by using the phrase "easy way out".* I know I'm scared to death when I have to do it. *The manager's last comment, by pairing fear with herself, makes her less aversive to her subordinate and an admission of fear on his part also less aversive to him.*

Subordinate: I know, I get a little uneasy about it myself. *The manager, in her last comment, has paired herself with a reinforcer to this subordinate; the admission of fear in oneself is reinforcing to many people.*

Manager: What is it about the situation that makes you a bit uneasy? *Good feedback exchange question. The manager didn't merely accept his self-deprecation and move on to other things; thus, she is telling him this is important to me.*

Subordinate: I don't really know. I'm sure Ed expects it.

Manager: You know, I feel at times you might be a bit reluctant to hurt someone. How do you feel about it? *Good gentle, feedback approach.*

Subordinate: Well, I think you might be right.

Manager (in a concerned, soft voice): Why? Why do you feel you might be a bit reluctant at times to hurt someone?

Subordinate: I don't really know.

Manager: I wonder if, at times, you might be anticipating their negative reaction a little bit. But I wonder if when we fire someone we often don't do them a favor. I know a lot of guys who have been fired and said it was the best thing that ever happened to them. In fact, by firing Ed, you might be doing him the greatest favor anyone has ever done him. It might take a lot of weight off his shoulders. Letting him go might lead him to reassess his lifestyle and maybe stop drinking so much. I wouldn't doubt but that if you fired him, he'd admire you more and thank you for it some day. *The manager is pairing the verbal equivalent of firing the individual with reinforcers, thus making this response less aversive to her subordinate.*

Subordinate: Well, I'm not sure what his reaction would be.

Manager (knowing that being labeled a "coward" and being interfered with is intensely aversive to this subordinate): I'll tell you what—I'll be in town on Friday next week; why don't we both sit down with him and do it? *The manager has punished her subordinate's concern over other people's reactions, which is appropriate here because his concern is based on fear, hence it is excessive. A confident person's concerns over the reactions of others would not be excessive and appropriate and should not be punished.*

Subordinate: That's all right, I'll probably get to it before Friday. *Punishment has reduced her subordinate's concern for others' reactions and led to avoidance behavior on his part; that is, he is committing to the action to avoid his manager's interference.*

Manager: Well, you're the boss and it's your ballgame. *Stops the aversive stimulus by reinforcing the response she wants. Hopefully, taking the action will result in a less than traumatic experience for the director. If it does not, if Ed reacts poorly (or even violently) to being let go, the likelihood of the director firing someone in the future is virtually nil. A person should never be surprised by being fired, because the feedback given the person should have been so frequent and indicative of the manager's feelings that it should be an almost foregone conclusion.*

Some managers may feel these interactions do not give the subordinate enough credit. They may feel that a more "rational, logical" approach would be just as effective and certainly more respectful toward the subordinate. In the example above, for instance, it might be argued that the manager should point out to her subordinate the low probability of a cure in cases involving alcoholics, the bad effect the alcoholic is having on others in the department, and the possibility that the stress of the man's responsible position is causing the alcoholism.

These arguments are absolutely correct. But this "rational, logical" approach actually accomplishes what we are suggesting in our use of behavioral principles—and accomplishes it in a less effective, less precise manner. Each "rational" suggestion pairs "keeping the man on his job" with stimuli that hopefully are aversive to the subordinate (low probability of a cure, bad effect on others, stress of job contributing to alcoholism).

The difficulty with the so-called rational approach is that it makes unwarranted assumptions about human behavior. It rests on the assumption that rational considerations trump emotional factors. Pointing out to an individual the "bad effects of an alcoholic on others in the department" may be quite reasonable. It may also have little impact on a subordinate to whom these "bad effects" are not even slightly aversive and may even be reinforcing. Those who espouse a rational approach to management are often assuming that stimuli that are reinforcing or aversive to themselves (such as "facts" and/or statistics) are reinforcing or aversive to everyone (at least, everyone who is "reasonable"). Much of this book has been devoted to showing that this is an "unreasonable" assumption and far from the truth. As Wardsworth taught us, "Feelings are the fathers of thoughts."

CONCLUSION: THE INFLUENCE OF AUTHORITY

Most people in positions of power use that power to retain their power. To this end, the vast majority of managers focus upward toward their superiors because that represents the greatest threat to the influence and prestige of their position. Effective managers focus downward toward their subordinates, recognizing the enormous impact their own behavior has on the behavior of their subordinates.

Our society is founded upon the concept of authority. Throughout life, we learn that doing those things that please our parents, teachers, policemen, government officials, and others in authority will lead to pleasant experiences. More importantly, we learn that *not* doing those things that please people in authority will lead to unpleasant experiences. Few, if any, people are in a stronger position of authority over us in our daily adult lives than are our immediate superiors in the work setting.

This phenomenon of "authority influence" has a critical impact on the profits of an organization. It starts at the top with the chief executive officer, whose attitudes, opinions, and philosophy quickly permeate the organization down to the lowest level. The chief executive who believes all decisions should be made in his office will selectively pair "decisions by others" with aversive stimuli and "following orders to the letter" with reinforcers in the presence of his vice presidents and department heads. The latter will, in turn, engage in similar behavior with their subordinates. Independent, decisive subordinates, those with good constructive initiative, those to whom merely "following orders" is strongly aversive must change or leave the company. Within a surprisingly short time, virtually everyone within the organization will adopt cautious, conservative behavior patterns, behavior that will eventually show up on the loss column of the profit sheet.

This impact is true of all organizations, be they governmental, academic, military, non-profit, or profit-making, regardless of their stated policies and philosophies. Indeed, behavioral impact will always trump stated policies and philosophies.

No decision an organization makes, consequently, is more important than the one involving the selection of its chief executive officer. This is not due to the impact the chief executive has on formulating policies and procedures; rather, it is due primarily to the impact she/he has on the behavior of other people in the organization. And the weakest area of any organization usually revolves around the fact that most CEOs have the board of directors in their "hip pocket". By having so much influence in the selection of board members (supposedly their bosses), they ensure their own survival – regardless of their competence.

We presently live in a world in which success, competence, good fortune, and confidence are aversive stimuli to many people when they occur to, or in, other people. We presently live in a world in which failure, fear, lack of confidence, dependency, hostility toward others, and misfortune are reinforcers to many people when they occur to, or in, other people. Who will change this sad state of affairs? The institutions of religion and government do not appear to have had much success.

Managers in private industry, however, are powerful authority figures who have the tools to change basic attitudes and behaviors. And we know that confident people who truly like and respect themselves are usually the most productive, constructive, objective, and generally effective people in an organization. To the extent that managers are successful in building the confidence of their subordinates, to that extent will they help the individual, their organization, and society.

There is a parlor game which asks each person to respond to the following question: If there were a nuclear holocaust (not an improbable event) and you were one of only several survivors, what technical skills would you want in the others? Most people name such professions as engineer, medical doctor, or chemist. Yet, because of the enormous influence she/he is capable of having on the behavior of others, surely the greatest need of all would be for an individual skilled in one of the most difficult arts known to humankind—an effective manager of people. After all, effective managers elicit the best from others in terms of productivity,

325

cooperation, and positive relationships. And they do this because their behavioral impact on others increases people's confidence, their liking and respect for themselves. And who wouldn't want an inner circle of friends and colleagues who are so confident that they want the best for us.

BEHAVIORAL DESCRIPTIVE TERM DEFINITIONS

I. APPROACH TO INTELLECTUAL PROBLEMS

rapid   - grasps and solves problems quickly.

accurate   - precise in his thinking; rarely makes
                        serious mistakes

efficient   - does not waste time or energy on
                        superficial irrelevancies; emphasizes
                        productivity

careful   - intent on avoiding mistakes

systematic   - works through problems in an orderly,
                        organized manner; does not go off on
                        tangents

thorough   - looks closely at all aspects of a
                        situation

theoretical   - generalizes from concrete situations to
                        broad, abstract principles

analytical   - breaks down complex situations into
                        their more simple components

logical   - thinking corresponds closely to reality
                        and moves rationally from given
                        premises to warranted conclusions

objective	- thinks in terms of the facts of a situation and considers both positive and negative aspects
comprehensive	- understands the ramifications and interrelation-ships
basic	- focuses on the lowest common denominator in problem areas
penetrating	- probes deeply into the relevant aspects of a situation
flexible	- thinking on an issue can be changed with new inputs
intuitive	- reaches quick, spontaneous conclusions with minimum analysis
venturesome	- not fearful of new or ambiguous areas; willing to try new things
creative	- solutions are constructive, but rarely thought of by others
constructive	- offers alternatives rather than merely criticizing the ideas or approaches of others
curious	- frequently asks questions; interested, easily stimulated; seeks to develop in-depth under-standing of matters

tactician vs. strategist	- focuses on daily, rather narrow issues vs. a more global, overall view of situations and their implications
alert	- responds to his environment
concise	- conveys information with minimum of verbiage, time and energy
organized	- moves through situations in a logical, one-two-three manner
planning	- anticipates needed actions and the consequences of decisions.
deliberate	- thoughtful hesitation before committing to a decision or action
risk-taking	- not fearful of mistakes; will jeopardize important things if the goal is worthwhile
good detail orientation	- watches nuances closely without bogging down in them

II.   APPROACH TO WORK RESPONSIBILITIES

mature	- does not overreact emotionally to situations; copes effectively with adversity; defers short-range gratification in favor of long-range objectives

patient	- attainment of goals not under a strong time urgency; deals effectively with frustrating circumstances
expressive	- feelings readily apparent
responsible	- accepts obligations and the praise or reprimands concerning those obligations as his own
optimistic	- readily sees the positive side of situations
dominant	- strong influence in determining interactions of others
aggressive	- action-oriented; attacks problems head-on; not fearful of using aversive critical stimuli to solve problems
open	- freely states what's on his mind
predictable	- adheres closely to consistent modes of behavior
cooperative	- minimal hesitation in offering aid to others and working with others on common goals; contributes his share in conjunction with others
enthusiastic	- readily expresses strong, positive feelings, especially through tone of voice and facial and body gestures

forthright	- leaves listener with few doubts as to how he feels on a given issue; direct expression of thoughts
dependable	- consistently meets commitments previously made
ambitious	- attaining positions of influence, power and prestige is important
impulsive	- jumps to a decision without giving the matter or alternative sufficient consideration
intense	- experiences strong feelings
competitive	- motivated by comparisons of performance or abilities with others
independent	- does not lean on others for guidance when personal resources are adequate to do the job
confident	- realistic awareness of his own abilities; minimal need to impress and sell himself to others; reasonably assured when dealing with people and/or problems
controlled	- overt expression of feeling kept to a minimum

determined	- perseveres in the face of obstacles; disciplined in following through on assignments he finds aversive
initiative	- initiates action without a push from others
decisive	- commits himself and others to a course of action, especially in ambiguous situations; has a healthy risk orientation

III. APPROACH TO OTHERS AND SELF

easy to know	- expresses attitudes and views, even at a personal level freely
conformist	- actions adhere closely to socially acceptable standards
warm	- expresses positive feelings at a personal level easily
sincere	- actions based on the issues, not on their impact on other people at the moment
engaging	- stimulating; elicits positive attention from others
self-centered	- overly concerned with personal considerations; insufficient concern with needs and desires of others

frank	- expresses views with minimal regard for personal impact on others
self-conscious	- overly concerned with how others see him
wears well	- liked by most people over long periods of time; not disruptive
persuasive	- emphasizes the positive aspects of his own ideas from other person's point of view in order to sway the other person's thinking
reserved	- monotoned and reticent expression of ideas and feelings; hesitant when meeting people
tactful, diplomatic	- rarely says anything that hurts people; expresses ideas in such a manner that others do not become overly emotional, defensive or sensitive
good listener	- responds in a pertinent manner to what others are saying
defensive	- responds negatively to realistic criticism of himself and/or his ideas
knows his potential	- does not set personal goals beyond his capabilities
capitalizes on his strengths	- seeks out responsibilities which call on skills in which he is proficient

is realistic about his limitations	- knows his shortcomings and is not hesitant to seek advice and guidance of others when needed
looks for self-improvement	- seeks out personal feedback from others and responds positively to it
accepts criticism	- responds positively to realistic feedback; considers and profits from criticism
has an intuitive understanding	- responds properly without a deep analysis of the "whys"
senses moods and their meaning	- responds appropriately to subtle clues in the behavior of others
helps others develop	- not fearful of giving feedback to others; provides growth experiences for others

IV.   APPROACH TO MANAGERIAL RESPONSIBILITIES

realistically critical	- sees both strengths and shortcomings of people evaluating subordinates in an objective manner
selects and promotes competent subordinates	- looks for people who are intent upon achieving practical results
fires incompetent subordinates	- not fearful of taking adverse action when necessary

develops subordinates	- accepts responsibility for the behavior of subordinates and gives subordinates frequent feedback and growth experiences
maintains a fast, enthusiastic orientation	- behavioral impact on subordinates encourages productivity and positive attitudes
communicates with subordinates	- freely expresses his ideas and elicits and responds appropriately to the ideas of subordinates
makes demands	- not fearful of asking for more effort when appropriate
practical results orientation	- influenced more by practical results than by such things as pleasing others, avoiding mistakes, etc.
autocratic	- not susceptible to the ideas and influence of subordinates; overly authoritative
laissez faire	- democratic style of management; if carried too far, can lead to abdication of responsibilities to subordinates, rather than appropriate delegation
lenient	- has difficulty seeing shortcomings in subordinates and using reprimands when necessary

ABOUT THE AUTHOR

David Thompson, Ph.D., is the President of MTR Corp, a management consulting firm based in Chicago (www.mtrcorp.net). He is the author of Psychology in Clinical Practice; Managing People, Influencing Behavior; and What You Fear is Who You Are: The Role Of Fear In Relationships (www.whatyoufear.com).

Dr. Thompson's primary professional interests are in the areas of managerial assessment, reinforcement theory, and management training and development. He holds a bachelor's degree from the University of Chicago and a doctoral degree in psychology from the Illinois Institute of Technology.